THE £5 VIRGINS

Books by Michael Pearson

The Secret Invaders

The Millionaire Mentality

The Million Dollar Bugs

Those Damned Rebels: The American Revolution as Seen Through British Eyes

The £5 Virgins

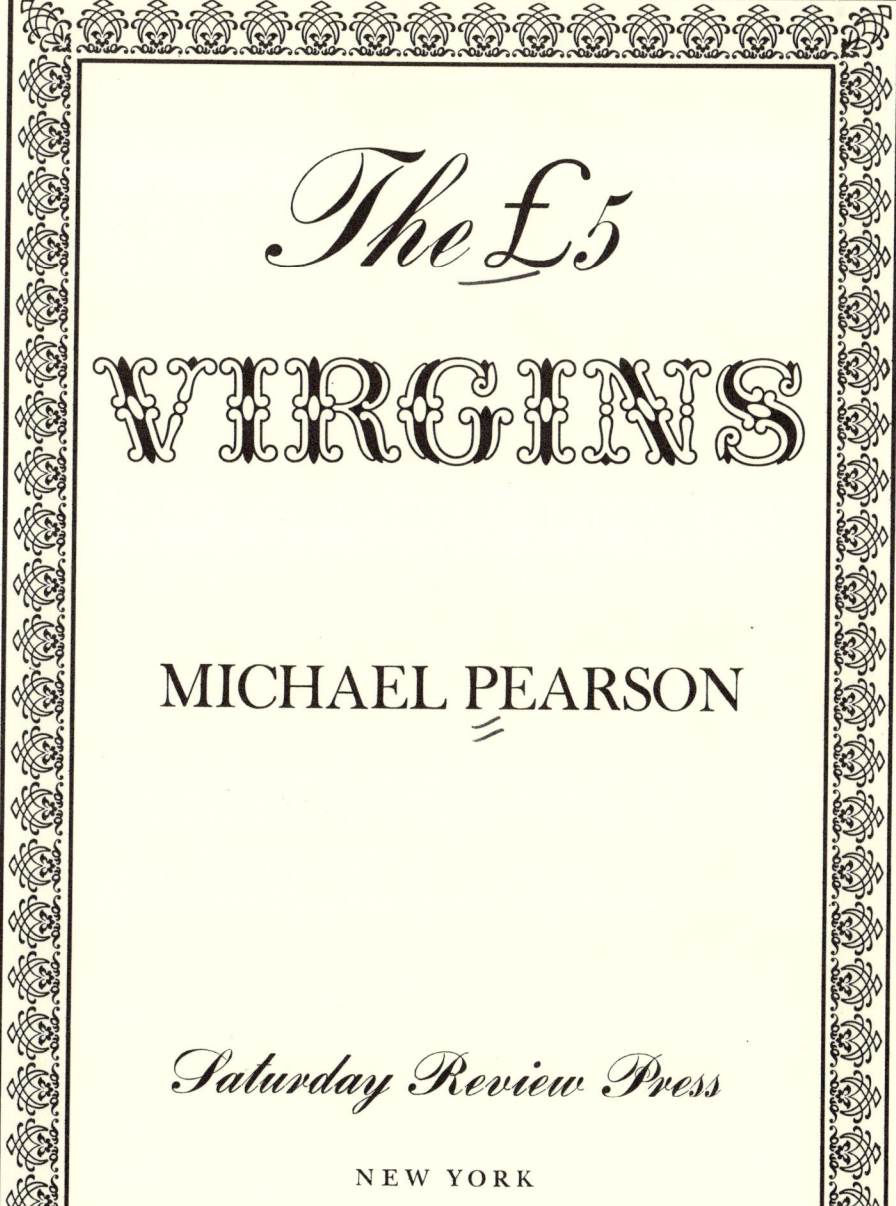

Copyright © 1972 by Michael Pearson

First American Edition 1972

Published in Great Britain as *The Age of Consent*

All rights reserved. No part of this work may be reproduced or transmitted in any form or by any means, electronic or mechanical, including photocopy, recording, or any information storage and retrieval system, without permission in writing from the publisher.

Library of Congress Catalog Card Number: 76-154279

ISBN 0-8415-0197-1

Saturday Review Press
230 Park Avenue
New York, New York 10017

PRINTED IN THE UNITED STATES OF AMERICA

For Tessa

Contents

		page
	List of Illustrations	9
	Preface	11
1	The Proposition	15
2	The Streets of London	23
3	Enter the White Knight	36
4	The Women in Revolt	58
5	The Hallelujah Evangelists Join the Battle	84
6	Attack on 'The Empress of Vice'	99
7	The Campaigning Editor	118
8	The Sensational Exposé	147
9	The Reaction	168
10	The Trial	190
11	A Society Outraged	212
	Bibliography	218
	Index	220

Illustrations

(following page 128)

KATE HAMILTON'S NIGHT HOUSE *(Mary Evans Picture Library)*
THE HAYMARKET AT MIDNIGHT *(Mary Evans Picture Library)*
A SPREE IN A RAILWAY CARRIAGE *(Mansell Collection)*
COURTESANS IN HYDE PARK
WILLIAM THOMAS STEAD *(Radio Times Hulton Picture Library)*
JOSEPHINE BUTLER *(Radio Times Hulton Picture Library)*
THE BOOTH FAMILY *(Radio Times Hulton Picture Library)*
AN AMOROUS YOUTH ON A JAUNT TO LONDON *(Mansell Collection)*
PROSTITUTE IN THE BURLINGTON ARCADE *(Mansell Collection)*
AN AWKWARD MEETING IN REGENT STREET *(Mary Evans Picture Library)*
POLICE INTERRUPT A PARTY *(Mary Evans Picture Library)*
WENTWORTH STREET, WHITECHAPEL
A SALVATION ARMY MARCH IN EAST LONDON *(Radio Times Hulton Picture Library)*
THE EMPIRE THEATRE *(Ronald Pearsall)*

Preface

The brothel—and the freelance prostitute—have existed throughout the history of man. But their relative significance in the societies they served has varied.

In Victorian England, for a few decades, sex-for-sale assumed a peculiar importance. It was a period when the enormous social and economic changes that have now materialised were in the early stages of development. For a whole range of reasons, the harlot—the 'gay' girl—became the focus of many of the issues that arose from the traumatic transformation the whole country was undergoing.

Britain, like America and other western states, was changing painfully from a nation whose roots were mainly in the land to one characterised by smoky, overcrowded cities. Its class divisions, that were soon to come under assault primarily as a result of the new conditions, were still rigid. Its wealth was still concentrated in a relatively small section of a people who accepted completely the concept, within a paternalistic property-owning society, of the dominant male.

As yet, there was little sense of social responsibility for the millions who lived in conditions of appalling poverty and overwork that are now regarded as no better than slave labour. Property was especially revered, as indeed it always had been, but there was a difference about the new situation. Whereas formerly most of the big landowners had accepted that the people who lived and worked on their estates had some rights to their protection and care, the middle class that had expanded on the profits of the Industrial Revolution felt no such obligation. Poverty was dismissed as a fact of life that was unlikely to change.

It was a strange society that worshipped the inherent 'purity' of women while accommodating the inherent 'evil' of men. It believed

Preface

that, since the modesty of ladies must be protected, natural male lusts should be serviced by the poor, who supplied most of the other basic needs of the middle and upper classes. It tolerated the view that a gentleman was entitled to take his pleasure providing he paid for it —even if this was by force from a very young virgin which, since this was the purest female available in a purity-obsessed community, he often did.

'A gentleman had better fuck them for money than a butcher boy for nothing . . .' wrote 'Walter', the anonymous Victorian author of a million words of sexual experience, about young working-class teenagers. 'It is the fate of such girls to be fucked young . . . It is the law of nature that nothing can thwart . . .'

It was a cynical comment—and, significantly, a justification for actions about which clearly he had an uneasy conscience—but it pinpointed brilliantly the attitude of a highly mercenary society that was trying to reconcile the worship of impossibly high ideals of womanhood with male sexual need. Under these circumstances, since society tacitly accepted that prostitution—like poverty—was an unalterable fact, it is not strange that it was shocked, not by shocking facts, but by their exposure to innocent sensibilities. This was hypocritical, but unquestionably logical.

However, marked as the period was by great change, new ideas were being explored. Ironically, many of them—involving such issues as industrialisation, poverty, class, the rights of women, the female sexual role, the laws of property and even human freedom—centred on the prostitute and the system that supported her.

This was why an exceptionally bitter struggle arose when several big groups of reformers, with varying aims, combined forces in 1885 to mount a sustained offensive against the organisers of prostitution in Britain and Continental Europe. For, in practice, these strident bonneted women and ardent bearded men were not merely pursuing the sex racketeers: they were assaulting society itself. They were campaigning against a standard of artificial morality that was accepted by most of the western world. They were rousing the women of Europe—and, later, the women of America—to mobilise against rigid and oppressive male attitudes, and demanding what was, in effect, a

Preface

new deal for the Second Sex. Most important of all, because of their assaults on these targets, they came into head-on combat with the ultra-powerful Establishment that consisted entirely of men.

The explosion when this apparently impregnable barrier was breached was enormous. The catalyst, which came after years of independent militancy, was a series of sensational newspaper articles —probably the first of the campaigning exposés of modern journalism —that bared to the shocked scrutiny of Victorian Londoners the sordid underbelly of their own society.

The social picture, and the attitudes that sustained it, revealed in this brutal and probably overstated probing were not unique to the British capital. They were shared by most of the major cities of America and Europe. It was because of this that the campaigners' astonishing victory reverberated round the world, causing drastic changes to laws and mores thousands of miles from the prostitute-crowded streets near Piccadilly Circus. Possibly it was because of this, too, that Victorian Society, smarting from this public self-examination, turned and savaged the young editor who had held up to it so traumatic a mirror—although his careless and sensational reporting certainly demanded some rebuke.

This book tells the story of this revolution and of the revolutionaries —in particular of William Thomas Stead, who, as the impulsive editor of *The Pall Mall Gazette*, played the major role in the explosive *dénouement*.

History has been surprisingly kind to Stead. Within a few years of his trial, which signalled a spate of public censure of him, he was re-vamped as a hero. Even most modern writers, who live in an age that would have shocked Stead just as much as his own, have portrayed him as a great journalist who conducted a noble crusade, disregarding completely the enormous professional errors he displayed in his articles. Although there is no doubt that his famous series did a lot to clean up the vice market—and achieved a much-needed increase in the age of sexual consent for girls—it did so by cheating.

The sex revolutionaries often cheated—sometimes without realising they were doing so. Obsessed as they were with their cause, they regularly distorted facts—some of which were horrific enough without

Preface

any promotional treatment. Zealously they operated on the assumption that the end—their end—justified any means they chose to employ.

Stead, however, was not just a revolutionary. He was the editor of an influential daily newspaper with some responsibility both to his profession and to his readers. As it was, burning with zeal for his mission, he played up—and even made up—his material to an extent that, if it happened today, would result in the instant dismissal of any junior reporter.

Yet journalism and the Victorians forgave Stead. Before he died, he was to achieve professional heights far above even those he had reached before his sex crusade. Certainly, with his overflowing emotional excess, he was a fascinating character and easy to forgive—a poseur, a terrible 'ham', but a man of great warmth and enormous courage. To join battle with the society in which he lived—and in which he was admired—involved an immense risk. However, his ardour does not absolve him from criticism, and this book attempts to view Stead and the other campaigners—less famous but just as active—in a perspective provided by nearly a hundred years.

Many people have helped me in the writing of the book. I would like to thank in particular the Principal Keeper of Printed Books and his staff in the British Museum for their great assistance. I am especially grateful, too, to Joan Bailey of the London Library who has been invaluable in tracing many of the works I have needed to consult. Charles Terrot, Lionel Playfair and Richard Collier, each of whom have written on the same subject area in books that are quoted in the bibliography, have also helped me a great deal.

I am grateful, too, to the Home Office for an opportunity of examining the files that are still 'closed' under the 100-year rule, and to the staff of the Public Record Office in London for their help in studying government and police records that are now 'open'.

I would like to express my appreciation to the librarians of The Society of Friends and of the Fawcett Society for their assistance in pursuing material on Alfred Dyer and Josephine Butler.

Finally, I would like to thank Sylvia Voller, as always, for her laborious typing of the notes and various drafts of the manuscript.

I

The Proposition

It was a good Spring that year. The blossom on the trees in the parks had flowered earlier than usual. And on Friday, 23 May, a pale sun warmed the congestion of hansoms, carriages and garish two-horse omnibuses that jostled their way through the Strand towards Trafalgar Square.

Benjamin Scott paid off his cab and walked down Northumberland Street, a narrow little alleyway opposite the side of the massive bulk of Morley's Hotel which with its symmetrical rows of blind-shaded windows, dominated the south east corner of Trafalgar Square. He was an old man—in his late seventies—white-haired, wing-collared, frock-coated, but he was energetic for his age and, on that Friday in particular, he was filled with an angry determination.

He entered the drab stucco building that housed the offices and presses of *The Pall Mall Gazette*, one of the most widely read of London's evening newspapers, and demanded to see the editor.

Thirty-six years old William Thomas Stead—red haired, bearded and characterised by an immense and voluble enthusiasm—had only been editor of the *Gazette* for eighteen months, but he had made dramatic changes. 'He was the first,' wrote novelist Matthew Arnold, 'to popularise the interview or to use illustrations in a daily paper . . . he caught the reader's eye with terse and picturesque headlines.'

He was to have plenty of scope for picturesque headlines in the proposal that his elderly visitor was about to make to him.

Benjamin Scott was Chamberlain to the Corporation of the City of London, but like so many of the late Victorians, he spent much of his

The Proposition

spare time working for social causes. Because of the prestige of his city appointment, he served as the spokesman for a group of reforming societies that, though they existed for varying purposes, were united in their determination to clear sexual vice from the streets of London—and, for that matter, from a number of other cities.

The struggle had been in progress for years—and there had been limited and momentary successes—but that May the conflict came to a climax. The vice interests and their sympathisers deployed their massive influence and coolly obliterated the opposition. An attempt by Scott's organisation to jail the owner of the most famous string of brothels in London failed abysmally—stifled in court, despite overwhelming evidence, by powerful friends. Only the day before the old man's call at *The Pall Mall Gazette*, a bill designed to tighten up the prostitution laws—and to raise the age of sexual consent for young girls from thirteen to fifteen—had been filibustered in the House of Commons by the lobby that supported the brothel operators. It had been a skilled operation of political tactics that had twice before checked government attempts to tighten the vice legislation.

Watching from the public gallery of the House of Commons, Scott had realised that he and his many thousands of supporters had gone as far as they could on their own. After years of aggressive campaigning, they had now been blocked completely by the solid opposition of men who held the key power in Britain. It was now clear to him that the only way that this barrier could be undermined was by a public exposure of the sexual underworld of London that would shock the legislators into action. In an age when sex was not regarded as a suitable subject for discussion, and certainly not in the press, it was a proposition that would have been rejected outright by every editor in London—with one remotely possible exception: William Thomas Stead.

Stead was a liberal humanitarian man, with a taste for hell raising. He was an ardent supporter of the movement for women's liberation and, as Scott knew, he sympathised strongly with the anti-vice cause. In fact, the next morning, when Scott was still considering what courses of action were open to him, the *Gazette* lashed out at the 'loquacious' Members of Parliament who had allowed the prostitution

The Proposition

bill to be 'talked out' and forecast that there was now little hope of it becoming law.

Stead had never met Benjamin Scott before—but he listened to him patiently. 'Only you,' said his visitor, 'can save this bill.' And he urged him to set up an investigation of sexual vice in London and to publish the facts that he uncovered.

The young editor remained grimly silent as Scott drew a horrific picture of the white slave traffic, of the systemised rape of child virgins, of girls who walked the streets under the constant surveillance of brutal captors.

Almost certainly Scott was overstating the situation, not in the sense that the things he described were not happening on some scale, for they certainly were, but in his suggestion that they typified the prostitution scene in London. But the Victorians could only see sexual issues in stark terms of black and white. Never before had female virtue been so highly romanticised. Virginity was 'a priceless pearl' and the loss of it a 'fate worse than death'. Virtuous women were not just human beings—they represented an ideal of purity that was in striking contrast to the natural impurity of men.

This was a result of what Hugh Kingsmill has described as the 'revolt against Hell'—a reaction against the Puritan doctrine of original sin, the theory that everyone was born wicked. The Victorians, with their hunger for rich emotionalism, could not tolerate so harsh and bleak a view of life. They adapted the rigid pessimistic Puritan theory into the more hopeful belief that, although a lot of people were wicked, this did not apply to everybody. It was too early, however, in the development of the philosophy for subtlety. They saw only two extremes. Those, who were not wicked, were angelic. To the romantic Victorian mind, there were no in-betweens—and the natural place for women was with the angels. If they lost their virtue, it must, by definition, be because they had 'fallen' victim to male lust.

In calling on Stead, Scott had chosen the right man. For Stead was the son of a methodist preacher. He had been brought up in a house in which Hell was seen as a permanent threat that needed constant alertness. Even within marriage, he had been taught, sex was uneasily close to sin and other types of pleasure—even theatre-going, playing cards or reading fiction—were highly dangerous areas. 'The Novel . . . ,' he related years later about his childhood home, 'was regarded as a kind of Devil's Bible.'

He was a highly intelligent, emotional man, conscious of the overwhelming need to reform Victorian England, devastated as it was by the appalling poverty caused by the Industrial Revolution. This, coupled with his religious background and the obsession with sex that it had developed, must have made the idea of attacking male lust—and upper class male lust at that—a most appealing proposition. Also, he had a flair for sensational journalism, and here was a subject area rich with human story angles.

However, as a proposition for a young editor, it was very dangerous ground. Although the militant reformers, such as Benjamin Scott, regarded women in much the same above-sex way as the rest of middle class Victorian Society, there was a big difference in their attitude to men. For while the militants believed that men, too, should be chaste, the ruling view of the legislators in common with most other people was practical. Men needed sex and, if 'modest' women were to be protected, there was virtually only one outlet—the prostitute. It was for this reason that the brothel operators were so strongly entrenched throughout the western world. For they had the support, not only of their influential clientele, but also of the moralists. 'The complete suppression of the brothels,' asserted the London magistrate Sir James Ingham a few months after the meeting between Scott and Stead, 'would lead to the more frequent seduction of modest women, the multiplication of kept mistresses and other evils'. By 'modest' women, of course, Sir James meant those of the higher classes.

It was a view that was constantly repeated in debates in Parliament and, as a logical extension of it, came the promotion for control—the idea that, since male lust was a fact of life, every effort should be made to curb its anti-social disadvantages such as disease. By the middle of the nineteenth century this thinking had crystallised into hard policy. Most of the European countries had followed the French lead and set up state-authorised brothels with regular medical inspection of the girls who worked in them. But there was a natural city-to-city movement in women, a kind of regular changing of the merchandise, so to

The Proposition

be truly effective, the system needed to be world-wide. It was with this aim that a big international organisation was campaigning to encourage those nations, who had not yet gone so far, to introduce similar laws.

As a result of the lobbying, Britain and many US states were actively considering this kind of formal control, and both nations were making the first tentative steps towards it. In the 1860s an experimental system of compulsory inspection of suspected prostitutes had been set up by Parliament in some of the English troop towns and, in two later bills, the territory covered by the acts had been gradually extended. In America, during the seventies, the city of St Louis had set up a trial official licensing system, that was being studied carefully by authorities in other states.

However, a new age was emerging and, along with other social issues, the role of women was being re-thought. Already, the early Suffragettes were stomping the United Kingdom and the American continent demanding the vote. To the new feminists, the concept of the prostitute, as a state-supported institution, was intolerable. By implication, it approved and even encouraged sexual licence by men.

The issue sparked the western world's first feminine revolt of any stature—the first militant reaction against male dominance. It was far more basic, and commanded more support, than the Suffragette campaign, still only in its very early stages, because it involved the ordinary women's own menfolk. The brothel—officially approved and regularly inspected—would offer even more of a standing invitation than the unofficial temptations already available to them. Also, in an age in which erotic pleasure was seen as a masculine province, the whole principle evoked a vivid image of sacrifice—an offering up of unwilling female bodies to evil-inspired male vice.

It was not strange that the rousing appeal to women—pioneered at the end of the 1860s by a quiet, slender blue-eyed woman of thirty-nine named Josephine Butler—produced a warm response. By the eighties, she was commanding a national female army that was operating at every level from the brothels themselves—where they stood at the doors urging the prostitutes to protest—to the lobbies of Parliament where they harangued the legislators.

The Proposition

By then, too, she had realised that, since the promoters of the state system operated at an international level, she must fight them on a world wide basis. The organisation, that she masterminded, now had headquarters in Geneva, from which it organised national campaigns against proposals for state brothels whenever they were made and maintained continual sniping in those places where the system was already established. Already, emissaries from Josephine had roused Purity Leagues throughout the US East Coast to the need for constant alert for any moves by their legislators to slip through seemingly innocent bills that contained brothel licensing powers. In Britain her army checked the troop town laws; and in Missouri the petitions of four thousand angry protesting women killed the St Louis experiment.

In 1885, the battle was still raging, and Josephine Butler's militant women gave Benjamin Scott an organisation with which he could exploit any campaign he could persuade William Stead to mount. In addition, the Booth family—who ran the newly-formed Salvation Army that was then attracting enormous crowds to its brassy evangelical meetings throughout the world—were eager to deploy their forces to support any attack on the brothel owners. The conflict had been joined, too, by a fervent group of Quaker ascetics.

The meeting on that May day between Scott and Stead saw the fusion of all the independent campaigns that had been in progress for more than a decade against organised vice. Although the personal risk for the young editor was very great, the pressure that Scott was levering on him was enormous, for his proposal was tactically logical. Deployed as the reform organisations now were, the chances of success for a newspaper campaign were, in terms of potential practical results, extremely good—especially since action on the more limited issue of child prostitution had now been urged by two parliamentary committees and a growing number of increasingly vociferous rescue societies. In other words, despite the immediate setback by the opposition group in the Commons, the timing for drastic measures was right.

Stead wrote later, that he believed at first that Scott was exaggerating the extent of the cruelties that he insisted were an integral part of London's industry in sex—which he undoubtedly was. But this suggests that the editor's reaction was cool and cerebral, which would have been quite out of character. Stead was a highly emotional, impulsive man—which contributed much to his great personal appeal—and he often had to discipline his enthusiasms. Benjamin Scott's account of the meeting suggests a much warmer response:

'Do you *know* any cases of child rape?' demanded Stead. His visitor told him about a witness whom he had hoped would testify in the prosecution of a brothel owner his society had recently promoted. In fact, it was not a very good example: the witness had failed to appear in court—bought off, so the reformers accused, by defense counsel—and the evidence that she could have given concerned events that were eleven years old. Still, she had been a servant in one of the defendant's brothels and had left, so she claimed, because of the rape of a thirteen-year-old country girl.

Despite the decade that had passed since the incident, the story deeply affected the young editor. 'Stead sprang from his chair,' Scott reported, 'and exclaimed: "That's damnable!" And, taking a walk twice up and down the room, it was a minute before he was sufficiently composed to resume the conversation. He then said: "Mr Scott, what on earth can be done to stop this sort of thing?" And I replied: "Why not issue a commission of enquiry?"'

Though this is probably nearer what happened than Stead's own version, the story does not quite ring true: the emotionalism of the sex reformers always led them to exaggerate. For, despite his apparent reaction of shock, Stead was already fully aware that young girls were involved in the open and rampant prostitution in London. Quite apart from the fact that it was obvious to anyone who took a walk, he had been under pressure barely a month before from Ellice Hopkins—one of the militant reformers—to act in the cause of 'these poor mites suffering these nameless horrors', and complaining about people 'who shuffle nervously into a pair of lavender kid gloves . . . exclaiming "Oh, it is such a delicate question that I cannot be mixed up in it."' He had long corresponded with Josephine Butler, who had made the issue of children in brothels the main pitch of a violent personal attack she had mounted successfully against the owners of the Brussels sex houses and the white slavers who supplied them.

The Proposition

There was no doubt that Stead was well-informed and had already been asked by others to bring the *Gazette* into action in the cause. But Scott's visit was different. For, in effect, he came to him with a formal request from *all* the reforming societies; and he came, what is more, after every other course that was open to them had been fully exploited.

Without committing himself to any dramatic action, Stead cautiously agreed to investigate the subject and—since he was a highly influential man—to explore what he might be able to do to help.

To do so, he did not have to travel far from his office off the Strand. For it is doubtful if the bustling streets of London had ever been so crowded with silk-dressed girls for sale.

2
The Streets of London

'From three o'clock in the afternoon,' Howard Vincent, director of the Criminal Investigation Department at Scotland Yard, told a committee of peers in 1881, 'it is impossible for any respectable woman to walk from the top of the Haymarket to Wellington Street, Strand.'

This flat statement summarised vividly the sheer volume of prostitution in late Victorian London—for the two streets were a considerable distance apart. Any woman who chose to make the trip would have had to walk the best part of a mile and, by the time she had completed it, she would have crossed most of the West End. On every corner there would have been 'gay' girls, their faces rouged and powdered, soliciting the passing men.

Furthermore, the route named by the police director did not include many of the areas where the women thronged the pavement in profusion. Lower Regent Street, for example, which reached south barely a hundred yards from Piccadilly Circus, was—according to a police survey—the regular midnight territory of as many as five hundred prostitutes. Pall Mall and St James', where tall stone buildings housed the big London clubs, provided the beats for many girls who greeted members as they stepped from the pillared entrances, with the standard invitation: 'Charlie, are you good natured, dear?'

A *Saturday Review* reporter wrote a vivid description of the streets near Piccadilly at night:

> The pavement is occupied in force by crowds of men and women who saunter about in the blaze of gaslight which issues from the aggregation of gin palaces and oyster shops . . . There is no room for any charitable self-delusion as to the character of the assemblage

of men and women or of the nature of the deities in whose service they are engaged.

'It is always an offensive place to pass,' commented *Household Words* about Coventry Street, which joins Piccadilly Circus to Leicester Square, 'but at night it is absolutely hideous, with its sparring snobs and flashing satins and sporty gents and painted cheeks and brandy-sparkling eyes and bad tobacco and hoarse horse laughs and loud indecency.'

The Burlington Arcade, a glass-roofed parade of little shops off Piccadilly, was a favourite contact spot—especially, as *The Saturday Review* put it, 'at late afternoon when the garish gas casts appropriate light on tawdry surroundings... the western counterpart of an eastern slave market'. Many of the shops had bed facilities in rooms above where the 'heavy chignoned' girls took their clients.

By the 1880s, parliament had succumbed to pressure from the Temperance movement and banned the serving of alcohol in public places after 12.30am. This had closed the famous night houses, where previously the high class prostitutes had been able to mix under social conditions during the early hours of the morning with potential clients. Forced to find new operating ground, they now thronged the bars of the music halls—the vaudeville theatres such as The Empire and The Alhambra in Leicester Square.

This had altered the venue of the higher class trade but it had made no difference at all to the scene on the West End streets. Because most of the night houses had been in or near the Haymarket, this short wide street near Piccadilly, only ten minutes walk from Stead's office, had always been the hub of the business in sex. Even after these establishments had been closed down, it still retained its traditional role.

Henry Mayhew, the nineteenth century authority on London, wrote about the girls in the area:

> in black silk cloaks or light grey mantles—many with silk patelots and wide skirts... We observe them walking up and down... often by themselves, one or more in company, sometimes with a gallant they have picked up, calling at the wine vaults or restaurants to get a glass of wine or gin, or sitting down in the brilliant coffee rooms, adorned with large mirrors, to a cup of good bohea or coffee.

In 1857, the medical journal *The Lancet* had estimated that one house in every sixty in the capital was a brothel and that one woman in every sixteen was a whore—which if true meant that there were roughly 6,000 brothels and 80,000 prostitutes in London, which conforms roughly with other sources. It is almost certain that, by twenty years later, the situation had not changed much. 'I should think that prostitution in England,' asserted Scotland Yard's Howard Vincent in 1881, 'is considerably in excess of the prostitution in other countries . . .'

There were several reasons for London's booming business in 'gay' women. Perhaps the most important was that they were a built-in part of metropolitan society. They were not, as they later became, furtive figures whispering their invitation from dark doorways. In the cheerful, overtly sexual atmosphere of the music halls, the 'men about town' socialised openly with them, and certainly without shame. In the streets, such as the Haymarket, they chatted and joked with them even when they were not planning to buy their services.

This social aspect of the capital was essentially a part of the life of men—as opposed to that of their wives—but it reached right up through society. At the highest echelons, the courtesans, with their carriages in Hyde Park, maintained publically cordial relations with aristocrats, who from time to time were criticised for this in the newspapers. Even the austere and fiercely moral Gladstone was friendly with 'Skittles' who, only a few years before, had been one of the most famous women in London.

At the same time, the police were apathetic. Admittedly, the laws were completely inadequate. The British age of consent at thirteen (and prior to 1871 only 12) contrasted with France, for example, where it was twenty-one. Abduction and procuration were virtually impossible to prosecute, unless the girls owned property. Technically, the police had no powers against the brothel owners. Only the local authority could bring action but, since they normally used the police for the investigation, this did not make much practical difference. Even then, however, the only charge that could be brought was minor—keeping a disorderly house—and designed more at protecting the neighbours than curbing anything that might be going on inside.

What went on inside often merited the attention of the police but they were not particularly concerned. They took the view that these were the facts of life and they had enough trouble as it was without trying to change human nature.

Prosecutions were brought from time to time—which if nothing else proved they could be—and brothel owners were sometimes jailed. 'The houses close down' explained Police Superintendent Joseph Dunlap resignedly, to a House of Lords select committee investigating traffic in young girls, 'then they open up somewhere else'—a statement that could hardly have been more lacking in sense of urgency. Certainly, the raising of the consent age would not have made much difference in the troop towns where the Contagious Disease Acts—the instrument of Parliament's experiment with state control—were in force. Girls of eleven appeared on the prostitute registers, but there is little evidence that the police were at all aggressive about charging the clients who broke the law every time they bought their services.

In practice, of course, there was a graft-supported tolerance, as there so often is, between police and offenders all over the world. 'Unless the public peace or order is infringed,' Chicago's police chief wrote to Howard Vincent at the CID, 'we do not interfere. We deal with it as an evil to be checked but which cannot, in the present state of Society, be exterminated.' He could not have expressed the policy of Scotland Yard more exactly.

The prostitution system operated in three main forms. At the top end of the trade were the introducing houses where clients met carefully selected girls who travelled to the brothel especially for the assignation. Normally, money did not pass directly between the sexual partners. The procuress handled all the sordid financial aspects.

It was all very delicate, though it was threaded with keen promotional techniques. Regularly, the procuresses would send notes to their clients inviting them to meet their latest personality from France whose youth and beauty they would extol in provocative and often French descriptions such as 'de la plus grande fraicheur' (in the absolute bloom of youth), as one madame described her newest offering.

The Streets of London

Beneath the surface of this service to the carriage trade, there was, of course, a sub-strata of perversion. The procuresses catered for all tastes.

The introducing houses, however, supplied only a very small part of London's sexual market. By tradition, most girls sought their custom on the streets. Some of them came from 'dress houses', where they paid an exorbitant rent for food, clothing and lodgings. Because they were perpetually in debt to the owners of the houses, they lived in virtual slavery. They were under constant pressure to work, and were kept under observation on the beat. However, although the clients they brought back would be expected to buy over-priced drink from the brothel proprietor, the girls themselves received the cash for their own services, which gave them a certain very narrow degree of independence.

Other prostitutes free-lanced, taking their pick-ups to the 'accommodation' houses which were everywhere throughout the West End—often shops or coffee houses which openly displayed notices worded 'beds to be had within'. The client rented the room as well as the girl.

Police evidence suggests that, by the eighties, this free-lance trade made up the biggest section of the industry. By then the dress houses—though they still existed—were on the decline. Certainly, most of the experiences recorded by 'Walter'; the anonymous author-voluptuary quoted at the beginning of this book, are in this rent-a-bed category.

In the eleven-volume *My Secret Life* 'Walter' methodically wrote down his impressions and thoughts after each experience with 1200 women from the streets of London and the brothels of Europe. It is often monotonous and distasteful but—although it is marked by fears about the size of his 'prick' and an obviously overstated enjoyment by the girls—it provides what is now accepted as a clearly authentic and valuable record of the Victorian sexual underworld and the people who frequented it.

His descriptions are often vivid, such as his account of a visit to an accommodation house one summer morning when he was in Regent Street:

> It had been raining and the streets were dirty. In front of me I saw a well grown woman . . . She was holding her petticoats well up

out of the dirt, the common habit of even respectable women though with gay ladies the habit was to hold them up just a little higher. I saw a pair of feet in lovely boots which seemed perfection and calves which were exquisite . . . Just by Beak street, she stopped and looked in a shop . . . I followed on, passed her, then turned round and met her eye. She looked at me so steady and indifferent . . . She turned and went on without looking round. Crossing Tichborne Street, she raised her petticoats higher; it was very muddy there . . . I followed her quietly, saying as I came close 'will you come with me?'

At first she did not reply, so he repeated his question and this time she answered:

'Yes—where to?'
'Where you like—I will follow you.'
Without replying a word, she walked steadily on until she reached the house, No 13 J***s Street. [presumably James Street.] She seemed in no hurry, nor indeed conscious that I was close at her heels, though she knew it. Inside the house, she stopped at the foot of the staircase and, turning round, said in a low tone . . . 'I won't let anyone come with me unless they give me a sovereign at least.'

Walter agreed and they went upstairs, accompanied presumably by the proprietor of the house, because he describes how he paid for the room before entering and locking the door behind him. The room was 'handsome,' furnished with a big four-poster bed, and a sofa in red damask. Between the gaslights on the wall, over the mantelpiece, was a mirror leaning outwards so that anyone on the bed or the sofa could see themselves. The rent was seven shillings and sixpence for a short time or a pound for the night.

At all levels of London prostitution, however, the most vicious aspect of the trade centred on children and young girls. Thirteen year olds—their faces coloured with cheap cosmetics—paced the pavements in great numbers alongside the more mature professionals. Although there had always been a market for young teenagers, the demand for them in the second half of the century appears to have grown sharply. 'Prostitution of these very young children,' said Police Superintendent Dunlap in 1881, 'is a new thing to me . . . I should say within the last two years.' The investigating committee of the House of Lords was

The Streets of London

astonished to learn from the CID's Howard Vincent that children went out onto the streets 'with the connivance of the mother', returned home at night, and made their contribution to 'the profit of the household'.

On one occasion, Dunlap—acting for the local authority—raided an apartment over a saddler's shop in Great Windmill Street, near Piccadilly Circus, to arrest a brothel-keeper. 'In each of these rooms,' he said, 'I found an elderly gentleman in bed with two of these children . . . I got into conversation with them. They knew perfectly well that I could not touch them in the house. The girls got six shillings each from the men who had also paid six shillings for the room.'

Inevitably, Walter included young girls—'juvenile punks,' as he called them—in his range of sexual experience and, as he got older, his need for them became unpleasantly sadistic. However, his description of a 'voluptuous evening' with a couple of young teenagers, though appalling in the picture it draws of social conditions, is completely revealing.

As usual, he was in Regent Street one evening when :

> three quite little ones passed me together. It was, though early, quite dark and so foggy that it was possible I might be mistaken. Were they modest or immodest? I chirped with my tongue, saying in a low tone 'come here' and I passed them and walked up ***** Street.
>
> That street was quiet. I walked quickly on in the fog, heard small feet pattering after me, turned round and there were two of them. We could not now see across the road for the fog . . .
>
> 'How old are you?'
> 'Fifteen.'
> 'Have you any hair on your cunt?'
> 'Only a little, Sir, but she has none—have you, Louey? . . . Come with us and we'll both strip naked.'
>
> While Louey kept watch for any approaching police in the fog, Walter 'felt' the girl. 'You let men fuck you don't you?' he said. 'Do they hurt you?'
>
> 'Not if their things aren't too big. I won't let them if they are.'
>
> 'My letch,' Walter recorded, 'was satisfied in ascertaining how small her cunt was and I gave her a shilling.'
>
> 'Oh give me another. You've been feeling a long time.'

The Streets of London

Walter left them to dine at his club, then returned and took them to a room in a local accommodation house. He was always keenly interested in the girls he hired—which despite his perversions and near-sadism, lends his revelations a warmth that pornography normally lacks—and he questioned them. 'Both had been fucked a year, they told me . . . they said they were not fucked every night but someone felt them every night. Sometimes two or three did. "Mother knows," said one of them . . . They often frigged gentlemen in the street, they told me.'

Eventually, he selected one 'almost hiding her little body with mine', and, inevitably as with all Walter's girls, she had to enjoy it. 'I fucked her slowly at first and the little one spent with me . . . Making her spend gave me much voluptuous gratification, she was so artless in her pleasure.'

Since working class girls in the nineteenth century rarely reached puberty until they were sixteen, his description of her enjoyment was almost certainly a wild exaggeration but, apart from this, the scene he draws and the dialogue he reports are clearly an authentic account of what happened—and what happened every night to young girls in London.

At one stage, he asked them 'to suck my pego for another shilling,' which they 'both refused but in five minutes acceded, tempted by the promised gift'.

Walter was playing a gentleman's game in a society that had seen the emergence of the British middle class with its reverence for wealth. Payment provided him with complete licence to use these girls how he liked. However, he was a thinking man, and the fact that he repeatedly justified his taste for very young girls throughout his memoirs suggests that he experienced a sense of guilt about this aspect of his sexual life.

The appeal of the extremely young girl as a sexual partner seems both repellant and strange, but it was logical against a background of Victorian culture. By definition, prostitutes were the exact opposite of the 'pure' women who were so honoured. Under these circumstances, it was inevitable that virginity—with its unique first time element of possession—should acquire an enormous market premium. In London

The Streets of London

in 1885, the going price for a virgin could be as high in the top brothels as £20 to £25—a fantastic sum against the cost of living levels of the time—and, although the rate dropped off sharply after defloration, young girls who had not long been seduced were much in demand. The pure, or the nearly pure, were often preferred to the expert.

The demand created a whole trade in girls. Many poor families put their daughters on the streets on a regular basis or, if their pride did not permit them to go so far, sold them for one night, after which they returned to more 'respectable' employment. Professionals developed skilled and practised techniques for supplying the voracious demand from the brothels.

No young girl was safe from the procurers. They waited like vultures at the railway stations. They took journeys on trains in the hope of setting up an acquaintance. They walked in the parks and got talking to young nursemaids pushing children in prams. They met the boats from Ireland and the Continent. They stood at the gates of the factories, and watched the girls streaming out after work and selected likely 'marks' as they called them.

Employment bureaux and even some employers—such as millinery shops—were often recruiting houses for the brothels, advertising jobs that were very different from what the girls expected. Much of the trade to the Continent—where the procuring laws were far stricter than in Great Britain—was handled in this way, with the girls under the impression that they were going into domestic service.

Virtually all the techniques were based on luring the prospect into a house. The procurers did this by winning their confidence, arranging for a trip to the West End and making sure that the girl lost her last train home. Then a bed for the night would be offered by a friend—almost always an apparently respectable middle-aged lady. Faced with inevitability of rape, some girls accepted the situation. Others fought and screamed and had to be either held or strapped down while the act was committed. Very young girls were sometimes chloroformed.

The situation—like so many others in Victorian England—was scandalous and in drastic need of correction. But it was, in fact, only one aspect of prostitution in London.

The Streets of London

In common with Charles Dickens and most of the Victorian public, Benjamin Scott and his campaigners saw the prostitute as a woman living in such utter degradation and misery and shame that suicide was never very far from her thoughts. This was just not true. Although some, of course, conformed with this picture, many of the girls on the London streets were there because the life appealed to them—appealed to them, at least, more than the alternatives that faced them in Victorian England.

Walter's impression of prostitutes was in striking contrast to the sad, downcast-eyes image of Victorian literature: 'I enjoyed their lubricity, their skilled embraces, their passionate fucking when they wanted it themselves... yet I was tired of their lies, tricks and dissatisfied money-grubbing, money-begging style.'

Walter is suspect as an authority—but he had strong backing in his basic reporting of the scene. Henry Mayhew, the leading authority on London life, mocked the ruling concept of the girls on the streets as social outcasts victimised by male lust, and emphasised that the idea that virginity was so priceless was limited to the upper stratas of the community. 'To be unchaste among the lower classes,' he wrote, 'is not always a subject of reproach. The commerce of the sexes is so general that to have been immodest is very seldom a bar to marriage.'

In 1890, a prison chaplain named G. P. Merrick conducted a survey of fallen women. 'I was of the opinion, as many people are,' he recorded, 'that the career of every woman of the streets could be written and summed up within a few words—seduced, deserted, cast off by relations. I thought that every poor outcast was the victim of some man's brutal lust and heartless abandonment. But ... I soon found, on the authority of the erring women themselves, that the common impression and my own were altogether wrong.' Of the 16,000 women the reverend interviewed, more than eleven thousand took the sexual plunge willingly and deliberately. Less than 700—only 4 per cent—conformed with the sex campaigners' view of harlotry in that they had been 'betrayed by gentlemen'.

Walter describes one encounter with a young girl who evidently had a cheerful approach to prostitution. Left at home in charge of the children while both parents went out to work, she would lock the youngsters in the house and make for the West End. Insisting that she was not 'gay' because she did not make her living by it—a subtle definition that amused Walter—she tried to explain why she sold herself:

'I buy things to eat . . . I buy foods and gives the others what mother gives me; they don't know any better . . . sometimes we have only gruel and salt; if we have a fire we toast the bread, but I can't eat it if I'm not dreadfully hungry.'

'What do you like?'

'Pies and sausage rolls,' said the girl smacking her lips and laughing, 'Oh my eye, ain't they prime, oh!'

'That's what you went gay for?'

'I ain't gay,' she said sulkily.

'Well what you let men fuck you for . . . Sausage rolls?'

'Yes, meat pies and pastries, too.'

Walter, being a man of his time, was not touched by the poverty she described—only by her quick humour.

Police Superintendent Joseph Dunlap explained to the peers investigating the white slave traffic, how many teenagers moved into prostitution in the West End. 'Little servant girls come out on errands,' he said. 'They see these girls walking about the streets, their equal in social standing. They see them dressed in silks and satins; they do not think of the way they get their money; they say: "You can go and dress in silks and satins while I am slaving." They talk to the girls and they are influenced . . .'

Even William Stead, who tended to overdramatise as much as Benjamin Scott, admitted that many girls fell because of 'the temptation that well-dressed vice can offer to the poor.'

The prostitution system of the nineteenth century—with its obeisance to male sexual need, its protection of 'modest' women, and its tolerance of cruel excess—was serviced by terrible poverty. For most women, the streets were an alternative to the treadmill of the factories, with incredibly long hours in awful conditions, or to domestic service—often working for a tyrant—which then employed almost as many people as industry.

The seduction that was the necessary evil choice open to a young girl —or to her parents—had to be balanced against the evils inherent in another: the death of children, for example, who fell asleep into the mill machinery.

Walter paid his two Lolitas half a sovereign each. However repugnant they may have found the experience—though habit must have planed down much of their sensibility—the pay was attractively high for half an evening's effort. At a time when the average wage for adult men was only 15/- a week, girls of this age would have had to work for many days in a factory, or weeks in domestic service, to earn as much. Mrs Armstrong, who was to prove so important in Stead's drama in 1885, said she expected her daughter, Eliza, to receive 2/6 a week as a servant.

The exposé, therefore, that Benjamin Scott was asking William Stead to publish involved a situation that was locked into a complex social structure. The revelations would be unwelcome to a very large number of people—to middle class parents such as the 'outraged mother' who complained to Josephine Butler's society about 'the uplifting of the veil which screens the indecencies of street life in crowded cities from the modesties of family life at home;' to prostitutes' families who might be robbed of income and forced to earn it in far harder and even more unpleasant ways; to the moralists who wanted to see lusts channelled away from 'modest' women; and, of course, to the clients, some of whom were powerful men.

It was a potential opposition that—because the suggested involvement of the *Gazette* added another dimension—would be more formidable than Benjamin Scott and Josephine Butler had fought hitherto. Later, Stead wrote that what finally determined him to go ahead was the link between the 'violation and trapping of young girls' with the quashing of the prosecution promoted by Scott's organisation against the London brothel-owner, and the 'foreign trade'.

In fact, by the date of that meeting in the *Gazette* offices, the most detailed and incontestable evidence that Scott was able to hand over to the editor was almost totally concerned with the 'foreign trade'. For many years, Scott had been a very active supporter of Josephine Butler and her campaign against state prostitution, but he did not become passionately militant, until a Quaker named Alfred Dyer displayed before him proof of a fully-organised white slave ring, that was shipping young girls to virtual imprisonment in the official brothels of Europe.

3
Enter the White Knight

ON a damp Sunday evening in the late September of 1879 Alfred Dyer, a publisher of religious tracts, learned almost casually that a young English girl was held captive in a Brussels brothel and 'was contemplating suicide as the only means of escape from her awful condition.'

Dyer was walking home with another Quaker after a Friends' meeting in the London business district of Clerkenwell. As the two men strolled through the streets of tall, grey, grimy buildings, his companion told him the story that he had heard from a debauched acquaintance who, on a recent trip to the Belgian capital, had visited an officially-authorised *maison tolerée*. The girl he had selected, Dyer reported later, 'had implored him with tears to aid her escape,' but 'he had left her to her fate, probably fearing that any attempt at her rescue would end in publicity.'

The news would have aroused the reforming instincts of any member of the many rescue societies that then existed, but its impact on Alfred Dyer was far more traumatic: for this thin, bony, ascetic of thirty-one was a religious fanatic who saw sin almost exclusively in terms of sex. To Dyer, engaged in a constant and bitter struggle with the Anti-Christ, the key area of conflict with his skilled and artful enemy lay in the lustful urges.

Although Dyer played a vital part in the campaign against the brothel operators, he alone among the sex reformers appears an utterly ridiculous character. All of them were genuinely, if a bit self-consciously devout. Stead was always dropping to his knees and praying before he entered 'the dens of iniquity' in search of copy. All of the campaigners, too, saw prostitution in wildly overdramatic terms.

But, even today in the perspective of history, they have retained a certain stature and, though their clichéd ardour and their purple phraseology can be tiresome, they command respect. They had great courage and, even if they cheated sometimes in their distortion of facts, they were cheating in what was probably a good cause.

Alfred Dyer had courage, too, and there is certainly no doubt about his missionary fervour in the cause of God but unfortunately—ferociously serious though he was—nature had selected him to be a clown. If there had been a banana skin on the floor of any of the Belgian brothels, into which he ventured with such tight lips, he would assuredly have slipped on it. Everything he did was clumsy which, perhaps, was not all that strange; for subtlety did not come easily to a man at grips with Satan in his home manor.

Dyer was an extremist in his horror of sex, even for that sex-taboo period, but a lot of his beliefs were shared to *some* extent by many Victorians. Masturbation, for example, was commonly regarded as an enormous sin, not only for the moral objections there might be to the practice, but also because it was believed to be physically harmful. The ruling attitude to male semen was not all that different to the general view of money. Because it was a life force, it should not be wasted which, in any kind of sex act that came to climax, it inevitably was. This was why the contemporary phrase for orgasm, used even by Walter who never for one minute considered curtailing his activities, was 'to spend'. Inevitably, Dyer took the theory far further. In *Plain Words to Young Men on an Avoided Subject,* he warned that self-abuse was mortally dangerous and quoted terrifying examples of boys who had so exhausted their strength by masturbation that they no longer had the will to survive the night.

Nothing that could be remotely stimulating sexually, no matter how mild the level, was acceptable to Alfred Dyer in his fevered battle with the devil. Even so apparently innocent a pastime as dancing—'promiscuous dancing,' he called it, as though it was some kind of orgy—was morally dangerous and should be rigidly avoided. 'The ballroom blunts the moral susceptibilities, fosters the sensual and ruins spirituality,' he declared stoutly. As evidence, he quoted the police chief of a great, though unidentified, American city who had stated

Enter the White Knight

that this was the cause of the downfall of three quarters of its outcast women.

Coarse jokes and 'veiled sentences of double meaning about women and courtship,' he asserted, 'are the revelation of the heart of a leper'. Art that featured the nude was merely 'an opportunity for gratifying the lustful eye'. The written word could be just as bad. 'Foul reading (no matter how fashionable the book or periodical) . . . is the gateway to foul deeds.' 'Fleshly poetry' was making 'the so-called leaders of society the tools of an aestheticism which has . . . the heart of a beast.' He could not even watch some little girls cavorting in the road to the music of an Italian organ grinder without brooding that 'the dance was an immodest one that had been learned on the boards of a theatre' and contemplating gloomily on the 'probable future of these children, the bloom of whose modesty had been destroyed ere they reached maidenhood'.

Dyer's attack on sin was not entirely negative. Dramatically, he urged every young man to become a 'white knight,' his symbol of a reverent attitude towards women. It is probable, though Dyer does not appear to say so specifically in his writings, that this phrase was derived from the 'White Cross' purity movement, active both in America and Britain. Again this conformed with the ideals and attitudes of many Victorians even of they did not see the situation in quite such unabashedly sentimental terms as Dyer, who explained that 'a white knight' is the man 'who delights to weave a crown of laurels to place on the brow of womanhood'.

Inevitably, for a man with these beliefs, the revelations about the English girl in the Belgian brothel—whose clients were the very antithesis of 'white knights'—induced in Alfred Dyer a terrible sense of shock that quickly became transformed into a personal call from God. He was consumed with a violent, angry determination to fight this evil. Immediately, he planned a crusade to rescue the girl from 'the deeper depths of sin'—and any other English girls who were in her predicament. And it so happened—since the white slave trade was specially prosperous at the time—that there were quite a lot of them.

Dyer—who was already a member of a City of London committee dedicated, under the chairmanship of Benjamin Scott, to helping

Enter the White Knight

Josephine Butler in her fight against state prostitution—lost no time in gathering the evidence. With what must have been some effort, he called on the man who had passed the information about the brothel to his Quaker friend and was given a full run down on what the girl had told him.

He had found her, he said, in one of the houses in the Rue St Laurent, a famous redlight street in Brussels. Her name was Ellen Newland, but because she was under twenty-one—minors being forbidden in Belgian brothels by law—she had been registered with the police under a false birth certificate of an adult woman.

Her story conformed with the stock Victorian picture of the 'fallen' woman. 'She was courted in London by a man of gentlemanly exterior,' Dyer reported, 'who promised her marriage if she would accompany him for that purpose to Brussels.' At Calais Station, on the way to Belgium, he had told her that he had mislaid all his money and would have to return to England to obtain some more. However, they had just met a friend of his on the platform and he suggested that she should go on with him to Brussels, where he would join her later. When Ellen objected, because she did not like the look of the stranger, he pushed her into the carriage, slammed the door behind her and the train started moving.

Ellen had been taken to the brothel in the Rue St Laurent and, horrified, had watched her escort being paid in cash for her delivery. She had been interrogated at the police station in French—which she did not understand—registered and examined by police doctors for VD. Her clothes had been taken from her and she had been given a seductive negligee-type dress worn by all the girls in the Belgian brothels.

Although the door of the brothel could be opened easily from the outside, it had no handle on the inside. The only way of opening it was with a key retained by members of the *maison* staff. By law—presumably to preserve the public decency—the girls were not allowed to show themselves at the windows. In theory, any girl was free to leave a *maison tolerée* when she chose—and notices on the walls of each brothel proclaimed this fact in four languages—but in practice, since the owners had paid for their merchandise, they rigorously discouraged any intentions to leave. Ellen Newland, in short, was a prisoner.

Dyer, however, now had enough facts to set up an investigation. He wrote to a non-conformist friend in Belgium, Pastor Leonard Anet, asked him to find the girl and do what he could to send her home. The pastor traced her quite easily, but by this time she was in the special prostitutes VD ward in Brussel's Hôpital St Pierre, held there under the authority of the Belgian Police des Moeurs (Morals Police) who controlled the brothels. Since she was now cured, she was about to be returned to the Maison Roger in the Rue St Laurent, but under pressure from the pastor, she was released and sent back to England. On the day after Christmas she arrived in London where Dyer met her.

Already, Dyer had been to see her parents, travelled to Brighton, where Ellen had been a maid, and interviewed her employer. 'I had received satisfactory replies to my enquiries regarding her character,' he recorded. It was, in fact, on her day off—when she had taken a trip to London to find a new job—that she had met the man who had persuaded her to cross the channel with him.

By then, too, Dyer had learned from Pastor Anet of another dramatic case that was far more flagrant. On an evening in October— soon after Pastor Anet had started looking for Ellen Newland—a young artillery lieutenant had just finished a spell of duty at the Barracks of St Elizabeth and was wandering along the Rue des Sables that intersected the Rue St Laurent. Suddenly, he saw a crowd surrounding a young girl who was crying hysterically. Dressed in a negligée, she was screaming that she had escaped from a house at Number 28 where she had been decoyed and held captive. The 'Gouvernante' of the house—the manageress—was angrily demanding that the girl should return at once, but she was prevented by the crowd from using force.

Further back up the road, another girl who had escaped at the same time—also in the uniform negligée—had not been so fortunate. Two of the strong women the brothels employed to control the girls, had caught her and were dragging her screaming back to Number 28.

Meanwhile, the men in the crowd round the first girl—including

Enter the White Knight

the lieutenant—agreed to protect her from the furious madame, set up a collection on the spot to provide her with funds, then conducted her to a local hotel, where they entrusted her to the manager until proper arrangements could be made.

It did not do young Ada Higgleton much good. That evening, a man named Henri Perpeté arrived at the hotel reception desk and said he was from the police department. He invited Ada to accompany him to his office to give her evidence on this sad affair. And that was the end of her brief spell of freedom. Perpeté was nothing to do with the police—though, even if he had been, the result would have been the same—and by that night Ada was back in a brothel. Not the same one, for enquiries were certain to be promoted by the lieutenant, but the *maisons* in the Rue St Laurent worked very closely together.

In London, however, Dyer had all the facts he needed to publicise the cross-Channel traffic in girls. With Ellen Newland back in England, he even had a real live 'white slave' that he could produce as proof for anyone who disbelieved him.

On 1 January, 1880, he broke the story that young English teenagers were being shipped into the Brussels brothels. He mailed a letter to all the London dailies, citing his two examples. The following morning, three of them—the *Daily News*, the *Standard*, and the *Daily Chronicle*—all ran it prominently.

Dyer's letter sparked a spate of correspondence in the newspapers. Among it was an angry denial from Edward Lenaers, chief of the Brussels Morals Police, insisting that all girls entered the houses of their own free will, and had to state this formally to a police officer before they were permitted to do so. The police chief had strong support—astonishingly, in view of the facts that were soon to emerge —from Thomas Jeffes, the consular official in the British Legation responsible for British subjects who might be in trouble. 'From the experience I have gained in these and other similar cases,' he wrote to the London papers, 'I can confidently assure the parents of all really virtuous girls that there is no fear whatever of finding their children in the same position as the girls referred to in Mr Dyer's letter.'

If Alfred Dyer, engrossed as he was with his battle with evil, over-

41

stated the situation—which he probably did—Jeffes quite clearly and rather strangely understated it. By this time, the chaplain to the British Embassy had reported a marked increase in the number of British girls in the VD ward at the Hôpital St Pierre where he had gone—so Dyer claimed—only as a result of Pastor's Anet's trailing of Ellen Newland. There was no doubt that Jeffes knew that British girls were in the Belgian brothels, and it followed logically that some arrangement must have been made to get them there.

Dyer, of course, suspected bribery but it was more probable that Jeffes, like so many Victorian men, had a paradoxical attitude to prostitutes. Although he probably accepted the current view that most girls 'fell' as the result of some man's brutal lust, once the damage was done they moved into a kind of sub-human category that merited little sympathy.

In evidence before the House of Lords Committee on the traffic in girls the following year, he explained that almost all of them were prostitutes before they left England, and knew the type of life that they were heading for. What took them by surprise was the complete lack of liberty that life in a Belgian brothel involved. But even if Jeffes was correct in his basic premise—and subsequent proof showed that he was not—he appeared completely unmoved by the element of imprisonment.

However, Jeffes' support of the Brussels police only served to convince Dyer that the white slave trade was being operated with the full support and connivance of the international Establishment. By then, Josephine Butler had sent him details of a case that had just been heard in the French courts. A man named Jean Sallecartes, who had six times been convicted of crimes by British courts including one revealing charge of beating up his mother, had been tried in Paris for abducting minors.

With the help of a friend, Sallecartes—whose name was soon to be well known to Dyer, and later to Stead, as a key figure in the white slave network—had been taking three girls across the channel to the French Port of Boulogne, in the steamer *Cologne*. Some of the crew recognised him from a previous voyage in another channel steamer. On that occasion Sallecartes had been with a couple of teenagers, but the captain had guessed the character of the trip and shipped the two girls home.

When the *Cologne* docked at Boulogne, the suspicious seamen tailed the two 'placeurs'—as the white slavers who handled the transport end of the business were known—to the town's red light district, grabbed the two men, handed them over to the police, and took the girls back to their ship for return to England.

The news of the Sallecartes trial, plus further information from Belgium, convinced Dyer that Ellen Newland and Ada Higgleton were not exceptions. The traffic in girls into the continental state brothels was on a large scale and operated by an organised vice ring.

Dyer's letters to the press had caused a temporary furore but, so far as he could see now that the dust had begun to clear, had provoked no action by the government to curb the trade. In truth, though, he was wrong. Lord Salisbury, the Foreign Secretary, had instructed British Ambassadors in several European countries, including Belgium, to seek formal co-operation from the authorities for an investigation by a British police detective who would soon be leaving for the Continent. The Belgian Minister of Justice had ordered a special enquiry into Dyer's allegations. The British Consul in Brussels had made a rather mild request that the Belgian authorities should prosecute those brothels that were harbouring any British minors—a possibility which the police, of course, hotly denied.

However, Alfred Dyer was completely unaware of this behind-the-scene activity that was resulting directly from his sensational January letter. He decided that, since the awful situation that he had revealed was being ignored in official circles, more drastic action was needed. So the 'white knight' decided to go to Brussels himself, enter the brothels in the guise of a client and rescue the girls he found.

For support—and to protect himself from blackmail—he persuaded another Quaker to go with him. This was George Gillett, described by one of the girls as 'an old gentleman wearing moustaches,' who, since he had married into the powerful Rowntree chocolate family, was one of the top members of the English Society of Friends. Gillett's role, as he testified later—apart from answering any accusations of immorality that might come from unsympathetic quarters—was to help his friend to get alone with any English girls so that he could discuss escape proposals with them.

And so these two devout English gentlemen left London for Brussels to pose as lecherous roués. Dyer reported his visit in very great detail in *The European Slave Trade in English Girls*. Even if Dyer's burst of publicity in January had not already alerted the Belgian police and the brothels network, the plan was completely absurd. No one could possibly have confused Dyer—with his pathological reaction to sex in even its mildest forms—with a man in need of a woman. The whole operation seemed doomed before it started. Yet astonishingly, clumsy and stumbling though it was, it served its purpose.

At six o'clock on the evening of 27 February, the two men strode resolutely up the Rue St Laurent—the street of 'licensed hells'—and stopped at Number 12 where, so Dyer had been informed, there was a girl who was keen to escape. They entered the house, sat down in the salon and 'to avoid the object of my visit being suspected' ordered some champagne—'which however being a total abstainer, I did not drink.' With the air of a sexual connoisseur, Dyer asked to see all the girls the house had to offer.

Whether or not the 'Gouvernante' believed he was genuine—which is hard to credit, though of course brothels had to cater for strange customers—she called the girls into the salon and Dyer, playing his part as a high liver, offered them all champagne. Then he asked which of them were English. Only one of them responded—a London girl named Louisa Bond—and Dyer indicated that she was his choice. Politely, he asked the others if they would mind leaving them alone and they all left the room except for a German girl called Matilda who, since she could speak English, remained to partner the moustached George Gillett.

Gillett, stoutly performing his role in the operation, gallantly asked Matilda to take him upstairs—though Louisa testified later that Matilda told her they did 'nothing more than drink champagne'. At last Dyer was able to tell Louisa the real purpose of his visit. Her story was similar to that of Ellen Newland. She had been working in a London store when she met a man who said he was a doctor. He made

Enter the White Knight

love to her and suggested she should go to Brussels with him to take up a very good job he could get her in one of the city's shops. Inevitably, she had ended up in a brothel watching the *tenant-maison* paying off her seducer for delivering 'the parcel'.

At Dyer's escape suggestion, so he wrote later, 'she became overcome with joy which, however, was in a few minutes dispelled by an apparent sense of agonised bewilderment as she began to realise her true position.' She could not leave the house in the *decolleté* outfit she was wearing. Her own clothes were locked up under the care of the management. In any case, any attempt to leave would be stopped by the men the brothels retained to deal with unruly clients, and Dyer would be 'half killed'. Dyer conceded that he and Gillett might not be strong enough on their own to handle a rough house, and suggested he should return with a larger party.

The two men left the brothel promising to return for her the following morning with friends. But, as they discussed the project on their way back to their hotel, the whole plan seemed a bit drastic—at any rate at that stage. As Dyer commented to Gillett, the Belgian officials had stated in the London press that they 'were desirous to give every facility to English girls to leave these houses'. Should they not give the authorities an opportunity of proving it?

The following morning, Dyer and Gillett, accompanied by a Brussels attorney named Dr Alexis Splingard, called on the Procureur du Roi —the official who was responsible for the morals police—and applied for Louisa's release from the brothel.

Since the whole issue of English girls in Belgian brothels was under official enquiry as the direct result of Alfred Dyer's allegations, the Procureur was not very sympathetic. 'The girl,' he said coldly, so Dyer reported later, 'has the right to leave the house at any moment.'

'Legally, that might be so,' answered Dyer, 'but practically she's the victim of intimidation.'

The Procureur shrugged his shoulders. He had no powers, he said, to grant the application. So Dyer reminded him of the statements in the British press that the Belgian authorities were willing to help protect British women. 'If you can't help me officially,' insisted Dyer, 'then I appeal to your courtesy as a gentleman to at least give me a

Enter the White Knight

private note to whoever does have the power to comply with my request.'

The Procureur stared at him stonily. 'How can I be sure that you're who you represent yourself to be?' he asked.

'I can, of course, prove his identity, Monsieur le Procureur,' Dr Splingard, the attorney, interposed.

The Procureur was not prepared to argue. 'You can apply to the local Commissioner of Police in the district,' he said, 'and he can help you if he chooses.' And the interview ended.

His attitude only served to strengthen Alfred Dyer's conviction that he was not only fighting the brothel operators of Brussels: he was in open combat with the police.

At the local police station he encountered an attitude that was even more aggressively unhelpful than he had met in the office of the Procureur. The deputy commissioner interviewed them and stubbornly refused to accede to Dyer's request. 'It is necessary,' he explained, 'to protect these houses on account of the capital invested in them by the owners.'

Shocked, Dyer insisted that he was not concerned with the brothels' return on investment but with an English girl who was held captive.

At last, the police official rose wearily to his feet and said he would go personally to the house and find out if she truly desired to leave.

'May I be permitted to accompany you?' asked Dyer.

'Oh no,' he answered, 'Your presence might influence her decision.' And he stalked out of the police station on his way to the Rue St Laurent.

After a few minutes, he returned, smiling broadly. Mr Dyer's story, he said, was completely untrue. He had talked to the girl, both in the presence of the *tenant-maison* and alone. On each occasion, she insisted that she was quite content, that madame treated her well and that she had no desire to leave.

Dyer faced the fact that the official channels were clearly closed. The only way of rescuing Louisa was by frontal attack. To deal with the problem of what she would wear—since she could not walk about the streets of Brussels in a negligee and slippers—he bought some walking shoes and a waterproof with which, as he later explained, in testimony, 'she could cover her underclothes'.

Enter the White Knight

That afternoon, the three men—Dyer, Gillett and Splingard—made their raid on the Rue St Laurent. As they marched into the house, one of them stayed by the door to stop it closing—since a key would then be needed to open it.

'The mistress,' Dyer recorded, 'was standing with another woman in the hall, her face white with rage.'

Dyer demanded to see Louisa. The madame refused angrily. 'If ever you return,' she warned, 'I can promise you that you will not be well received'—which Dyer took to be a threat that she would have them beaten up.

In fact, Louisa was watching—for later, in testimony before the Procureur, she recounted the occasion—but Dyer could not see her, or else he might have grabbed her. As it was, he had no alternative but to retire with what dignity he could retain.

As the three men walked down the road away from the house, one of the brothel's strong arm men ran after them and brandished his fists. 'If you come back,' he threatened, 'I'll break your heads open.'

Dyer was not beaten yet. He drove to the British Legation and demanded to see Sir Saville Lumley, the minister, claiming his protection for a British subject whose life 'he had reason to fear was in hourly danger'.

Only five days before, Sir Saville had written to the Foreign Office in London reporting that the Brussels inspector of police had stated that 'illegal and arbitrary detention in tolerated houses in Brussels was materially impossible as the girls residing are visited twice a week by a doctor and frequently by the Inspector himself.' [The full background story of Dyer's visit to Brussels is in Sir Saville Lumley's correspondence with the Foreign Office, now in the open Home Office papers in the Public Record Office in London.] Apparently, it never occurred to Sir Saville that the Inspector—whose control of the brothels Dyer had criticised in his letters to the press—might himself be involved in the vice racket.

Clearly, the minister saw Dyer as a religious fanatic—which he was —but it so happened he had stumbled on a real white slave ring, that truly needed urgent attention. At any rate, the angry Quaker got short shrift at the British Legation. Sir Saville refused to see him and one

Enter the White Knight

of the legation secretaries referred him to Mr Maltby, the vice-consul.

Dyer was furious. 'If this young woman is the victim of violence,' he warned, 'the responsibility will rest with the British Minister'—a threat which must have nagged Sir Saville, for that afternoon he saw the Minister of Justice who ordered an immediate inquiry into the case of Louisa Bond. The anxiety in official circles was indicated by the fact that the investigation was held the following day even though it was a Sunday.

But, as before, no one explained this to the frustrated Alfred Dyer who, in the belief that nothing was happening, stalked out of the legation and hurried to the consular office to see Mr Maltby.

Mr Maltby, however, always left his office at 4.0 pm for his home in the country. It was then after 5.0. Still utterly determined, poor Dyer took a cab to the village where Maltby lived. 'Oh,' said the vice consul, 'you should have applied to the Minister.' Then when Dyer explained that he already had, Maltby referred him to the pro-consul, Thomas Jeffes. 'This is really his department,' he said.

It was not Alfred Dyer's day. For Jeffes, of course, was the official who had written to the press following Dyer's publicity campaign in January, assuring the parents of virtuous girls that they had no need to worry. And, to be fair to Mr Jeffes, Louisa Bond was not, by definition, a virtuous girl. For she had been seduced before she arrived in Brussels. At any rate, when Dyer arrived at his house, he told him he would 'communicate with the proper authorities in the morning'.

'But the girl ought to be removed immediately,' insisted Dyer angrily. 'Her life's in danger.'

'Mr Dyer,' answered the pro-consul coldly, 'I have no power to have her removed.'

It did not seem as though Alfred Dyer's conflict with the Devil was going too well. He faced a wall of opposition. Together with George Gillett, he visited other houses but, although the girls seemed unhappy, he was not able to persuade any of them to make a break for freedom. At Number 109 Rue de Pacheco, for example, Ann Jones told him that 'she did not wish to escape because she thought her case was hopeless and would not know what she would do if she did.' He was

Enter the White Knight

not much more successful at 5 Rue de Persil where he found two English girls, Anne Williams and Louisa Hennessey. They would have welcomed the chance to escape but they did not trust the two strange men who, as Louisa later related, 'came with a waterproof and tried to persuade me and Annie Williams to go. They said they would see us safe back, but Madame said they wanted us to go to worse places than hers. I thought this might be true. She said the police were after them.'

However, with the help of Pastor Anet, the two men discovered Adeline Tanner in the prostitutes' ward of the Hôpital St Pierre, although she insisted that she had never had VD.

Adeline's story was horrifying, and there was certainly no doubt in her mind about her desire to escape. She had been transported to Belgium as a virgin—taken, in fact, by the *placeur* Jean Sallecartes who was now in a French jail—but a vaginal malformation had made the sex act impossible for her. Several men had paid for the privilege of trying but at last the brothel had sent her to the Hôpital St Pierre for an operation to make her usable as a prostitute—an operation, so she claimed, that had been conducted with great callousness. The other inmates of the ward, she said, had been appalled by the sound of her shrieks. Adeline had not yet been cleared by the doctors, but, when she was, she would return to the brothel that had bought her in the Rue St Laurent—a move which, of course, the two crusaders were determined to stop.

Dyer and Gillett had now faced the fact that their raiding techniques were impractical. Their only hope was to set up so much pressure through official channels—in particular the Home Office in London—that the Belgians would be forced to arrange the repatriation of the English girls concerned.

Their big fear was that their activities might already have endangered the lives of the girls—and they were right. Ada Higgleton, the girl who had made the dramatic break for freedom the previous year, had disappeared. Soon, too, all trace was to be lost of Louisa Bond, the girl who had 'trembled with joy' at the prospect of escape.

Dyer and Gillett saw everything to do with prostitution in horrific magnified terms, and their claims were challenged constantly by the

Enter the White Knight

British legation staff in Brussels. In some cases—such as Adeline Tanner who, claimed Thomas Jeffes, had never had an operation and whose screams could not, therefore, have been heard throughout the hospital—the conflicting versions could have applied to different girls. In any case, there can be no doubt that, however much Dyer's fevered, sex-obsessed imagination embroidered the facts, the operation of the Brussels brothels and the trade that supplied them was vicious and desperately in need of a clean-up.

When, at the end of 1880, the Home Office sent a London lawyer named Thomas Snagge to investigate, he reported that cases of direct cruelty were not numerous because it was:

> in the interests of the proprietors of the houses to reconcile the girls to what is in fact a life of dismal bondage, accompanied by dissipation and drink. From the point of view of the procureurs young girls are a form of merchandise to be acquired by industry and disposed of at a market price per parcel—'par collis'. Three hundred francs 'par collis' appears to be the ordinary tariff. From the point of view of the brothel keepers, the girls form a costly portion of their stock in trade; they are like stock upon a farm, kept in good condition more or less and prevented from straying or escaping.

The girls saw little of the money they made since they were kept in a permanent state of debt; for the *tenants-maison*, in addition to charging them for clothes and lodging, also debited them with their purchase price. Also, if they had arrived with false birth certificates—as most of the English girls had—they could hold over them the permanent threat of prosecution and jail for misrepresentation.

The supply organisation was run on the same cattle-trading lines. The 'packages' were ordered by the brothels from London and other European cities. The placeurs went out and found girls who met the specifications and shipped them to their destination.

There were some young prostitutes in Brussels who had truly left England for the Continent to take up genuine jobs as domestic servants or—as in the case of the convent-raised Mary McLoughlin—as nursery governesses. Even though the nuns themselves had vetted Mary's employer, she had ended up in a brothel in the Rue St Laurent. Monsieur Paul, who ran a 'straight' employment agency in the Belgian capital, also supplied the voracious demand for livestock in the state-approved sex houses.

Some reports suggested that there were auctions in Brussels but, apart from veiled statements to this effect by Adeline Tanner and the sex reformers—who cannot have been too sure of their facts or they would have played them up—there is little evidence to support this. Clearly, there was a lot of movement of girls between the brothels—but then it was probably sound business to vary the merchandise.

Other reports indicated the development of a whole range of techniques for 'breaking girls' into the life—especially if they came from respectable homes—but, in the closed brothel system, this would not seem to have been necessary. They arrived, as was testified in the Brussels courtroom, crying and shocked—young girls in a foreign country, imprisoned with other women who had long resigned themselves to their situation. If they refused to comply with the demands of clients—of clients, at least, who did not enjoy resistance—then they were beaten. In court, Emily Ellen, a twenty-two-year-old British girl, stated that she was thrashed—and one of the others testified that she saw her sobbing. This was not contested under cross-examination by Ann Josephine Parent, the 'Gouvernante' of the Rue St Laurent house that had bought Emily. 'She was naughty,' she said as though this explained everything. 'She would not lie down when a patron was in the room,' added another member of the management.

Josephine Butler described what one girl, sent to the Butler home by Pastor Leonard Anet, had told her.

> The keeper of this house in Brussels, enraged with her because of her persistent refusal to participate in some exceptionally base proceedings among his clients, had her carried to an underground chamber, whence her cries could not be heard. She was here immured and starved and several times scourged with a thong of leather. But she did not yield . . . all the time strengthened and comforted by the thought that Jesus had himself been cruelly scourged . . .

The story is typically overplayed, but the report of the punishment was probably true. 'Yielding' in a brothel was always a matter of degree. If the *tenant-maison* relinquished a girl of his own free will, it would not have been because she did not yield but because she was not suitable material, for the proprietors assessed their new girls with the same kind of careful study that a racehorse trainer views his two-year-olds.

Walter, in *My Secret Life*, gave a client's eye view of the European brothels that was, of course, very different to the tortured picture drawn by Alfred Dyer and the other campaigners. It was probably just as distorted but it provides a degree of balance.

He was not very impressed by the Brussels *maisons*—though he noted that one was a 'splendidly furnished house'—because none of the women were 'really handsome . . . and all were bawdy beyond my requirements'. However, his vivid descriptions of the sex houses in other continental cities, which were run on the same lines as those in Belgium, give an impression of what, from a voluptuary's viewpoint, the Brussels houses were probably like.

Although he had an unpleasant taste for young teenage virgins—that grew more insistent in his middle age—he did not indulge in the more wayout kinds of sadistic perversion. Walter needed none of the padded rooms that Josephine Butler was always describing so vividly. In fact his relations with the girls in the brothels suggest a degree of friendliness that contrasts with the misery image of the 'licensed hells' that the reformers repeatedly evoked. On those rare occasions, for example, when Walter could not 'perform' the girls were tender, co-operative and constructive, suggesting sometimes quite inventive ways in which his problem might be overcome. The implication in these accounts—which seem genuine if only because they reveal normal human weakness in a type of literature that usually displays the author as a man of almost superhuman virility—is that the girls went well beyond the normal call of duty.

The truth is probably that, although some of the brothels' clients were sadists whose tastes had to be catered for, most of them just came for sex in its milder form. Few of them can have been quite so single minded in their sex obssession as Walter, but their attitude was probably as unthinking. The pictures he draws of the Continental brothels—usually French or German—illustrate what was almost certainly typical of the average client's attitude and experience.

The scene as he arrived always made a great impression on him,

Enter the White Knight

the moment as the *sous-maitresse* opened the door of the room where the girls were waiting and called out sharply: 'Salon, Mesdames!' He wrote of a visit to one of his favourite spots in France:

> I have often been bewildered in my choice at a bawdy house, and more so, I think, when the ladies were naked than when clothed. Here they were clothed but . . . all were more or less *décolleté*, their breasts were seen nearly to the nipples . . . The majority had the most lovely, though not flashy or stagey, boots on and the display of calves was fine.
>
> They did not all stand up but most sat down, as if they had taken their places on chairs for the evening . . . At last, almost at hazard and in spite of my looking round till my eyeballs seemed to ache, I patted a not very tall girl on her lovely shoulders and left the room with her.
>
> She was an exquisite creature with cheeks like a rose, though her skin had a darker hue than our English women. She had eyes like a gazelle and dazzling teeth. In our bedroom, in a second, she sat on my knee and I glued my lips to hers. On a gesture which she understood, she threw off all clothing but boots and stockings and stood naked, a sight of glorious beauty. She was but eighteen years old . . . From neck to breasts, breasts to armpits, armpits to cunt, my fingers ranged and my lips followed . . .

He was a strange mixture of connoisseur and romantic—seeing what were probably rather tawdry women in near-poetic terms—and, of course, utterly juvenile. On one occasion, when visiting a French brothel in which the women in the salon were naked except for boots and stockings, he played a game throwing coins into the middle of the floor. His description has a cartoon-like quality. He stands there, in his frock coat, probably a little drunk, giggling lasciviously as the naked girls scramble for the coins 'in a naked heap . . . white breasts flashing, glimpses of dark hair . . . oval buttocks, hairy triangles of all colours at the bellies'. Then he thinks of a new game and he makes the girls sit round the room with their thighs open. He tries to pitch the one franc pieces between them and, if the girls can catch them with their vaginal lips, they can keep the coins. He describes how they keep calling to him: 'Ici, Monsieur! Ici, Monsieur!'

Louisa Hennessey, the frightened girl who readily believed her madame's warning that Dyer and his whiskered friend were only trying

Enter the White Knight

to get her out of the Paradis brothel in the Rue de Persil in order to sell her to a worse establishment, gave a highly detailed description of her procurement and of life in the Belgian houses—and provided the evidence that later was to jail Madame Paradis.

Louisa was seventeen—over the age of consent in Britain, but too young to be admitted legally to a Belgian house. On her day off from her job as a servant in the north London district of Hampstead, she went to the west end, window shopped, and bought herself a seat at the Princess Theatre, probably a vaudeville show.

As she left the theatre, a man and a woman approached her. To the teenager, who had only recently come to London from the country, they looked respectable. The woman started talking to her and invited her home to supper—home being conveniently nearby in Berwick Street in Soho. By the time the meal was over, it was too late to get back to Hampstead and they suggested that she should stay the night. It was the usual technique.

Soon after she had gone to bed, the man—who, it so happened, was the ubiquitous Jean Sallecartes—arrived home with another girl, Louisa Bond, whom later Dyer was to try so hard to extricate from the house in the Rue St Laurent.

The Sallecartes played it gently. Over breakfast, the next day, they told her about an attractive job that was available in a French hotel and agreed to arrange transport. She went willingly. Louisa Bond—according to the story she told Dyer—thought she was going over to take up a position in a store. Sallecartes took them to Ostend where Madame Evariste Paradis 'collected' them. She took them back to Brussels although they did not realise they were in a brothel until the following day. Louisa Hennessey recalled:

> After breakfast Madame asked me to get on the table so that she could examine me. An English woman ... and the housekeeper were present. I understood then what she meant. I said: 'Madame, I have been deceived. I want to go back to England.'
>
> The English woman said: 'You can't go back now. The man has taken the money for you and gone away.'

Meanwhile, the other girl lay on the table as she was told and all three women examined her. 'She did not resist,' reported Louisa.

Enter the White Knight

'After this, I felt resistance was useless. I got on the table and submitted. They were strong powerful women and could have used violence.'

In Louisa Hennessey's case there can have been little danger of disease, for she was a virgin. For some reason that Louisa did not know, Madame Paradis decided to initiate her into the prostitute life in a brothel in Antwerp. There Louisa was issued with negligée and boots and told to sit with the other girls in the salon. She must have been pretty, for she was selected very fast by a client—possibly because she was a virgin. He took her upstairs and locked the door.

Three days later, when she was in the salon, the housekeeper came in and told her to go up to a bedroom. When she saw that it was the same man waiting for her, she refused to stay. The housekeeper warned her that Madame would be 'very cross'. The client just told the housekeeper to bring up two bottles of champagne.

Louisa's story—transcribed verbatim for pre-trial proceedings—reveals a picture of a very simple country girl probably young for her age only just in puberty, frightened and dazed by the incredible change in her circumstances. Because she needed to be led by somebody, she accepted the domination of Madame Paradis—which is why she readily believed her when told that Alfred Dyer aimed to sell her.

It is clear from her account that, apart from her violation, she was treated fairly easily in Antwerp. The one man who had her as a virgin is the only client she mentions. When Madame Paradis had her sent back to Brussels, she was not thrust immediately into the routine of the brothel. She was allowed, accompanied, to sit in a cafe—probably a kind of advertising—but at last she was put to work:

> The house was darkened. I did not look out of the windows (which was forbidden by law). I never went out but once. Men came to the house during this time every day and all day, even after we were in bed. I was compelled to receive these men. I do not remember who the first was. I resisted at first and screamed but no one took any notice. There were eight or nine other girls there. The men were shown into a room . . . the girls were named and they had to go in and the gentlemen chose who they wanted . . .
> An English gentleman came one night (before Dyer) and asked

me if I would like to go back to England. Madame heard me say yes. The next morning a note came asking me to meet him at the railway station. I never got the note until it was too late. Madame read it to me and then gave it to me. She said: 'You don't want to go do you?' and she tore the note up...'

After a few months Louisa became pregnant which the artful Madame Paradis exploited for a short while—'Men wanted me while I was in this condition'—and then sold her to a brothel in The Hague for 1200 francs, carefully omitting to mention anything about her future confinement. When the owner of the Dutch house discovered the truth, she sent Louisa back to England, vowing that she would make Madame Paradis pay for the trip.

So Louisa found herself back in Britain—in a London workhouse, where she had her baby and where she was eventually found by a social worker who knew Alfred Dyer.

This, then, was the literal slave trade situation in Brussels which Alfred Dyer was determined to change. The consular officials must have known about it but they were career diplomats: it was not their job to police Brussels—merely to deal with problems involving British subjects as quietly and as tactfully as possible. If a serious complaint about a girl arrived from Britain, the police co-operated and she was deftly shipped home.

From the British consul's point of view, Alfred Dyer had thundered into this delicate situation like a rogue elephant in full charge and caused a lot of harm. The Quaker publisher had done all that was necessary—in terms of achieving results for the girls in Brussels—when he broke the story in January. It alerted the authorities—and the British consul—to the fact that the system needed tightening. Even before Dyer arrived in Belgium on his crusade, new regulations had been instituted, requiring all English girls to be screened by the consul, to ensure that they were over twenty-one and knew what they were in for, before admission into a brothel.

But the sex reformers were not concerned solely with practical improvements for the girls. They wanted to break up the system on the continent. They wanted to clean up the streets of London. And the only way they had any hope of achieving this was through publicity. Ironically, the Brussels police presented them with their opportunity.

Dyer's visit clearly caused them irritation and, perhaps, alarm. For they reacted with a sudden display of defensive spirit. Thomas Jeffes had arranged in a private deal with them for Adeline Tanner to be returned to England when she was released from the Hôpital St Pierre. Now, following the Quaker's intrusion, they changed their mind and informed the pro-consul that they were prosecuting her for misrepresentation.

Furthermore, her trial was hostile. 'I don't want to hear any of your lies,' the Juge d'Instruction told her in English and sent her to jail for two weeks as an example to other girls.

Meanwhile, the investigation by the Procureur du Roi, into the case of Louisa Bond at Number 12, Rue St Laurent, supported the official cover-up. Clearly terrified, she insisted that she had never agreed to Dyer's escape proposal and would never wish to leave the kind madame in whose care she now was. Immediately, the Procureur released a statement to the Belgian Press to show that Alfred Dyer's allegations were nonsense.

However, if the police were congratulating themselves on their successful defense against the determined campaigners from Britain, they were about to be jolted abruptly out of their sense of security. For Josephine Butler—who had now mobilised her army of women to fight state prostitution throughout the world—had just obtained evidence against them that did far more than merely prove that Dyer was not talking nonsense. It was so damning that it scandalised Europe, and provided a high point to a campaign that this quiet but fluent woman had now been waging for more than ten years.

4
The Women in Revolt

'If . . . I felt sure HE means me to rise in revolt and rebellion (for that it must be) against men . . .' Josephine Butler wrote in her diary in an old lined exercise book, 'then I would do it with zeal, however repulsive to others may seem the task.'

It was September 1869—ten years before she learned the explosive story of the other side of Dyer's crusade from a disgusted detective of the Brussels' police. In a sense, that September was the beginning of the chain of events that ended with the jailing of William Thomas Stead, then a young clerk in the office of a Newcastle merchant.

Parliament had just ratified the third of the Contagious Diseases Acts which—as part of an ever-growing experiment—imposed an inspection system on suspected prostitutes in yet more of the English troop towns. The news of the bill—passed quietly without any publicity while she was on vacation in Europe—came to Josephine as the same kind of flash revelation that had sent Dyer hurrying off to Brussels. For, as she saw it, a Belgian type system of state prostitution was being foisted secretly, by a machiavellian political lobby, on an unsuspecting British public—one more move in an international conspiracy to make it world wide.

It was more than a decade since Josephine, as a newly married wife, had been one of the first to grasp the cause of women's liberation. At the time, she was a pretty girl of twenty-four with pale blue eyes, slender Grecian features and brown hair that she wore drawn back from her forehead and gathered at the neck. Her husband was a don at Oxford where the faculty was entirely male and mostly unmarried.

Josephine had been brought up in a home that was exceptionally liberal. Her landowner father had been a political reformist, campaigning actively on such justice-seeking issues as the abolition of slavery and the extension of the franchise.

By comparison, academic Oxford was an inverted and intolerant society. The young wife was appalled by the arrogant and bigoted male opinions she heard exchanged between her husband's colleagues in her drawing room—especially on the subject of women.

The climax of her growing sense of indignation came with the launching of Mrs Gaskell's best-selling novel *Ruth*, which shocked Victorian England because its heroine was a girl who had been seduced and left to bring up her child alone. To most of the Oxford dons it was immoral to portray 'a woman of that sort' as a sympathetic character. To Josephine, this was a social view that, considering the role played in the situation by men, was scandalously unjust.

Soon after the tumultuous publication of *Ruth*, however, she encountered a girl in the same position as that of the book's main character, *and* close to home. For the girl had been made pregnant and abandoned by a member of the faculty. He was wealthy, respected by the other dons and, true to form, indifferent about the girl or the child.

Distressed and determined to do something to help, Josephine approached 'one of the wisest men—so esteemed—in the University, in the hope that he could suggest some means . . . of bringing to a sense of his crime the man who had wronged her.' She was shattered by the professor's reaction to her approach. 'It would only do harm to open up in any way such a question as this,' he told her. 'It's dangerous to arouse a sleeping lion.'

Appalled by this harsh and unfeeling view, Josephine swept angrily from his room, haunted—so she wrote later—by 'the terrible prophetic words' of Blake:

> The harlot's curse from street to street
> Shall weave old England's winding sheet.

From that moment, she became a militant. Because the flagrant injustice she saw around her was primarily sexual, she campaigned in the sexual area. While the first suffragettes were demanding the vote, Josephine was demanding in essence what women liberationists were to call for a hundred years later: the removal of the 'double standard,' a sharing by men of the consequences of sex, and a common morality for both male and female.

Why, demanded Josephine, should it be the woman who always paid the price—a price that was appallingly high? If women were expected to be chaste, why should not this requirement be demanded of men as well? Why should a girl be regarded as 'fallen' while her sexual partner—often older and more experienced and wealthier—was barely criticised and, in some circles, even admired for his actions?

Inevitably, her concern for seduced girls led her to investigate prostitution and she soon discovered that the ravages of the prevailing masculine philosophy on sex were far greater than she had realised.

Driven by a need to do something about it, she was frustrated at first by the fact that the topic was considered unsuitable for discussion. 'Silence,' she recalled years later 'was thought to be the great duty of all on such subjects.' Also, because of her husband's academic position, she could not flout society's conventions too wildly.

For this reason she worked privately for a while—as did many charitable women—at rescuing the 'fallen'. The only difference was that Josephine took them into her home, setting up the basement as a shelter. Poor George Butler found himself sharing his house permanently with a group of broken down prostitutes—one of whom, soon after Josephine began active work, was so riddled with syphilis that she soon died.

The crisis—the instant when Josephine realised that the limitation of private rescue work was not enough for her—came in 1869, as the Butlers were on their way home from vacation on the Continent. When the cross-Channel packet docked at Dover, a telegram was waiting for her. It carried the news of the passing of the Contagious Diseases Act —*and* the first appeal to her from a political feminine group that shared her views on state prostitution to lead British women into action.

It was a dramatic moment. For Josephine did not see the issue of State brothels as a practical domestic English matter. Her feelings about it were almost religious. She viewed it as an evil ideology, promoted by skilful and pitiless tacticians, and her attitude to it was

The Women in Revolt

much the same as that of many people fifty years later to communism. She saw its agents everywhere, often working subtly and in secret, and achieving steady progress throughout the world. Wherever it appeared, she felt, it must be fought vigorously, for distance was no defense against ideas. The main promoters of the system in Britain were basing their arguments on army experience in Malta and the Far East.

She believed that the title of the bills—the Contagious Diseases Acts—had been chosen deliberately so that they would be confused with animal care legislation with a similar name. Queen Victoria, it was rumoured, had signed the first of the CD bills in the belief that it was concerned with cattle—which, in a manner of speaking, it was.

What is more, even though Josephine's vivid campaigner's mind often distorted the facts, her suspicions were fully justified. There *was* an organisation—with an able lobby working on a large body of sympathetic male opinion—dedicated to the setting up of official brothels on a world-wide basis with the laudable aim of stamping out disease, that was not only sometimes fatal but was also hereditary.

The European-based Association for the Control of Prostitution by Government Regulation had established a British HQ three years before and now had forty-three branches throughout the country—all of which were constantly pouring out propaganda, urging the extension of the CD acts beyond the troop towns to the whole of Britain. Soon, its agents were to move to America.

The Association had big support, for their argument was logical. If state brothels could curb disease, then it was vital that the system should be international. Otherwise, an infected girl in a city such as London or New York, where there was no control, could move into an official brothel in Paris or Brussels and start off an epidemic before the disease was spotted. It was, however, a theory that stemmed straight from the farmlands where the movement of cattle was restricted during outbreaks of foot-and-mouth disease, and it classified prostitutes as a kind of sub-human section of the community. 'Prostitutes', commented one mid-Victorian writer 'should be treated as foul sewers are treated, as physical facts and not as moral agents.'

Furthermore, by definition, a system of control involved the police and, for its experiments, Britain had borrowed the continental idea of

The Women in Revolt

a special plain clothes force of 'morals police' who could arrest any woman 'suspected' of being a prostitute, insist on her being medically examined (if she was menstruating, she was imprisoned until her period was over) and placed on a special register. Since police are not always the most subtle of men, inevitably they made mistakes—even arresting virgins and respectable middle-class mothers—and interpreted their instructions too liberally. Sometimes, the keener officers would even try to pick up girls in the street and, if their advances were welcomed, took this as proof that they were for sale.

It may have been a way of curbing disease—though the abolitionists, as Josephine and the reformers came to call themselves, were always producing statistics to suggest that it did not—but it did so at the cost of maintaining a permanent secret spy system. No young girl, flirting with her boyfriend, could be sure that a plain clothes man might not emerge from the shadows and demand her inspection. In any event, Josephine Butler was not interested in the practical advantages of a system that involved what she regarded as sacrificial slavery. Sexual abstinence, she argued, would curb disease far more effectively.

For three months, following the telegram at Dover, she agonised, pondering whether the keen desire she felt to lead a woman's movement was, in fact, a call from God. Somewhat self-consciously, she recorded in her old exercise book some of the prayers she composed during her spiritual struggle. Then, late one evening, she wrote her husband a letter—presumably because she could not bring herself to talk to him—asking his permission to campaign in public. She walked along the passage to his study where he was working. 'I hesitated, and leaned my cheek against his closed door; and as I leaned I prayed.'

With an effort, she opened the door, handed him the letter and left the room. After a few days, during which 'he looked pale and troubled' —as well he might, for she was asking a lot of him—he gave her his blessing. 'Go, and God be with you,' he said.

It was all very stark and studied. Clearly, as the Victorians so often did, Josephine saw herself playing a part in a melodrama. She stands in the front rank of social reformers but, although she achieved enormous social progress, it is hard to avoid the conclusion that she was a bit of a showoff.

However, she struck no studied attitudes in her campaigning which was hard and basic. During the first week in 1870, she was the main instigator of the Ladies National Association for the Repeal of the CD Acts—which was to work alongside a National Association, with male members, that had been formed a few days before. It was the nucleus of the woman's army. Even before the ladies organisation was set up, the first shot in Josephine's campaign was fired. On New Years Day 1870, the *Daily News* published a 'solemn protest' signed by more than 120 women including such prominent figures as Florence Nightingale, Harriet Martineau and Ursula Bright.

The protest demanded the ending of the laws governing the troop town experiments 'because it is unjust to punish the sex who are the main victims of vice and leave unpunished the sex who are the main cause both of the vice and its dreaded consequences . . . because by such a system the path of evil is made easy to our sons . . . because the conditions of this disease in the first instance are moral not physical . . .'

The declaration—made, as it was, by so many women of standing —took an England, recovering from its end-of-year revels, by surprise. It sparked the feminine revolt. Throughout the country—undaunted by the *Saturday Review*'s sneering denunciation of them as 'frenzied, unsexed and utterly without shame'—thousands of women joined the Ladies Association, filling public halls in angry meetings demanding the repeal of the acts, police action against the white slavers that the new laws encouraged by providing an official market, and, on grounds of equality, medical inspection for both sexes. 'What,' demanded Josephine scathingly at one meeting of 4,000 women, 'do the acts do for fallen men?'

In particular she directed her appeal for support at working class men—many of whom had got the vote for the first time under the Reform Bill only three years before—since it was *their* wives and daughters who were most likely to receive the attention of the Morals Police or, for that matter, to 'fall' into prostitution.

This was sound policy and she won big support—especially since the issue of class was basic to the whole area of prostitution. 'Ladies of high rank' commented several men to her—and she repeated their remarks joyfully on public platforms—'would not feel the acts because the police would not take *them* up.'

Enthusiastically, throwing off years of restraint—and discovering at the same time that she was a born public speaker—Josephine left no angle unexploited. 'I cannot doubt,' she declaimed in March to a large audience of sympathetic women, 'that all of you suffer a pang of heart every time you remember that there is a permanent class of harlots among us, that among that class are thousands under the age of fifteen, a large proportion of them orphans, many of whom have been sold into this awful slavery by wicked relations or traders in vice.'

Grimly, she told her horrified listeners of a friend who had overheard a man at a party remarking lustily: 'Now we shall have the same facilities that we have in Paris!' And the massed female shout of 'Shame!' that the anecdote evoked throughout the hall must have confirmed Josephine's conviction that it was possible to mobilise women against what she regarded as this base and anti-christian side of male nature.

Meanwhile, in the troop towns—where the acts were in force—Ladies Association field workers were standing at the doors of the medical inspection centres urging the women as they came out, 'most of them . . . crying', to sign petitions to Parliament. Under the guidance of Josephine's angry feminists many of them refused to submit to the doctor's inspection, forcing the police to take them before the magistrates and offending Victorian sensibilities by insisting on their cases being heard in open court. When they were convicted, as they almost invariably were, they would shout out in the courtroom: 'What does the Queen think of our being sent to prison rather than expose ourselves in so revolting a manner?'

This was rich stuff for the Victorians. Naturally, it got no publicity in the general press—which was where Josephine wanted it—but, month by month, news of what was happening in the action centres, together with the reports of major speeches, was sent out to activists throughout Britain in the Association's journal, *The Shield*. And—way north in Darlington—among these activists were the wife and mother of William Stead, even though he had not yet met Josephine Butler, who was later to become so close a partner

Not all the women in the troop towns objected to the new system. To the disgust of Josephine and her campaigners, some of the prostitutes welcomed it. 'They call themselves "Queen's women",' she reported angrily. 'They walk in silks and satins and assume an arrogant manner. When warned of the sin in which they are living by one of the National Association agents, they answer: "Oh, it's quite different now. We don't need to be ashamed." '

This of course, was one of Josephine's main arguments: although on the one hand state control created a class of unhappy slaves, it gave some regular prostitutes a sense of respectability. She could never consider the possibility that some prostitutes did not find the life all that uncongenial—to Josephine they were all 'fallen', all 'outcasts'.

During the early months of Josephine's campaign, there was a great deal of heady activity but not too much in the way of result. By and large, the press took no notice, except for the occasional derisive comment. Friends in the House of Commons promoted a bill to repeal the acts but it was effectively quashed by the promoters of state prostitution.

In the troop towns, the new laws were executed rigorously by the authorities. Thousands of women were inspected—often pretty roughly with the speculum, the metal instrument used for internal examination —and placed on the registers, which meant that they had to report back to the doctors twice a month. Those who *were* diseased—though they were very few—were obliged to enter the VD wards of the local hospitals.

The examinations were not as private as they were intended. Crowds of mocking men would watch the women going into the medical centres for the inspection sessions, that were held at regular times. Children played in the streets at games of doctors and prostitutes. However, fear of the morals police, and of possible confinement in near-prison conditions, did have the effect of cleaning up the streets. In Castle Street, in the port of Plymouth, according to a local Police inspector, every house was once a brothel. 'They used to sit about on the stones there by the dozen.' Now, he reported proudly, the street had only one brothel and three prostitutes.

From the point of view of the supporters of the system, there were other advantages. Dr Richard Acton, the leading nineteenth century authority on prostitution, reported how the brothels were especially full on the day following inspection. Also men, seeking sex, began to make special trips to the troop towns on the theory that they could indulge their tastes there, with less fear of 'picking up a dose'. 'Devonport,' reported one disgusted Ladies Association member about the Plymouth suburb that was the home of a Royal Naval dockyard, 'is a venereal elysium.'

Meanwhile, the authorities took somewhat reluctant action when necessary against the abolitionists. They sent a few of them to jail for short periods for persuading women to break the law by refusing inspection but, in general, they tolerated them. They regarded them, as they viewed the Suffragettes, as the lunatic fringe that should not be made the object of too much attention.

It soon became clear to Josephine and the abolitionist leaders that what the movement needed to be taken seriously was a confrontation with the government—some action that the press would be forced to report. In the autumn of 1870, they got their chance.

The Liberal administration planned to appoint a new and experienced soldier as Under-Secretary to the War-Minister. The man they had in mind for the job was General Sir Henry Storks, who had just returned home from commanding the British military base at Malta.

To take up the post, however, he had to be elected a member of parliament. When a by-election was announced at Colchester—due to the death of the resident member—Sir Henry was nominated by the Liberal party with some confidence since they already held the seat.

But Colchester was one of the troop towns covered by the CD acts. The morals police were walking its streets. The daughters of voters were being compulsorily inspected. The Ladies Association members were campaigning. The brothels—so the theory went—were being

The Women in Revolt

made safer to patronise. And Sir Henry Storks, who had operated rigid inspection systems of the prostitutes available to his troops in Malta, was on record as a hardline advocate of state prostitution.

The abolitionists made careful plans to defeat the general by putting up their own candidate. They knew they could not win the seat, but they *could* possibly divert enough Liberal votes to hand it to Sir Henry's Tory opponent. Even this would not advance their cause in immediate practical terms—since he, too, was in favour of the controlling acts—but the rejection of the Government man would force the recognition of state prostitution as a political issue.

It was a rough election. Josephine and her ladies, starting off each day with big prayer meetings, toured the town distributing handbills quoting a public statement by Sir Henry—which he must now have been regretting—that he would not limit inspection merely to prostitutes. He advocated its extension to soldiers' wives.

The general's men—supported, according to Josephine, by a group of brothel operators—retaliated with violence. They broke up the meetings held by Dr Baxter Langley, the abolitionist candidate, and drove him from the platform. They posted on the walls about the town exact descriptions of Josephine's dress so that she could be recognised by Liberal supporters and mobbed. As a result, she had to wear different clothes every day.

One evening, because they could hear an angry crowd outside, Josephine stayed in the hotel while Dr Langley and his male colleagues went out to address a meeting at a nearby theatre. 'The mob,' recorded Josephine, 'were by this time collected in force in the streets. Their deep-throated yells and oaths . . . sounded sadly in my ears.' In fact, as the woman who was causing all the trouble, she was one of the main targets. When they had broken up Dr Langley's meeting, the crowd advanced in force upon the hotel.

The manager, pale and scared, hurried in to her and asked her to go to an attic. 'His words,' she recalled, 'were emphasised at the moment by the crashing in of the window near which I sat.' When, soon afterwards, her men colleagues returned from their meeting bleeding and bruised, the hotel management decided that Josephine and the abolitionists were too much of a liability, and asked them to leave.

Josephine tried several other hotels but they all recognised her and refused her admission. At last, she succeeded in getting accommodation in one, without giving her name. But, in the middle of the night, the manager awoke her. 'I find you are Mrs Josephine Butler,' he said. 'The mob outside have found out that you are here and have threatened to set fire to the house unless I send you out at once.'

He smuggled her out a back way and at last she found a small inn —*The Cock*—whose owner was sympathetic to the abolitionists' cause. He gave her a bed but warned her: 'Don't let your friends call you by name in the streets.'

The next day, a public meeting for women only was planned. Josephine went, with a bodyguard of twenty-four men, 'in the guise of some of the humbler women going to the meeting. I had no bonnet or gloves, only an old shawl over my head, and looked quite a poor woman.'

Since it was a meeting for women only—which the Ladies Association favoured, as the subject was less embarrassing for the audience if no males were present—the mob was restricted to the street outside the building. Josephine pushed her way through the catcalling men without being detected. She conducted the meeting against the noisy background of the restless crowd in the street outside. Then she was warned that they knew now that she was in the building, and were threatening to manhandle her as she came out through the entrance. On the urging of the other speakers, she escaped through a back window.

It was Josephine's first taste of action—and it was highly successful. Sir Henry Storks was badly defeated.

For the first time, women—though helped admittedly by men—had exploited political power as a sex in a sexual area of conflict. The press, as it had to, covered the victory. The government reacted sharply to this strange new development and promptly adopted the usual delaying stratagem that governments often deploy when threatened with social dispute. They announced that a royal commission would investigate the operation of the controversial acts in the troop towns—a move which brought a howl of abuse from Josephine and her militant women. For she was concerned with principles, not with operation. The commission, she told a big audience at Bradford:

> may arrive at the conclusion that the health of one sex is possibly benefited by the wholesale sacrifice of the other . . . but . . . the people . . . will instinctively feel that, for the Government to spend the national money in preparing prostitutes for men, is the beginning of a course which will undermine the national virtue . . . they will shun the polling booth as they did at Colchester.

After public attacks such as this, it was hardly surprising that the twenty-five-man commission—characterised later by Benjamin Scott as a 'packed jury', for there was only one member of it on the side of the abolitionists—gave Josephine a somewhat chilly reception when she was called to give evidence before them in the tall ceilinged committee room of the House of Commons.

It was a historic confrontation. As she took her seat in front of the long row of frock-coated bewhiskered politicians, she was in the heart of enemy territory, the bastion of deeply-entrenched male prejudice. She, an unescorted woman, was there to discuss a subject that these stony faced men considered revolting for a woman even to think about—let alone talk about openly. They reacted to her as a political committee of the twentieth century might react to a woman using four-letter swear words.

Emotionally dedicated as she was to her cause, it must have required great courage for Josephine to sit there in the witness chair facing her hostile interrogators—for that, in fact, is what they were, even though they were supposed to be conducting an impartial enquiry—and waiting for the questioning, that was to range way beyond the limited issue of state prostitution to encompass the whole question of the social role of women. At least, however, it gave her an opportunity to put the views of militant feminism on official record.

Perhaps it was because she was tense and nervous that she moved soon into the attack. In answer to a gently sardonic question by chairman William Massey on her views on the working of the acts, she refused adamantly to give an opinion. 'I've no interest in the operation of the acts,' she snapped. 'It's nothing to me whether they operate well or ill but I will tell you what you wish to know as to my view on the principle.' When pressed to answer the question, she retorted: 'We claim that a law shall not be made which teaches . . . that impurity of life is not a sin but a necessity. We claim that a law shall not be made whose practical effect is . . . to offer protection and immunity to the sinner in the practice of his sins.'

With a display of urbane tolerance, which must have angered her, the chairman said: 'Supposing these acts were repealed, you could suggest no mode by which the state could interfere and regulate or check this evil?'

'Seduction must be punished,' Josephine flashed back. 'At present for the purposes of seduction, and of seduction only, our law declares every female child a woman at twelve years. I am ashamed to have to confess to such a shameful state of the law before you gentlemen . . .'

Unperturbed by the row of supercilious masculine faces in front of her, she lashed out at male morality: 'A higher public standard as to the vice of men, that is the thing in which we women are most interested; we have had enough to do with the reclamation of women. We know about that. We know now that nothing can be done until the vices of men are attacked and checked . . . Whereas all legislation hitherto . . . has been directed against one sex only, we insist that it should be directed against both sexes and whereas it has been directed against the poor only, we insist—and the working men insist—that it should also apply to the rich profligate.'

Josephine was at war with men as a sex, but rich men—such as the men she was addressing—were the target at which she directed the main force of her scorn: 'It's quite the fashion I find in London among the upper classes, to talk of this subject as though women were tempters, harpies, devils, while men are wholly innocent . . . Legislation following up this idea has in almost all cases been protective for men and punitive for women . . .'

She scanned the silent hostile faces. 'It cannot be said, that there is no such thing as seduction of young girls by gentlemen of the upper classes. It cannot be said there is no such thing as profuse patronage of houses of ill-fame by rich profligate men.'

This was courageous talk. She was tramping on delicate ground and the chairman cut in. 'To descend from the high views you have opened [opined],' he said, mockingly, 'from your extensive experience of these women, do you think they are tempted into a career of vice *always* by seduction?'

Josephine conceded that awful social conditions were also a big cause. She spoke movingly of incest by drunken fathers, of families who slept five in a bed, of the seaport towns where 'there is a mass of people, boys and girls who begin to be unchaste and vicious from their earliest years. There is the commencement at once from the huddling together of poor people, like beasts. If you look at their lives, you can scarcely wonder at it.'

But she was not going to be side tracked from her running theme against vicious rich men. She had traced the history of many girls in 'the fashionable houses', she told the commission, 'and a very large proportion of them have been brought down by seduction—a real passionate affection or a fancied love affair which has ended in this unhappy way.'

Again, the chairman switched the subject away to less sensitive and more general areas, speaking of prostitution and disease as 'an unhappy fact for which as yet no remedy has been found'. And once more Josephine attacked. 'When we deal with robbery or theft,' she asserted, 'we deal with it as an unhappy fact which exists do we not? We deal with it for its repression. But in dealing with prostitution under these acts, we heal those who are diseased in order to facilitate the practise of vice.'

One of the commission asked her: 'In your experience of fallen women, have you found in practise that they have been utterly degraded and have lost all womanly feelings?' and she rounded on him angrily. 'I have not found loss of womanly feelings in one,' she said with rebuke, 'except in garrison towns and that is lately. I'm astonished that such a question should be asked of me—a woman.' Then, under further questioning, she reluctantly conceded: 'The women of Paris, I should say, have no consciences left. It is like talking to a dead person because they have no notion of right or wrong. They are reduced to the level of brutes which is what I suppose,'—and she looked at her questioner pointedly—'certain gentlemen desire they should be . . .'

Sarcastically she taunted her interrogators—who must by now have been even more astonished that George Butler should allow his wife to even think of the subject, let alone discuss it with such aggressiveness —about the 'double standard'. 'You know very well,' she said, 'that young men go through two or three years of profligacy or, as it is mildly expressed when applied to men, to "sow their wild oats," . . . it is exactly the same with these women. And yet you never hear anyone say: "Have you found any conscience in these men or are they entirely unhumanised? Have they any spark of modesty or manliness left?" '

The transcript of the commission evidence makes moving reading. Josephine, speaking alone on a forbidden topic to a hostile group of important men, made many mistakes and grew highly emotional—mostly because she felt their handling of her was unfair, as indeed it was.

They questioned her harshly when she suggested that the police overstepped their instructions, and queried her acceptance of the stories told her by immoral young girls rather than the versions supplied by the authorities. They taunted her about one particular case that she had pressed personally at the Home Office—and, as she did so often, overstated—only to find that she had been misled by the girl who complained of her treatment. 'They all claim to be virgins,' as one doctor had said.

They read to her letters she had written—one of which apologised to the Home Office for her error—that she had believed to have been sent in confidence. And, even though she insisted angrily that she should have been given an opportunity to prepare herself for detailed questioning, they grilled her relentlessly on her public statements.

Sitting there in the centuries-old mother of parliaments, they pitted the whole weight of authority against this slender, courageous woman whose beliefs on sex—though open to argument—were very clear. Yet despite the unequal nature of the confrontation, through it all came ideas that were very new—ideas that women were the equal of men; that cruel and immoral behaviour should not be tolerated in a person merely because he was male; that compulsory inspection of a girl was so gross an invasion of privacy that it contravened the basic right of citizens laid down by Magna Carta; that women should be educated because otherwise 'they had a vacant mind'; that the uncontrollable need for sex by men was a myth or, if it was not, then a woman, too should not be condemned for 'sowing her wild oats'.

Even a hundred years later Josephine's testimony makes strangely crisp reading, but it had little impact on the members of the commission. 'An active and influential organisation was arrayed against the acts,' they reported. 'Most of these (their) statements . . . were perversions of the truth, but they had their effect . . .' On Josephine's assertion that men too should be medically examined, they commented:

> We may at once dispose of this recommendation so far as it is founded on the principle of putting both parties to the act of fornication on the same footing by the obvious but not less conclusive reply that there is no comparison to be made between prostitutes and the men who consort with them. With the one sex, the offences are committed as a matter of gain, with the other it is an irregular indulgence of a natural impulse.

All the same, even though they urged the extension of control, they did recommend some improvements, such as raising the age of consent and limiting the powers of inspection.

The report did not deter Josephine and the abolitionists. They stepped up the pace of their attack—and presented a formal petition to parliament bearing the signatures of a quarter of a million women. They campaigned vigorously at the hustings and, on one occasion, almost caused the defeat of a cabinet minister who was defending his seat. When a woman who was not a prostitute—though she was living with a man—committed suicide after rough treatment by the morals police, the Ladies Association howled its denunciation of the system from public platforms throughout the country.

Meanwhile, Josephine rallied powerful support. Firstly the Quakers. Following an address by her at their annual general meeting in 1872, they formed a committee to attack state regulated vice—a committee, of course, of which Alfred Dyer was to become a prominent member. Later, a campaign group, mainly business men, was set up in the City of London under the chairmanship of Benjamin Scott, who had an official position in the City administration. Dyer, in his role as a man of commerce, was a member of Scott's group, too.

The Women in Revolt

By 1875, Josephine's militant campaign was beginning to have its effect. Although motions for repeal of the acts, covering the inspection system in the troop towns, were always defeated in parliament, the abolitionists were beginning to gain more supporters. Several top Liberals had moved over to their side, mainly because the compulsory controls did not appear to be reducing the incidence of disease.

Even Gladstone was beginning to favour repeal. The Liberal leader's attitude to the acts had been strangely paradoxical. He devoted hours of his spare time at night to walking through London's West End, urging the street girls to give up their profession—an activity that laid him wide open to attack by his political enemies, especially by Disraeli who exploited it artfully with Queen Victoria. However, for all his personal campaigning, he kept his feelings out of his statesmanship. It was Gladstone's government that introduced the 1869 CD Act that had sparked off Josephine's 'Great Crusade' as she called it.

Meanwhile, the state prostitution lobby was also highly active, pushing a proposal from the Continent that all the seaports in Europe and America should have a common system of control. This was truly dangerous, since the CD Acts already covered some of the main seaports.

At last Josephine realised that, since pressure was being applied on an international front, it was no longer enough to fight the sex war solely on home ground. She must attack it at source, where it was deeply entrenched, as well as in those areas, such as England and America, where it was being promoted. With the help of the Quakers, who had branch societies throughout the world, she led a newly-formed international federation of abolitionists in the European countries. When she learned that the promoters for control had started work in America, she sent two men across the Atlantic to rouse US women to the danger.

As in Britain, opinion in America—under the urging of police and doctors—was moving towards the idea of licensed prostitution. In seven states, politicians who favoured control had made attempts—so far unsuccessfully—to push regulation measures through the legislatures. In California, a bill with this aim had seemed, at one stage, as though it was going to win a majority vote—until the quick-thinking wife of one of the state senators persuaded her husband to introduce another bill with exactly the same wording, except that the word 'man' was substituted for 'woman'. It was a deft and successful move. In Washington, DC, control legislation was promoted on three separate occasions—only to be killed in the voting.

By 1876, the only American city in which official brothels had been permitted to operate was St Louis—and the technique by which the experiment had been promoted through City Hall was precisely the kind of stealthy operation that Josephine was always warning the women of the world to guard against. A clause in the city charter, that gave the municipal authority the power to suppress brothels, was altered quietly to include the two words 'or regulate'. Before the Purity Leagues and the women's organisations realised what was happening, the system was already a fact. The women of the city rebelled. Four thousand of them petitioned the Missouri State Senate who conceded to their pressure. In 1877, the St Louis experiment was stopped.

Josephine's two representatives, working closely with the Quakers and the Purity Leagues, moved up and down the eastern seaboard from Washington to Boston, urging action. As a result of their endeavours, the wording of a Board of Health bill that was then before the House of Representatives in Congress was changed. It concerned sanitation, but Josephine's men—who suspected the hidden presence of the enemy—insisted that it carried ample power for setting up a system of inspection and licensing. In fact, it was almost certainly a false alarm, for the man who drafted the bill agreed quite happily to the suggested changes, and insisted that his purpose had been misunderstood.

The anti-vice men, however, were ever-alert and distrusted politicians. They were campaigning among innocents who—unlike the women of Europe and, presumably, St Louis—did not yet realise the dangers, as they wrote to Josephine, of this 'plotting . . . against the morals of the whole republic'.

However, even if they chased some shadows, there was no room for doubt about the threat in Philadelphia. There, the medical journals were urging a current annual conference of physicians to make an official demand for the introduction of a prostitute licensing system in Pennsylvania. Acting under the guidance of Josephine's advocates, the Women's Christian Association set up an aggressive lobby and forced a defeat of the motion.

Meanwhile, in Europe, Josephine was travelling from city to city demanding the abolition of state vice systems and advocating attack on the authorities that administered them. Under her urging, national societies in each country promoted complaints whenever they could against the morals police.

As a result of abolitionist activity, the Municipal Council of Paris mounted a committee of inquiry—made necessary mainly by the usual complaints that the police were hounding innocent women. Josephine travelled to France to testify. The inquiry did not produce all the results that would have satisfied her, but it did lead eventually to the sacking of the two top officials in the morals police that regulated the French brothels. This was a great victory for Europe's campaigning women because it was the morals police that they regarded as their immediate target.

At the same time, Josephine was in close combat with the police in Britain whom she was convinced were in collusion with their colleagues in Europe—and early in 1880 she believed she had grounds for proving this.

From a very early stage in her campaign, Josephine had come in contact with Colonel Howard Vincent, head of the CID at Scotland Yard. In March, 1880, Dyer's exposure of the case of Adeline Tanner had given her ample material to start bringing pressure to bear on Vincent. For Adeline stated that she had been procured and shipped to Brussels by a 'white slaver' named Max Schultz—who was a kind of partner of Jean Sallecartes and the reported lover of Josephine Ann Parent, who managed one of the houses in the Rue St Laurent. Schultz, who was Dutch, was based in London. Back in January, Josephine had learned that the authorities in both Holland and Belgium had made application to London for his extradition. Immediately, she began to bombard Vincent with demands for his arrest.

Somewhat lamely, the CID chief replied that his men had been out looking for him but had failed to find him. So Josephine, through her underworld contacts, discovered where he was living and telegraphed his address to the CID. Promptly, Vincent stationed detectives on round-the-clock surveillance of the 'placeur' but claimed he could not arrest him since he had committed no extraditable crime.

Josephine, utterly sceptical, planned a new tactic. Early in May, one of the abolitionist MPs stood up in the House of Commons and asked if it was true that the Belgian authorities had applied in vain to the Home Office for the extradition of Max Schultz. The same day, Josephine wrote a sharp letter to the Home Secretary, Sir William Harcourt, hinting that the CID were tied in with the vice ring. Angrily, she pointed out that Schultz, anxious because of the police surveillance, had now escaped to Paris.

At all levels, scenting victory, this determined woman increased the tempo of her campaign. Vincent, mindful that Dyer had been able to exploit the stonewalling he had encountered in Belgium, decided to attempt conciliation with Josephine.

Ever since the beginning of March, Chief Inspector Greenham of the Metropolitan Police had been touring the brothels of Europe to investigate officially Dyer's allegations of a white slave traffic in English girls. As the result of Foreign Office requests at government level, the inspector had been given every assistance by the morals police in every country he visited.

His report implied that the allegations by these campaigning religious fanatics overstated the situation to an extent that was absurd. Although the statistics he gave portrayed a sex-for-sale situation that was staggering—Amsterdam, alone, maintained 186 brothels containing 1,064 women, which put Brussels with its 19 houses or even Liege with 29 establishments fairly low down the scale as sin cities—he found that there were only 33 English girls in all the countries he visited. Of these, only one—Adeline Tanner in the Hôpital St Pierre —wanted to return home.

Howard Vincent invited Josephine to Scotland Yard to read the paper the inspector had written so that she could report to the annual meeting of the international federation of abolitionists that was soon to be held in London. Clearly, since the campaigners had already caused the sacking of two French police chiefs, he did not underrate them.

As a ploy it failed. She did not believe a word of it. For one thing it quoted Louisa Bond as telling the inspector that Alfred Dyer at one stage in his escape proposals, 'took me round the neck and kissed me and . . . said that his poor dear wife was at home praying to the good God that he should succeed in his mission. I asked him, if he and his wife were so good and religious, why he acted towards me like that . . .'

'It is impossible,' Josephine wrote later to the Home Secretary, 'to reconcile the report with statements made by honourable men who had a knowledge of the state of things in Brussels.' By then, as it happened, she was in a very strong position. She had stumbled on evidence, during a subsequent visit to Brussels, that utterly demolished the inspector's report. It came to her in the form of a visit to her hotel by an ex-member of the Belgian police department with an offer—apparently dictated by his own conscience—to reveal the whole inside story of the tie-up between the authorities and the brothels.

Everything that Dyer had said, Josephine's new informant assured her—and she translated it into English on pale blue paper that is still on file in London—was correct. Louisa Bond—the girl whose rescue was the main purpose of the Quaker's crusading visit to Brussels—had certainly wanted to escape from the brothel at 12 Rue St Laurent. But, following Dyer's official complaint, Schroeder, the deputy chief of the morals police, warned her what to say when the matter was investigated. 'The brothel keeper himself,' Josephine was told, 'said to me that he had so thrashed the girl that she would no longer have any thought of escaping.'

However, the Procureur du Roi had been more concerned by the visit of Dyer and Splingard than his unco-operative attitude suggested. He had sent for Schroeder: 'You have no minors in these houses have you?' he demanded.

'Not one, not one,' the official assured him.

But Schroeder's boss—Edward Lenaers, the head of the police des moeurs—realised the danger behind the questioning of his subordinate. He told him to tour the brothels immediately by carriage and bring all the minors to his office, so that they could be transported out of his jurisdiction. It was with some relief that the Brussels police learned of the imminent visit of Scotland Yard's Chief Inspector Greenham, for this would give them a perfect opportunity to portray Dyer and Splingard as 'imposters'.

Much of this, as Josephine conceded in her statement to the Home Office, could have been exaggerated, but the Belgian detective had given her two hard facts: Madame Humbeck, the owner of two houses in the Rue St Laurent, had died the previous autumn. In her will, she had left her establishments to a senior official of the morals police. In addition, the son of the department head, Edouard Lenaers, ran a wine business that supplied the brothels. Josephine herself had checked out the will—which was a matter of public record—and it was clear evidence that the links between the morals police and the houses they were supposed to supervise were far too intimate.

Triumphantly, Josephine sent her evidence to the Home Secretary in person and demanded an enquiry. She chose her moment carefully, for by then the Belgian authorities were pressing the British Government to take action against their militant sex campaigner.

On May 1st, in the abolition journal *The Shield*, Josephine had alleged in highly provocative terms, that big business was done in the provision of children as sexual partners: 'English girls from 12 to 15 years of age, lovely creatures (for they do not care to pay for any who are not beautiful), innocent creatures, too; stolen, kidnapped, betrayed, gone from English country villages by every artifice and sold to these human shambles.'

Asserting that this was an undercover trade, unseen by normal patrons of the brothels, Josephine described the 'padded rooms with mattressed floors and walls to prevent the cries of tortured girls from being heard outside'. 'The secret is known to none except the wealthy debauchees,' she declaimed, adding that 'these infants seldom live more than two or three years after their capture, rarely so much.'

This was typical Josephine in wild flight. For even if it was true —though it bears all the signs of exaggeration—she quoted no evidence, as Dyer had done, no names of girls, no addresses, no details. Her stated source was Alexis Splingard, who apparently had conducted a private investigation, but even *his* evidence was mainly hearsay or surmise.

Josephine's revelations caused uproar in Europe. Newspapers in Belgium and France ran the story prominently. English newspapers rebuked her. The Belgian authorities furiously denied the truth of the allegations, and the Procureur made a formal demand to the Home Office in London under the extradition arrangements, that Josephine should be made to repeat her statements on oath before a magistrate.

Many people urged her to decline. Pastor Anet was warned in Brussels: 'Take care what you do, especially in the matter of children found in these houses.' Benjamin Scott was cautioned by letter from Belgium: 'Do you know that you are walking into the jaws of Hell? You know not the depths of the bitterness and hatred you are raising against yourselves.'

'That is true,' Josephine wrote back to Scott with her usual display of studied courage when he passed on the warning, 'but the cry of the children is sounding in our ears.'

She swore the deposition but, when she forwarded it to the Home Office, she enclosed with it the damning statement she had taken from the Belgian detective in Brussels. He was, she declared, prepared to face the men he accused at a public enquiry but, she asserted, it was clear that this should not be held in Belgium.

It was now October and another important move by the abolitionists in their war on the Belgian brothels and the white slavers that supplied them was moving to a climax. During the summer, since the authorities in both Belgium and Britain were so apathetic, Josephine's international organisation had decided to mount a private prosecution in Brussels against the brothel owners for prostituting girls under the age of twenty-one.

On 13 December, in Brussels' main court house, twelve owners and managers of the city's brothels filed into a courtroom and took their places in the dock. The ubiquitous attorney, Alexis Splingard, rose to address the judge in a new role as prosecutor. Waiting to testify outside were four girls, who had now travelled to Brussels from England, under drastically different circumstances to their previous visits. Among them were Adeline Tanner, Ellen Newland—Dyer's original white slave exhibit whom he had used to break the whole story of the girl traffic the previous January—and Lucy Nash, one of the two girls who had made the dramatic break for freedom that he had publicised at the same time.

Quietly, under Splingard's examination, the girls told their stories, depicting vividly the whole way in which the Belgian state brothels operated. The beatings, the supply techniques, the prison-type conditions were given big coverage by the Brussels newspapers. Two days after the start of the trial, Splingard sent Josephine a triumphant telegram: 'All convicted.'

But it did not end there. The Brussels municipal council announced that it would hold an inquiry into the suggestions of police complicity with the brothel owners. Among the witnesses called before it to give evidence was the editor of *La Nationale*, one of Belgium's national dailies. The newspaperman read Josephine's deposition as part of his testimony—then front-paged it in *La Nationale*.

It caused an even bigger sensation than the trial. The editor's life was threatened openly by the vice interests; his offices were besieged by a brothel-paid mob. But it ended the career of Lenaers and Schroeder—the two men who until then had run the police des moeurs.

Three months later, there was a second trial of brothel operators, this time mounted by the Belgian prosecutor himself. For by then, Louisa Hennessey—the girl who had become pregnant and been sent back home by an Antwerp brothel—had been found with her baby by an associate of Alfred Dyer in a workhouse on the outskirts of East London. Also accused was Jean Sallecartes, the man who had shipped her to Belgium, although—since he was still in prison in France—he was unable to attend court. As in the previous case, all the accused were jailed.

The sex campaigners had won a substantial victory. State brothels still existed in both Belgium and France, but—with the sacking of the leading members of the morals police in both countries, coupled with the clean-up of the houses in Brussels—the system that Josephine hated was at least being run legally. The white slave traffickers, operating out of London, had taken a battering, although the lax British laws, which had enabled them to supply the Continental *maisons*, still remained unchanged.

The abolitionists concentrated their attack once more on England. In March, 1881, Benjamin Scott wrote to Lord Granville, the Foreign Secretary deploring the fact that the convictions in Belgium had failed to 'arouse the attention of public men in promoting action in this country'.

When this produced no more than a formal acknowledgement, Josephine travelled to the capital and warned Granville in a personal letter: 'I shall be in London for three days and will wait those three days outside your door, until Your Lordship chooses either to hear our petition, or to order my removal!' Granville sent for her at the Foreign Office, and smiled as she was shown into his room. 'No need for your three days' siege,' he said. 'I have already given notice that I shall move on May 30th for a Committee of the House of Lords.'

For ten months, fourteen peers studied the evidence and heard testimony from police, magistrates, doctors. Alfred Dyer gave evidence. So, too, did George Gillett, who had gone with him to Brussels on his crusade, and Benjamin Scott and Thomas Jeffes, the British pro-consul who, despite the trial in Brussels, still insisted that the whole thing was exaggerated. The main witness was Thomas Snagge, a London attorney whom the Home Office had sent to Belgium to attend the trial and to carry out his own investigation. Snagge supported most of the allegations made by the reformers.

In 1882, the Lords committee published their report. Asserting that a scandalous situation existed—both in England and in the traffic of girls to the Continent—it silenced the critics of the sex campaigners who had long mocked that their allegations were products of fevered, sin-obsessed imaginations. The report urged tough new laws to control abduction and brothel-keeping and recommended that the age of sexual consent should be raised to sixteen.

As a result, the government introduced the Criminal Law Amendment Bill, designed to effect many of the committee's proposals, but, although this passed through the House of Lords, it was always filibustered by the brothels lobby in the Commons. If the administration had been truly determined, they could have pressured it through but, busy with other legislation, they did not give it high priority. The electorate was all-male, and it was hardly a vote-catcher.

However, in 1883—while thousands of Josephine's women knelt in prayer for the whole day in halls and homes near Parliament—the House of Commons suspended the compulsory inspection system that was central to the experiment in state control of prostitution. It was passed by only one vote, and it was not complete repeal. It could be reversed at any time, and the brothels lobby declared this as their dedicated object. At least, however, from Josephine's point of view, her women had succeeded—if only temporarily—in checking the ideology.

But the situation in the streets of London remained unaltered. Young teenagers still touted for custom. The brothels still operated with little control. Perversions were still catered for. Girls were still abducted and placed in English sex houses. And there was truly little to stop the white slavers, who supplied the foreign market, from moving back into the city's streets once the dust had settled.

Three years later, in 1885, the sex campaigners decided to become more militant—and their success, which was far greater than their achievements in Brussels or Paris, astonished even them. By then, however, they had the backing of a powerful international organisation of drum-beating and uniformed evangelists. The Booth family, who ran the Salvation Army, had at last singled out the promoters of prostitution as a prime target.

5
The Hallelujah Evangelists Join the Battle

The Booths, a brilliant, passionate and fantastically successful family of hell raising preachers, were in the business of saving souls. Sexual lust—which was the focal objective of Josephine Butler and her reforming women—was for them only one of a whole range of sins that people must avoid to find Salvation. In fact it came way below drink and tobacco in their scale of priorities for campaign targets. As the Booths saw it, these were far more dangerous because they were openly socially acceptable. Pubs, unlike brothels, were sanctioned by law. And liquor, in particular, had dire practical results, quite apart from its other devil-inspired effects such as drunkenness and alcoholism: it syphoned off the pittance wages of working-class men, that were badly needed for semi-starved, ill-clothed families living like animals in the slums.

However, there came a moment in 1885 when the Booths were shocked into directing the whole weight of their dynamic organisation at breaking the power of the brothels and forcing a change of law. This sudden switch in campaign emphasis brought them solidly behind Josephine Butler and her army of women because, temporarily at least, their prime targets became the same. For this reason, the Booths as well as Josephine were to play a key role in the social explosion that reverberated round the world.

The Salvation Army—with its uniforms, its bands, its ebullient Hallelujah preaching techniques—was very new. Only a year before Alfred Dyer rushed off to Brussels on his brothel crusade, the Booths transformed their 'Christian Mission' with its unorthodox campaigning of God to the masses, into a military-style organisation—a concept that was to provide the dynamic which was to propel it into a vast world-wide operation with nearly half a million officers. By 1885, when the Army was only seven years old, it was still small by comparison with what it was to become, but already in Britain its preachers were urging crowds of sinners to seek salvation from platforms throughout the country. Overseas, its bands were thumping the beat for marchers in the streets of cities as distant as New York and Philadelphia, Paris and Bombay and Sydney.

Its founder was a tall, bearded, hollow-cheeked evangelist named William Booth, who was fired by an explosive and inexhaustible energy.

As a young man, with obvious and dramatic talents for the pulpit, he had been a Wesleyan preacher, working the circuits in the north of England. He had chafed against the organisational restraints that had been placed on him and, particularly, against the rigid class barriers that were upheld in the Methodist chapels.

To him, it was the poor, forced into sin by their miserable condition, who were most in need of salvation—but the practical facts were forced on him when he had just started his ministry. In a burst of youthful enthusiasm, he had taken a crowd of working men, that he had collected in a pub, through the main door of the chapel to the communion rail. He was roundly rebuked by the preacher. As he surely knew, he was told, the poor should enter by a side door and sit on benches where they could hear the service but could not see it— nor, of course, be seen by the middle class worshippers who owned their pews.

He broke away from the Methodists when he was thirty-two and campaigned through the sprawling rat-infested slums of East London, declaiming his message outside pubs—where, since he was trying to put them out of business, he was hardly welcome—urging their customers to seek salvation. 'There is a heaven in East London for *everyone*,' he would roar, 'for everyone who will stop and think and look to Christ as a personal saviour.'

Londoners needed some convincing. Dockland stretched east along the Thames from London Bridge. Behind it lay the awful product of the industrial revolution—mile after mile of narrow streets of squalid tenement hovels, that housed whole hungry families in each room. Hundreds of sewers flowed into the Thames. Cholera was a constant threat. Sickness gripped the under-nourished, overworked millions. They died in the streets.

Drink provided the escape from reality and fanned the violence that always grows in the frustrations of poverty-rooted overcrowding. And it was readily available. There were 100,000 pubs in the city. Every East London road had more gin-shops than any other business. A promotion feature was penny glasses of gin for children.

It was not strange that prostitution did not rate all that high in William Booth's scale of priorities when he stalked the gas-lit roads of Whitechapel and Stepney. Up in the West End, sex-for-sale provided overtly flagrant cause for social campaigning. But here in the slums, it had nothing to do with the sight of six-year-old children lying dead drunk in dark alleyways, of vomiting women, or fighting men.

Booth preached wherever he could—in the streets, in old warehouses, in empty buildings and, often, in a tent that his small band of converts, many of them reformed drunks, would help him erect. In his flowing black coat and wide brimmed hat, with his bible clutched under his arm, he drew big crowds. His son, Bramwell, described:

> His splendid head and profile, his outstretched arms . . . his erect and yet supple figure, swayed at times like a tree in the wind, all gave the most casual listener the impression of something quite out of the ordinary . . . his opening was customarily quiet, almost lamblike. It was in astonishing contrast—his striking and aggressive appearance and the gentleness with which he began to talk . . . Sometimes, even at moments of great tension, his manner would be very subdued . . . At other times . . . head, arms, hands, feet, the whole frame would vibrate and tremble . . .

Inevitably, speaking to the truculent angry mobs, his meetings were stormy. Often he would return late at night to his lodgings in Hammersmith on the other side of the city, with his face bruised and bloody from flying stones.

'The sins of London,' commented one of his family about his rigid determination to bring salvation to the slums, 'didn't shock him. They seemed to tear at his heart with claws that drew blood.'

The Hallelujah Evangelists Join the Battle

By then, he was married to Catherine, a slim dark girl whose youthful shyness was to crack with maturity to reveal a campaigner with almost as much evangelical sizzle as he had. Like Josephine Butler, Catherine was an ardent feminist. Early in their marriage, Booth commented in support of a Wesleyan Minister who had made some disparaging comments in public about women as the weaker sex. He never did it again. His demure young wife rounded on him angrily. 'That . . . a woman is in any respect except physical strength and courage inferior to man, I cannot see cause to believe,' she raged, 'and I am sure no one can prove it from the word of God.'

Booth conceded her point but he had been brought up in a world of male domination and, even though he paid lip service to sexual equality, the advanced thinking of his progressive young wife took some getting used to. 'I would not encourage a woman to begin preaching,' he wrote to her on one occasion, 'although I would not stop her on any account . . . I would not stop you if I had power to do so, although I should not like it.'

In the event, she gave him no alternative. Booth was preaching in chapel one Sunday morning when, as Richard Collier records in *The General Next To God*, he:

> glimpsed a perplexing sight: abruptly his wife had left her seat and was walking slowly towards him down the aisle. A stifled buzz of comment arose from a thousand voices . . . At once, all solicitude, Booth was at her side. 'What is it, my dear?' Like all the rest of the congregation; he concluded that Catherine was ill.
>
> 'I want to say a word,' Catherine heard herself reply, her voice made higher by nervousness. Booth himself was so astonished that he could only announce meekly: 'My dear wife wishes to speak.' Then he sat down.

Catherine had stood up in her pew as a result, so she claimed, of an overwhelming compulsion to preach. Fears that she would 'look like a fool and have nothing to say' she rejected as devil-inspired. 'I have never yet been willing to be a fool for Christ,' she told herself, according to Collier, 'Now I *will* be one.'

'I dare say,' she told the congregation, 'many of you have been looking on me as a very devoted woman, but I have been disobeying

The Hallelujah Evangelists Join the Battle

God . . .' Although she had insisted on a woman's right and duty to preach, she told them, she had ignored the divine revelation to her to do so.

Booth was astonished and impressed to observe that many of the congregation were so moved by her that there were tears in their eyes. Promptly, he realised the scope for exploitation of his wife as an evangelist. As soon as she had finished, he stood up. 'Tonight,' he declared, 'my wife will be the preacher.'

The idea of a woman preacher was revolutionary for mid-Victorian society. In a slightly different way, Booth attracted the same kind of criticism that George Butler was to be subjected to when Josephine decided to lead the campaign against state prostitution. In traditional Methodist circles—which still employed him—it was greatly deprecated.

It was, however, the beginning of a man-and-wife team of formidable power. For their techniques—and often their congregations—were different. Booth himself was a declamatory speaker who used shock tactics to rouse his audiences. Catherine spoke more quietly, more intellectually.

'To many who did not know her by sight but only by reputation,' wrote Bramwell Booth about his slim quiet-mannered mother who would grow passionately angry as she spoke of sin, 'her first appearance was a complete surprise. "What a slip of a thing," they would exclaim. Her first sentences, always spoken with great deliberation and with careful modulation of voice . . . created interest and curiosity and soon she was carrying her audience with her in her developing argument.'

The Booths enlisted their children early in the cause of the family campaign, as they toured the country. Bramwell was only seven when Catherine 'urged him very seriously to decide for Christ'. The little boy—who, despite his upbringing, could have hardly understood the question—did not reply. So his mother pressed him 'as to whether he would accept the offer of salvation or not.' He turned and looked her 'deliberately in the face'. Then, tautly, he said one short word: 'No.'

Catherine was certainly not taking that for an answer, although she was prepared to give him a little time. For months as 'sin was revealed to me,' he was subjected to the silent pressure of his parents' loving patience . . . during which they did not say much to me, except when alone, and they led my thoughts rather away from myself and my struggle.'

Bramwell's seven-year-old resistance soon gave way, and he accepted salvation and made his parents happy. And to be fair—even though it might seem that he was absurdly young to be forced to take such deep and truly complex decisions—he never looked back, which was why he came to be sitting with William Stead in the dock of the Old Bailey.

The Booth's concept of running their campaign like a military operation was brilliant. With its uniforms—designed for both sexes—and its blood red standards and its army-phrased general orders and its hierarchy of ranks, it gave its followers a sense of corporate unity and organisational pride. It provided their audiences with a show which, in an age when there was no television and relatively few books even for those who could read, was an attraction even to hopeless sinners. The marching to the rousing, booming bands—which came only with the military packaging—gave an audience-participant symbolism to the advance to salvation. And, of course, it put the campaigning right where it should be—in the streets.

William Booth was a great showman. Already, even before the army was formed, he had developed clever techniques for using the human enjoyment of singing. Most of his hymns were rousing and jubilant—as was fitting for people rejoicing that they had found salvation—and there was no question of his converted sinners not knowing the tune. For he put his martial Christian words to well-known songs, many of which—such as 'Here's to good old whisky' and 'Champagne Charlie is my name'—were directly linked to drink. When one of Booth's lieutenants suddenly realised with horror where he had heard the music of a hymn before, the General growled at him: 'Why should the Devil have all the best tunes?'

One of the Booths' strengths lay in their use of women in the Army. Like Josephine Butler—although possibly it had needed Catherine to strip away the last lingering traces of sexual prejudice from her husband—the general, as he became known, fully appreciated the

The Hallelujah Evangelists Join the Battle

latent power that existed, in a male-orientated society, in wives and daughters. Also, he came to realise that they were a rich source of often highly inspired preachers with an enormous emotional impact on their massive audiences—and how invaluable they could be to an organisation that was beginning to operate on sensational publicity. 'The best men in my army are the women,' quipped Booth. Certainly, since women preachers were still a rarity, they attracted the crowds.

Ironically, when William Crow, a Newcastle printer with an eye for a catch line, dubbed two 'lady preachers' as 'The Hallelujah Lasses' in a handbill he was printing for the Army announcing their arrival, Booth was furious. It was only when telegrams came pouring into his East End HQ in Whitechapel with the news that Rachel and Louise Agar—the 'Lasses'—were attracting enormous crowds that he had to admit that maybe the title had some merit. 'Lass,' of course, was the expression of affection used by Newcastle men, as well as by Scotsmen, about their womenfolk.

Among the thousands of people who were impressed by the Hallelujah Lasses as they swung out through Northumberland from Newcastle was a red haired young man who had just taken over the editorship of the Northern Echo at Darlington. It was Stead's first contact with the Army and the sight of the Agar sisters trumpeting their evangelic message with such vigour and success made a big impact on him—so big, in fact, that when he went to London he contacted the Booths and became friendly with William's son, Bramwell.

Most talented of the other Hallelujah Lasses was Kate Shepherd, a seventeen-year-old girl who, operating in the coal mining district of the Rhondda Valley in Wales, led a revival for the Salvation Army that had a fantastic impact. F. de L. Booth-Tucker, an Army leader and Booth's son-in-law described her impact:

> For hours together in the open air under the shadow of the Welsh mountains the people by the thousands would hang upon her lips. And when, with lifted face and closed eyes, standing in her cart-pulpit she burst into a torrent of prayer, it seemed as if a pin-fall would have jarred upon the breathless silence of the audience.
>
> Kate's power in prayer was unique. It was not so much what she

The Hallelujah Evangelists Join the Battle

said, as the *way* she said it. 'Oh Lord, you know they are mis-er-able!' she would begin and the heart of every sinner in the congregation seemed to echo, almost audibly, 'You know we are miserable.'

The prayer finished, the clear, sweet voice would ring through the air in some popular refrain adapted to spiritual words, which were heartily taken up by the crowd. And then followed . . . appeal upon appeal for every sinner to decide then and there the question of his soul's salvation. 'Won't you come? You'll be sorry for it some day! Yes, you will!'

And the large, dark earnest eyes, brimful of tears enforced the argument with a pathetic power . . . hundreds upon hundreds of the roughest class flocked like little children to the penitent form.

The 'Hallelujah Lasses' deployed contrasting styles. By comparison with the deep emotion that Kate Shepherd could stir, Lieutenant Eliza Haynes became one of the most famous women in Britain through a jaunty publicity stunt. Because the Army attendances at Nottingham were low, she marched through the streets of the town with streamers floating from her hair and a placard on her back bearing the words: 'I am happy Eliza.' Soon, she was leading a crowd that gathered behind her, growing bigger all the time—mocking, jeering, laughing at her but, accompanied by the brassy oom-pah of the band, they were joining in the singing of a Salvation song to the tune of 'Marching through Georgia'.

Her promotion stunt created a national catch phrase. From then on, all the Salvation Army's women were known as 'Happy Elizas'. Vaudeville songs featured them. Small boys, in the candy stores, would ask for 'an 'aporth of 'appy Elizas'.

The dramatic results of the girl's publicity in the form of attendances encouraged Booth's male preachers to adopt similar sensational tactics. Lieutenant Theodore Kitching, who addressed big audiences at Scarborough in Yorkshire, took to riding in to town on a donkey draped with crimson, ringing a bell. One officer walked to his meetings barefoot, dressed like John the Baptist in a goatskin. Another, who had been in Dartmoor Prison, wore an arrow-patterned convict's uniform and fetters as he urged the crowds to seek their salvation. Even Bramwell—by then a slim, rather handsome brown-eyed boy, with a dark

The Hallelujah Evangelists Join the Battle

bushy beard—often opened his meetings by rising from a coffin, born by six men, demanding: 'Death, where is thy sting?'

Inevitably, these brash techniques invoked a stream of criticism, but William Booth was convinced that almost any method of attracting audiences was permissible. The important part was getting people to listen so that his preachers could get across their message of salvation. 'What matter if the dish be cracked,' Catherine Booth challenged their critics, 'so long as it serves you with a good joint?'

Inevitably, the Army's noisy campaigning incurred the disapproval of the prim Victorian Establishment—and especially of the churches. Lord Shaftesbury, the great reformer, even described it as 'Anti-Christ'. Ironically, the traditional clergy found themselves ranged alongside the brewers, whom they condemned from their pulpits, against Booth—even though, despite his unorthodox techniques, he, too, was selling religion. But it was rough-and-ready and unformalised by sacraments or ritual—'corybantic Christianity', as one cleric jeered. All that was demanded of his converts was that they should advance to the Penitent form, confess to sin and seek salvation by leading a new life in future, a life, that, by Booth's definition, excluded liquor and tobacco—and, it went without saying, extra-marital sex.

Unfortunately, in practice, the General was in competition with organised religion. Although he did attempt at the beginning to direct his converts to the churches—which later evangelists such as Billy Graham made a rigid rule—these respectable middle class houses of worship were not adequate for the ordinary people who made up most of Booth's audiences. Certainly, they did not offer the colour or the excitement or, as it turned out, the drama of the Army's street campaigning.

However, it was the alcohol interests who organised the most serious opposition to the crusading soldiers—for the success of Booth's campaign, with its built-in demand for abstention from liquor, was affecting their business. 'We have thousands of converted drunkards in our ranks, who for years spent the chief of their earnings at the public house . . .' declared Catherine. 'We know as a fact that numbers of houses which used to do a roaring business are now on the verge of ruin . . .'

In specific areas the damage to the pub trade was enormous, at least for a while. As a result of seventeen-year-old Kate Shepherd's spellbinding, one pub in the Rhondda Valley sold only three pints of beer in a whole week. In Newcastle the Agar sisters were offered £300 to leave town.

In an attempt to shatter Booth's movement, the brewers and the publicans promoted the 'Skeleton Army'—big gangs of paid toughs who broke up his meetings and attacked his 'troops'. Displaying black flags, featuring the skull and crossbones in mocking mimicry of the Salvationists' blood red banners, they singled out the women for special attention. They hurled paint at them, pelted them with earth and stones and even dead cats, and treated them with the same booted violence that they directed at the men. After a riot in Clapton in East London, one girl died from a damaged womb following a kick in the stomach. In Whitechapel, a 'skeleton' group roped some Hallelujah lasses together—then showered them with live coals. From a ship moored at Gravesend, drunken seamen fired rockets at a group of Salvation girls singing hymns on the dockside. At Worthing—where a Salvation Army unit was led by an attractive twenty-three-year-old named Captain Ada Smith—the rioting of 4,000 'Skeletons' became so serious that the authorities had to call in the cavalry to restore order.

What made this militant opposition even more serious than the immediate damage it caused was that the 'Skeleton' army had the support—both financial and moral—of many 'respectable people', and often of the authorities. Even the police—who were supposed to be controlling the disorder in the streets—were among the public subscribers to the Skeleton funds. As a result, although Booth's soldiers were committed to a policy of non-violence—and, under attack, of non-retaliation—they were often jailed by magistrates on charges of participating in riots of which they had merely been the victims.

For the first four years of the 1880s the bitter violent war progressed. The peak year was 1882 when 660 salvationists were injured and 86, including 15 women, were sent to prison.

By then, Booth's men and women were under assault in streets that were many thousands of miles away from the Army's HQ in London. For he had begun to internationalise his movement.

The Hallelujah Evangelists Join the Battle

Three years after Josephine Butler's emissaries had begun to campaign up America's east coast, urging the women to fight the threat of state prostitution, George Railton, one of Booth's top officers, walked down the gangplank of the SS Australia onto a New York jetty accompanied by seven 'Hallelujah Lasses'. They held their first meeting right there on the dockside, singing their salvation songs to music that the Americans would recognise—'The old Folks at Home' and 'My old Kentucky Home.' They had adapted their crimson flag, too: in one corner was a tiny stars and stripes.

It was not long before the violence of the British streets was being repeated in America—with the support, as in England, of the police and authorities. Young Captain Ada Smith, who had led the salvationists through the battles of Worthing, was beaten up by a cop in Hazleton, Pennsylvania. In Colorado, the Salvation campaign was fought with gun fire. In Iowa, one of the Army's officers was condemned to a chain gang for open-air preaching.

In Australia, India, Canada and Europe Booth's officers, with the help of their bands, were proclaiming their simple message of salvation in the face of violent persecution. In Switzerland, his daughter Kate was jailed after a series of riots organised by the drink interests and also by the brothels, for many of her converts were prostitutes.

The Booths had much in common with Josephine Butler. Both their organisations were dedicated to sexual equality, to giving women a true social status as opposed to the phoney and unrealistic 'angel' image which Victorian society, with its obsession with sex as sin and its concept of treacly romance, had imposed on them. Both were in head-on conflict with the Establishment, and were fighting the hypocrisy that it fostered. Both, too, were engaged in what essentially was a class war, not only because most of the people who stood to benefit from their campaigns were in the working classes, but also because the social reforms they sought were completely in the hands of the middle and upper classes who held the monopoly of administrative power.

Strangely, although the Salvation Army marched regularly through areas of rampant prostitution, the Booths, with their militant trumpeting evangelism, did not begin to realise the ramifications in the vice trade until 1884—and even then they were curiously unwilling to believe it. One reason for this, of course, was that their sights were set on higher objectives. They were not merely social reformers: they were selling God. They dealt in prayer and hymns—not, like Josephine, in political lobbying nor, like the Rescue Society, in the practical reforming of fallen women.

In fact, when the suggestion was first mooted that they should set up a shelter for prostitutes who were keen to grasp the Army's offer to help them 'come to Christ,' William Booth promptly vetoed it. He was running a corps, not a string of homes. But he was on weak ground. In practice, for the salvation of the girls to be effective, they needed to get away from their immediate surroundings for a few days while they found other employment. Otherwise, the pressures on them to revert were too great.

For this reason, Booth's women officers often gave them a bed in their homes for a few nights and one—a baker's wife named Mrs Cottrill—took the problem so seriously that she turned her East End cottage into a permanent shelter. It was far too small to cope with the number of girls who sought to save their souls and eventually, somewhat reluctantly, Booth agreed to the Army setting up a proper home. In charge of it, he placed Florence, the young, rather plain, bespectacled girl officer whom Bramwell had married two years before.

Florence was horrified by what the girls told her about their lives. 'Mrs Booth,' recorded Bramwell, 'cried herself to sleep night after night,' despite the fact that her husband, who had been in the battle long enough to grow a little sceptical, warned her that the accounts were 'probably exaggerated; that the credibility of these folks were not to be trusted too readily...'

But the fact that she was so upset—and her insistence that there was a highly active white slave traffic—led Bramwell to investigate. Among the calls he made was a visit to London's Guildhall to see Benjamin Scott. 'I can well believe all you've heard from your wife,' the old man told him, according to Booth's memoirs. 'It's a disgrace to civilisation. I only hope something can be done.'

'Something will,' answered Bramwell angrily.

But nothing was—the work pressure at Salvation Army HQ was

The Hallelujah Evangelists Join the Battle

too heavy—at least not until one morning a few weeks later. That day, when Bramwell arrived at the Army's new building in Queen Victoria Street, he was told that the caretaker had opened the doors of the building at 7 o'clock that morning, to find, sitting on the doorstep, a young girl in a red silk dress. Immediately, Bramwell sent for her.

She was a country girl of seventeen—and a typical example of the trade that Florence had been describing to him. She had answered an advertisement for a maid to work in a London house only to discover too late that it was a 'decoy ad' for a brothel. The staff—following the same system employed by the Brussels 'Maisons'—had removed her clothes and issued her with the red silk dress.

One night, when a client made excessive demands, she fled from her room and barricaded herself in the kitchen. Defiantly, she refused to unlock the door on the orders of the madame and, through the wooden panels, she heard her say: 'Leave her there till morning; she'll come to her senses when she wants her breakfast.'

Desperately, agonising what to do, the girl considered the chances of escape. Even if she could get out of the house, she was still faced with the problem where to go: she did not know anyone in London. Then she remembered that upstairs in her trunk was a red hymn book that had been given to her when she attended Salvation Army meetings in her home village. On the cover was the address of General Booth. She waited until the house was silent during the early hours of morning. Then she crept up to her room, collected the hymn book and, as she recorded, 'crept to the door, opened it and stole softly away, not even daring to close the door'. Since this is quoted from the girl's own statement, it must be presumed that this English brothel did not employ the same system as the Brussels brothels which had doors that could not be opened without a key from the inside.

Walking through the dawn light of that cold morning in early Spring, she asked a patrolling policeman the way to Queen Victoria Street and he directed her. It was three miles from the brothel—which was in the Thames side district of Pimlico—and the walk, in light slippers, took her an hour and a half. There, at Salvation Army HQ, she curled up on the stone step until the doors were opened by the caretaker.

The Hallelujah Evangelists Join the Battle

'The story,' recalled Bramwell, 'was hard to believe, but there was the girl . . . and there, moreover, was the dress, which obviously was not such as a mistress would provide for a domestic servant.'

Immediately, young Booth sent an officer to the brothel in Pimlico to collect her trunk. At first, the madame said she knew nothing of the girl, but, when he warned her that the Salvation Army had her in their protection and that they would enforce the law if necessary, she conceded and allowed him to remove the luggage.

For Bramwell, the incident was traumatic. He had accepted that the vice trade existed and needed action but, hard-worked as he was it had still remained something of an academic problem. Now he had actually seen a terrified young country girl, who was very different from the prostitutes he saw around the streets. He told Florence to bring some of her girls up to Queen Victoria Street from her shelter in the East End, so that he could interview them. One of them was fourteen—and pregnant. Like the teenagers that Dyer found in Brussels, she had been picked up in the streets by an amiable motherly woman. From then on, it had been the same old story.

'I resolved,' wrote Bramwell, 'that, no matter what the consequences might be, I would do all I could to stop these abominations, to rouse public opinion, to agitate for an improvement in the law . . .'

He went back to see Benjamin Scott. Then he called on Josephine Butler. She was quite clear as to where they should concentrate their attack for it to be at all effective in practical terms. As she had already written to Bramwell's mother, Catherine: 'We have the votes of the people . . . we need to reach the upper classes and government.'

It was to blast a breach in this citadel of power that the committee, which Scott and Dyer had promoted to fight the trade in girls, decided on drastic action. Their purpose was to scandalise the world of Victorian respectability—the world in which gentlemen conducted family prayers every morning and patronised brothels at night, the world in which women were not expected to know about anything associated with sex outside the marital bed . . . upper class women of course, not the thousands of other women who existed, as Walter made so clear, for the varied pleasure of gentlemen.

Quite simply, the plan was to set up an investigation to get the evidence to prosecute the most celebrated procuress in London—a woman who owned a string of famous brothels where, with tact and delicacy, she supplied the sexual needs of some of the richest, most aristocratic and most powerful men in Britain. As a scheme, it was audacious and, in view of the woman's immense influence within the Establishment, was almost certainly doomed to failure. Ironically, however, it was her deployment of this influence that backlashed and provided the main catalyst in the series of explosions that ripped apart the superficial social fabric of Victorian England.

6

Attack on 'the Empress of Vice'

Early on the sunny morning of 2 April, a highly polished brougham stood behind a sleekly groomed horse before a row of terraced cottages in Church Street, (now Old Church Street), Chelsea.

It was a pleasant little road with trees, white-specked with spring blossom, lining the pavement—a quiet, respectable residential area of the inner suburbs of Victorian London. It was the last place where a stranger, strolling along the street for the first time, would have expected to find a brothel—or, to be more exact, the head site of a chain of brothels.

However, this apparently innocent environment was—according to the prosecution counsel—the whole point of its location. By contrast with some sex establishments in less reputable parts of the capital—such as Norton Street, for example, where the girls displayed themselves naked in the windows to stimulate custom—Mary Jeffries ran her business with subtlety and discretion.

Her more nervous clients could, in fact, enter one of the cottages in Church Street and, if they wished, leave from another—for they had internal communicating doors. The girls, who would often arrive in the carriage that was now waiting in the street, were the *élite* of their profession: young, attractive, elegantly dressed and vivacious—entertaining sexual partners for well born gentlemen who were happy to pay the very large sum of £5 a time for their services.

Mary Jeffries, herself, lived in the end cottage of the block, number 125, which was on the corner of an intersection of Church Street and Elm Park Road. It was from the front door of this cottage that at about 9.30am she emerged, followed by two pretty, young girls, whom she described as her 'nieces', and stepped past the waiting coachman into the brougham.

Despite her prominence as a procuress—or, as she was labelled by Benjamin Scott's committee as 'an Empress of Vice'—she was an old lady. Seventy years old, thin and straight-spined, she had narrow lips and a rather bony face, the skin drawn tight over an aquiline nose. She was on her way that April morning to Westminster Police Court to answer charges—promoted by Scott's committee—of keeping a bawdy house. But, even though technically she could be jailed for the offence, she seemed to have no anxieties about the result of the case. 'Nothing can be done with me,' she snapped at the crowd of reporters waiting on the pavement as she stepped down from her carriage, 'as my clients and patrons are of the highest social order.'

Followed by her 'nieces', she swept into the courtroom where, presumably because of her influential friends, the magistrate did not ask her to enter the dock, the box-type stand in which defendants in British courts normally faced their prosecutors. Instead, to the fury of the watching Alfred Dyer, a seat was placed for her deferentially on the floor of the court. It was from there, as she scanned the courtroom imperiously, that she would have seen among the waiting witnesses the face of Jeremiah Minahan, the man who was to be her main accuser, the man who was, in fact—with the help of Dyer and Benjamin Scott—the principal cause of her having to attend this ridiculous trial at all.

It was two and a half years, since Mary Jeffries had first met Minahan. At the time, he was an Inspector of the Metropolitan Police, newly appointed to T Division that was responsible for Chelsea. He was, a strange character. Some writers have suggested that he was mentally unbalanced, but this would seem to be going too far. Certainly, he did not share the well-bribed, easy-going attitudes of his brother police officers to the trade in sex to the upper classes—a divergence for which he was, in effect, to be driven out of the Metropolitan Police. But this independence of outlook could merely have been because he was an honest man with principles—probably a rare phenomenon in London police circles—even if he exercised what appears to have been an unwavering zeal for duty, with a remarkable lack of tact.

A momentary glimpse of his character was revealed in the Jeffries trial. Defense counsel Montagu Williams was pressing him rigorously to give answers of 'yes' or 'no' to a line of questions. When the magistrate suggested gently that the aggressive interrogation was defeating its own purpose, Williams answered: 'I like it (the evidence) *my* way.'

'And I'll have it *my* way,' said Minahan firmly—which was an astonishing manner for a police officer, who must have been accustomed to hostile cross-examination, to address counsel.

Minahan was utterly uncompromising—a rigid man with firm religious beliefs and, it would seem from his energetic reaction to this aspect of human weakness, a violent aversion to sexual sin. The picture that emerges from his testimony and other sources is of an overzealous, humourless officer, striding through the district he was in charge of policing, determined to be diverted by no one from his duty.

It was, in fact, when he was on his rounds in his new district in the summer of 1882 that he noticed Mrs Jeffries on several occasions—not only at the block of cottages in Church Street, but also at houses in two other streets in his territory: Thurloe Place and the Fulham Road. At first, so he indicated in testimony, he did not realise who or what she was. Then his suspicions were alerted by the number of hansom cabs that were always arriving and departing from her houses. 'I have seen them there at 11 in the morning and 11 at night,' he said, referring to the cottages in Church Street. 'I have seen a cab waiting outside from 11 at night until 5 in the morning.'

Clearly, Mrs Jeffries—who was accustomed to cordial relations with the local police—saw this new grim-faced inspector, whose disapproval of her was patently obvious, as an uncomfortable new arrival, if not an actual danger. For she tried to make a friend of him. One August evening, as he was striding briskly towards Church Street along Elm Park Road, she was in her garden on the other side of a low wall. 'Good evening,' she said to him pleasantly. 'Where's my friend, Mr Chennery?' Chennery was a sergeant in Minahan's division. When the new inspector responded with a frigid reply, she remarked: 'You haven't been here long have you, Inspector?'

Then, according to Minahan's testimony, she decided to confide in him, presumably in the hope that this would soften him. 'I keep my houses in good order,' she told him, 'and it's no good the Police watching me. The Police have watched me before and they always find that I conduct them well.' By this, she meant presumably that she operated them with discretion without causing complaints from the neighbours—which, under the law at the time, could have been the only grounds for charges against her.

She then elaborated on her business. She named some of her clients —an allegation by Minahan that does not conform with her reputation for discretion—and some of the girls she introduced to them. 'It was at one of my houses,' she said, 'that the celebrated Mabel Grey was seduced.' Mabel Grey was a well known courtesan and Minahan had seen pictures of her in shop windows. Mrs Jeffries, so Minahan insisted, even revealed such intimate details of her operation as her prices and the cut she took for management: £2 out of the £5 paid by the clients. She told him that she maintained eight houses in London as well as running a healthy export business in girls to Paris, Brussels and Berlin.

While she was talking to him, Minahan was given a glimpse of the vice trade in action. A servant arrived at number 125, accompanied by a girl. 'Make haste,' said Mrs Jeffries to her, 'there's a gentleman waiting at St James' Villa.' St James' Villa was a cottage further up Church Street.

Then, the procuress, as Minahan put it, 'offered me gold' although, because she held it between her fingers, he 'could not swear whether it was a sovereign or half a sovereign'. True to character, he refused it indignantly. 'Oh,' said Mrs Jeffries, 'you're not like my good friend Mr Chennery or the other inspectors.'

The meeting can only have ended on an icy note. Minahan stalked back to the police station to report this scandalous conversation to his superior, Superintendant Fisher, only to find his zeal met by a sharp rebuff. 'You'd better be careful what you're saying,' warned his chief. When the other officers heard that he had refused Mrs Jeffries' bribe, so Minahan testified, they made a 'laughing stock' of him.

Minahan was not unused to being the odd man out. He had been

Attack on 'The Empress of Vice'

transferred from his last division for making allegations, considered to be ungrounded, against his brother officers. Now, however, in the face of rigid opposition, he had no choice but to drop the matter of Mrs Jeffries—at least officially. But she had made a vigilant enemy who was merely biding his time.

For six months, the inspector took no further action, but her thriving business in sex clearly continued to anger him and he spent much of the time compiling a dossier of evidence. He took careful note of the numbers of men arriving at the cottages in Church Street and of the girls who came separately to meet them either by hansom or in Mrs Jeffries' brougham. On one occasion, this stern and puritanical police inspector was engaged in his persistent surveillance when he was actually addressed—'solicited', as he described it, though this would seem to have been an exaggeration—by one of Mrs Jeffries' girls. 'How do you do, Ducky?' she said, and, with a provocative wiggle of her bustle, she walked jauntily into the cottages.

By April 1883, the inspector was ready to move once more into the attack against the procuress who was so well protected by his colleagues in the police. This time, he submitted a report *in writing* so that his superintendant would be forced to refer it to higher authority; and, in it, he laid out the results of his surveillance that he had recorded carefully in a notebook, kept in a drawer of his desk. He also described what had happened when he had first reported verbally on Mrs Jeffries, making the indignant point that his chief had 'seemed much annoyed with me as did also my brother officers'.

The superintendant was not the only officer to be annoyed with him. When Minahan was summoned to Scotland Yard, Colonel Labalmondiere, assistant commissioner of police, picked up his report, noted with horror the words 'brothels for the nobility' and glared at this impudent inspector. 'That is a highly improper observation for a responsible police officer to make,' he declared.

This time, there was no question of transfer. He was demoted to sergeant ostensibly for making unfounded charges against police officers. Also, so he claimed, his notebook—containing the detailed record of his surveillance of Mrs Jeffries' houses—was stolen from his desk.

Attack on 'The Empress of Vice'

Minahan went down fighting every foot of the way. He appealed over the heads of the police chiefs to the Home Secretary who investigated his case personally—and then supported the demotion, since the ex-inspector's allegations—as he told the House of Commons later—were completely groundless. Mrs Jeffries appeared to have won.

Bitterly, Minahan resigned from the police force, and sent copies of his report to three national dailies under the title: 'How an inspector of the Metropolitan Police was Punished for Faithfully Performing his Duty to the Public.' All the papers ignored it, so the crusading inspector decided to have it printed for private distribution. And at this point his luck changed. For the printer he chose—unwittingly, according to his testimony, though the coincidence is hard to believe—was the firm in Paternoster Row, Clerkenwell, that was run by Alfred Dyer and his brother. Perhaps he had heard of Dyer's campaign against the organisers of prostitution. If so, he displayed a sense of tactics that had been quite lacking in his earlier behaviour.

The meeting took place in early 1884, more than three years since the combined campaigns of Dyer and Josephine Butler had climaxed triumphantly in the Brussels sex trade trials—three years, of course, during which the two bills, promoted half-heartedly by the government to tighten up the prostitution laws, had been blocked by the brothels lobby in the House of Commons.

Alfred Dyer, goaded by the sexual sin he saw all around him on the London streets, was tortured by a sense of frustration and impotence. There seemed to be nothing further he could do—*until* the sudden appearance in his office of Minahan, a casual customer calling with some copy to print. It must have seemed like a Heaven-sent answer to his prayers, for it opened up a whole new avenue for action. Here was a man with inside information about Mary Jeffries, the owner of the most celebrated chain of brothels in London—a man, what is more, who had already been savaged by the Establishment for daring to suggest that her activities should be curbed.

Dyer must have rushed out of his office as soon as the ex-Inspector left, hurried by cab to see Benjamin Scott at the Guildhall and—although there is no record of this—told him with the restrained excitement of a Victorian gentleman of this big new opportunity that

Attack on 'The Empress of Vice'

had suddenly been presented to them. For in March, the London Committee for the Suppression of Traffic in English Girls—formed after Dyer's crusade to Brussels in 1880—offered the now unemployed Minahan a job as an investigator at a salary of £2 a week.

His brief was to get the evidence to prosecute the woman who—in addition to himself—had been the prime cause of the smashing of his career.

Under the law that then existed, prosecution for keeping a bawdy house could only be mounted on the complaints of two ratepayers—people who paid local property taxes—in the parish where the brothel was situated. This was going to be hard enough to organise in the face of the pressure that was sure to be levered on anyone willing to bring charges. But, before this could even be attempted, a dossier of incriminating facts would have to be prepared that would make the case unbreakable. Furthermore, since publicity was the main purpose of Dyer and Scott, the more lurid the evidence that Minahan could find the more valuable it would be for the committee's attack on the upper classes and the moral standards they sustained.

In the moral backlash that followed the fantastic success of the purity campaign, Mrs Jeffries has been portrayed as one of the most evil women of the nineteenth century. There is, however, very little factual evidence to indicate that she was particularly vicious. Stead suggested in the *Pall Mall Gazette* that a flogging house in St Johns Wood—equipped with all kinds of equipment as well as whips and scourges—was owned by her but, although he wielded some pretty wild slashes at the peddlers of vice, he was careful not to state this categorically.

According to Minahan and others, she admitted sending girls abroad, but there was nothing to suggest that this was done under the repressive conditions that were a built-in feature of the normal white slave trade operated by such men as Jean Sallecartes. Nor did anyone accuse her of running her houses under the prison-like conditions of the continental brothels or even of the Pimlico house from which the silk-dressed teenager escaped to Salvation Army Headquarters. Mrs Jeffries' girls came and went quite freely.

Almost certainly, the truth is that the class of business she ran—with high prices paid and high value demanded—could only be operated by willing girls with a flair for the profession. No doubt she catered for perversions but even Minahan, for all his keen personal motives, could only find one rather old case of her arranging for the seduction of a young virgin, which suggests that it was a comparatively rare occurrence.

What little is known about her background comes primarily from Charles Terrot in *The Maiden Tribute*. His main source, as he kindly revealed subsequently, although he did not quote it in his book, was the late Rosa Lewis, celebrated proprietor of the Cavendish Hotel near Piccadilly and mistress of Edward, Prince of Wales (later Edward VII).

According to Mr Terrot—and presumably Rosa Lewis—Mary Jeffries began her professional life as a girl in a very famous top class Mayfair brothel called Berthe's. Clearly, she was intelligent—and probably skilful as a prostitute—and eventually, as she grew older, she became number two in the hierarchy, second only to Berthe herself.

Berthe, however, had scruples about the way she ran her business. No perversions were catered for and certainly no children were ever provided. It was this aspect, reported Mr Terrot, that struck Mrs Jeffries as a serious omission when, on a visit to Paris, she found that some of the French houses did a booming business in off-beat sex. She returned to London, obtained financial backing from some of her clients, and set up in opposition to her previous employer with a policy of supplying sex in whatever form her clients required it.

Without question, she was highly successful, though whether she made a speciality of perversion must remain a little suspect since Rosa Lewis—though a contemporary source—was a very old lady by the time Mr Terrot interviewed her, and her allegations were not backed very substantially by the terrier-like probing of Jeremiah Minahan.

In fact, the sex campaigners—who could not believe that any woman could sell her body willingly—were not so much concerned with what Mrs Jeffries' clients did when they were in her house as with who they were. Evidence of perversion would be useful—and their imaginations always saw it as being far more widespread than it probably was—because it would add an additional horror dimension to the vice picture, but the key to their whole thinking lay in the quality of her clientele. It was because her patrons were so eminent that they exemplified the whole idea—which was the reformers' main ideological target—that there was nothing wrong with a gentleman visiting a brothel. Throughout this new stage of their campaign they flaunted the threat that they would name names—and, at one stage, they did.

However, if Minahan was not too successful in ferreting out evidence of perversion—which anyway was not relevant in a legal sense—he did come through with some hard facts to support a prosecution.

He approached George Bellchambers, Mrs Jeffries' coachman who had just left her employ, and found him willing to talk. The brougham was a central part of her operation, both for communication and transport. When telegrams or letters arrived at Church Street from clients who wanted to make dates, Bellchambers would be sent off in the carriage to arrange for the women to keep their appointments. As a result, he knew all the addresses and, of course, the names of the girls. Then, Mrs Jeffries would send him with notes to the fashionable clubs where her clients were staying or dining—the Turf, the Guards, the Army and Navy, the Bachelors, the Marlborough. In the afternoon or evening, he would often collect the girls from their homes and bring them to the houses in Church Street, Thurloe Place, the Fulham Road, and to an address that Minahan did not appear to have known about previously, the Brompton Road.

On one occasion, when Mrs Jeffries was alone in the carriage, Bellchambers recalled, she had been in particularly talkative mood. On her orders, he had reined in beside the S-shaped lake in Hyde park called The Serpentine. 'She told me that she used to supply the King of the Belgians and get £800 a month,' the coachman later related in court, 'she told me she trod on the toes of Madame James, who lived at Lodge Row, and took His Majesty away from her'.

Later, Mrs Jeffries must have had moments of reflection when she wished she had not been so open with her servants. Certainly, she should have been more circumspect in the way she parted company with them—for they were the main means that enabled Minahan to effect her ultimate downfall.

Attack on 'The Empress of Vice'

For example, Elizabeth Bromwich, her cook at number 125 Church Street for seven years, gave him a colourful rundown on what happened when clients arrived. She would often answer the door and show them into the drawing room where Mrs Jeffries would greet them and introduce them to the girls, who would normally arrive after them. The money was usually left unobtrusively on a small table in the dining room. Mary Miller, a housemaid, worked even closer to the patrons, for she made the beds after they had finished with them. She confirmed what Minahan had already observed from external surveillance: some clients stayed all night, others were there for as short a period as an hour or even thirty minutes.

However, Maria Watt, another servant, provided the most vivid evidence that must have aroused all Alfred Dyer's campaigning instincts when Minahan repeated it to him. For she had been present when a thirteen-year-old girl—introduced as one of Mrs Jeffries 'nieces'—arrived at Church Street. She must have been the daughter of a poor relation, for she was dressed in hobnailed boots and plain country clothes. Her 'aunt' promptly took her out shopping and bought her a dress that was more suited to the requirements of the Church Street cottages.

The next morning, when Maria took the child her breakfast, she was crying. A man, she said, had hurt her badly in the night and Mrs Jeffries had given her £15. Maria had promptly given notice and told her employer she ought to be horse-whipped. Mrs Jeffries had tried to calm her, explained that what the child had said was nonsense and offered her a glass of wine; but the servant was adamant and left the house that day.

It was a fine story, just what Benjamin Scott and Alfred Dyer needed, apart from the weakness in it that Mrs Jeffries had given the child so much money. The main snag was that it had happened eleven years before—which was not a great deal of help in a prosecution for the present offence of keeping a bawdy house.

However, the Minahan dossier—and his list of witnesses willing to testify—grew bigger. He talked to some of the girls whose services Mrs Jeffries offered to her clients, and he succeeded in gaining the support of a couple of neighbours who cannot have been too happy

Attack on 'The Empress of Vice'

with the noise of hooves and cab wheels in the street at all hours of night. But the most important facts he recorded were the names of the clients that he obtained from the coachmen and the servants, such men as Lord Fife, Lord Douglas Gordon, Lord Lennox, Lord Hailford and, one that was truly explosive, the Prince of Wales—although later Mrs Jeffries strongly denied that His Royal Highness was one of her clients.

At last—and it must have been at about the time Bramwell Booth interviewed the fugitive from the Pimlico brothel—Scott and Dyer decided that they had enough evidence to mount the prosecution they had now been planning for a year.

On the evening of 25 March, Inspector Patrick Cronin, of Minahan's old T Division, called at 125 Church Street, told Mrs Jeffries that he had a warrant for her arrest and asked her to accompany him to the police station for the pre-trial formalities.

The hearings before a magistrate—which, like a Grand Jury investigation in America, were held to establish if there was a case for trial —lasted for three days. Two of Mrs Jeffries' coachmen, three of her servants and two of her prostitutes gave evidence as well as the butler of the house across the road from her cottages.

The magistrate placed a strict ban on the mention of the names of the clients, but naturally there was no restriction on witnesses from revealing the identities of the women they enjoyed.

Defence Counsel Montagu Williams tried hard to suggest that nothing had been proved against his notorious client who had run her houses for years without complaint. It was, he implied, all a conspiracy organised by fanatics. The magistrate, however, was not convinced. He sent the case to the higher court, the Middlesex Sessions, and on 5 May, Mrs Jeffries, stood formal trial before a jury—at least she did in theory.

Clearly, throughout this period, the authorities had viewed the proceedings with a degree of concern. The police were under implicit criticism and there was an obvious danger of scandal if any witness should forget the instruction not to mention names. Already, a comment had slipped out on the witness stand about the King of the Belgians—which was threatening to cause diplomatic repercussions.

Furthermore, the angry members of the reforming societies and the Methodists—who, even if they had not approved William Booth's novel techniques, were fully behind the war on vice—were becoming more outspoken in their public speeches.

Then there was an unfortunate incident on the final day of the preliminary hearings of the Jeffries case that cannot have made the Home Office officials too happy. In the daily routine business that the Magistrate was handling before the brothel proceedings came on, a woman appeared before him complaining that her sister had been decoyed by a London employment agency into the Albion Hotel in Le Havre, France, which she had now discovered to be a 'gay house'. The attorney for Scott's London Committee was waiting in court and the magistrate referred the woman to him. Scenting yet new material for the campaign, Scott wired the British consul in Le Havre, with a request to investigate.

The next day, T. D. Dutton—one of Mrs Jeffries' attorneys—appeared in court on behalf of the Albion Hotel, Le Havre, and produced a paper signed by the decoyed girl, stating that the whole allegation was nonsense. 'I was never in a more respectable house,' she had written. But by then, as the result of intervention by the British consul, the girl was on her way back to England. In London, at Scott's request, Minahan took her statement. She had, she insisted, been forced by the Albion Hotel management to sign the denial that Mr Dutton had produced in court. In truth, however, the hotel was a brothel.

Two days later, the morning papers carried a triumphant letter from Scott, quoting a statement by the British consul that 'This is not the first case where I have had to act on behalf of girls engaged at the Albion Hotel under false representations.'

The fact that Mrs Jeffries' attorneys should be appearing—with false statements signed under pressure—for an immoral continental house supplied by the white slave trade held an unfortunate hint of vice ring connections.

From an official point of view, the purity movement was getting far too much publicity. It was perhaps for this reason that the court police on the day of the Jeffries' trial were particularly officious. When

Attack on 'The Empress of Vice'

Alfred Dyer arrived with two journalists, one police constable told him that he had orders to admit no one. Another insisted that the public gallery was full whereas, in fact, it was completely empty—as Dyer discovered after arguing his way into the courtroom.

Another reason why the public was being discouraged from attending the case was that there was a plan to carve it up—which Alfred Dyer detailed in his campaigning journal, *The Sentinel*. At 10.30, Montagu Williams—so Dyer reported—entered the court and asked Mr Edward Besley, the Prosecuting Counsel, to retire 'for a private consultation'. For half an hour, proceedings were held up while the two counsels conferred with the judge.

When Williams returned to the court, he told Mrs Jeffries: 'Say you are guilty,'—which accordingly she did when the clerk asked for her plea. Then to Dyer's horrified astonishment, his committee's own counsel—briefed to prosecute a procuress—proceeded to make a speech in her favour. He was not the same attorney who had acted for them in the magistrates' court—and they soon regretted the change. By contrast with their former advocate, who had fought Williams aggressively and accused police witnesses of attempting to screen Mrs Jeffries, Besley said that there was no proof of any breach of the peace—even though, as Dyer wrote angrily later, he knew there was a witness waiting in court to swear that he had repeatedly complained about her to the police. 'The case really resolves itself,' said Besley, 'into allowing people to assemble together for improper purposes. Undoubtedly, they were free from scandal in the ordinary sense of the word.'

After a prosecution like this, Mrs Jeffries hardly needed a defence. The judge fined her £200 and bound her over to keep the peace for two years against sureties by herself of £400 and by another citizen of £400. This meant that, if she was convicted again within that period, a further £800 would be forfeited. Either way, it was a ludicrously small punishment for a confessed crime that often carried a sentence of jail. It was quite clear that Mrs Jeffries' powerful friends had pulled her out of the fire—quite obvious that, in order to avoid the need for unwholesome evidence, a low penalty deal had been agreed by the judge in return for a plea of guilty.

Attack on 'The Empress of Vice'

It was an age of hypocrisy and of privilege, but there were limits even in Victorian society. The affair had been handled in a way that was blatantly cynical and exceptionally clumsy. Although there were signs of nervousness in Whitehall, the Establishment seemed strangely insensitive to the groundswell of public opinion that, roused by reforming societies throughout the country, was turning slowly against the sexual underworld that so far—when it was aware of it at all—it had completely tolerated.

The focus of the public sympathy that was developing—guided by the reformers—was the prostitution of children and very young teenagers.

The House of Lords committee had made a special point that this needed early legislation. Even the royal commission, that had been so hostile to Josephine Butler, had urged action on the age of consent. Throughout 1884, memorials had streamed into the Home Office demanding action to stop the traffic in young girls. These did not come only from militant organisations such as those run by Benjamin Scott and Josephine Butler, but from a whole range of rescue societies of one kind or another. Many of them were headed by influential people—men such as Lord Shaftesbury, president of the Young Women's Christian Association, and Cardinal Manning, who insisted that something must be done to curb the procurers who waited on London docks to prey on the Irish girls who arrived on the ships from Dublin.

Against this background, the Jeffries case, with its obvious distortion of the normal legal processes, was particularly significant. It provoked sharp criticism in the London press, whose editors normally took the view that commercial sex was not a suitable matter for a daily newspaper. The *Morning Mail* attacked the sentence as a 'mere mockery of justice' and described the way in which it had been hushed up as 'a disgrace to all concerned'. *The Daily Echo* demanded that the government should set up an 'impartial investigation' into Minahan's charges of collusion against the police.

'The inferences,' wrote the infuriated Alfred Dyer in *The Sentinel*, 'point to a state of moral corruption, heartless cruelty and prostitution of authority, almost sufficient even in this country to goad the industrial classes into revolution . . .'

'Oh God,' cried C. H. Spurgeon, one of the Booth's leading preachers, addressing a big meeting in London's Metropolitan Tabernacle, 'have mercy upon the land whose judgement seats and palaces are defiled with vice.'

Another impassioned speaker, James B. Wookey—who had resigned from the Salvation Army to concentrate his efforts on the narrower sexual objectives of the Gospel Purity Association—went far further in his public lashing of the lustful upper classes at the country town of Luton near London and provoked a big scandal. 'We have in England,' he declared to his large audience, 'nearly 150,000 fallen girls who gain their daily bread by leading a life of sin and shame . . . Yet male traitors, but for whom these girls might still have been in the bright sunshine of those summer days when not a cloud passed by to darken them, are allowed to walk out amongst the pure as if there was nothing in their soul and body murdering life of which they need be ashamed. Nay more, they are oft times found sitting in Parliament making laws by which we have to abide. They have occupied the chief places in courts of justice.'

This was strong meat for a public speech, but Wookey was merely warming up his audience. Drawing for them a vivid picture of the trial 'of an old woman of infamous character' for 'keeping a number of human slaughter houses', he claimed to have seen Minahan's dossier of evidence, and told his thousands of shocked listeners that he was not surprised to 'see that among this crowd of male debauchees the names occur of not a few of exalted rank'. Then, at the top of his voice, he listed them, ending with his punchline that he knew would have an enormous impact—the name of Mrs Jeffries' most eminent alleged client, the Prince of Wales. It caused a sensation in the crowd in the Luton Corn Exchange—*and* in the papers that carried the story.

Meanwhile, the tempo of the various anti-vice campaigns—all of which had been stimulated by anger at the result of the Jeffries trial —was steadily rising.

The Criminal Law Amendment Bill was once more under debate in the Lords before being sent down to the lower house where, twice before, it had been filibustered. This time, it was having a fairly rough mauling even by the peers. The proposed age of consent had been forced down from sixteen to fifteen with the argument that there was a big danger that gentlemen would be exposed to blackmail by precocious hussies—which, as it was to turn out, they would.

It was to toughen the lobbying of the bill that, two days after the Jeffries trial, a large meeting was held in the Princes Hall, Piccadilly. Most of the men on the platform were parliamentarians who were promoting the change in law. One of the speakers, however, was a woman, Ellice Hopkins, who had already written to Stead urging him to take action. Personally, she declared, she had found in a public jail at Leith, Scotland, a seven-year-old girl who had been raped by a group of men. One of them had been arrested, but was freed by the judge at the trial on the grounds that he had not committed the crime alone.

This was nothing to do with the law—even then it was a clear crime —but with the attitude of male judges.

There was a further instance of this a week later: at the Middlesex Sessions, P. H. Edlin, who had given Mrs Jeffries so mild a sentence, tried the case of a man named Barrett. He, too, was accused of keeping a house of ill fame. But he did not have the same kind of friends as Mrs Jeffries. The judge—who must have had no political sense whatever—ordered him to jail for six months. The contrast in the two sentences by the same judge only served to emphasise the rigging of the Jeffries trial. On 21 May, James Stuart—one of the MPs who had supported Josephine Butler in her fight against state brothels—tabled a question in the House of Commons asking the Home Secretary to investigate.

The following afternoon—the Friday before the national holiday that the British always celebrate at Whitsun—the Criminal Law Amendment Bill was debated in the Commons. At one stage, Cavendish Bentinck—who had led the opposition to all the proposed vice laws—tried to stop the debate on technical grounds. There were less than forty members in the house needed for a quorum, he argued. But a head count proved him wrong. For almost an hour, the speakers debated the bill. Then Cavendish Bentinck rose again and complained at great and deliberate length that it was quite wrong to discuss a subject such as this without the presence in the house of the Law Officers.

He saw to it that he was still speaking when the clerk stood up and announced that it was 6.50pm, the hour at which the session had to end. There was, therefore, no time for a vote. Once again, Cavendish Bentinck had killed the bill.

To Benjamin Scott watching in the public gallery as the wigged speaker of the Commons rose from his deep leather wing chair to leave the chamber, it seemed that all his years of effort to change the vice laws had collapsed. With a general election imminent, it was obvious that the Criminal Law Amendment Bill was now dead. It would have to be taken up and promoted by a new government and possibly a new party.

The CD acts had merely been suspended and, as Cavendish Bentinck was to write in a letter to the *Pall Mall Gazette* a week later, if the House of Commons was now asked to vote on the main issue of state prostitution it would back it with a big majority. Obviously, it would not be long before his assertion was put to the proof.

Worst of all, the campaign to jail Mrs Jeffries—that had taken more than a year to promote—had fizzled out like damp gunpowder. It had attracted some criticism of the legal establishment and given some of the more sensational of the anti-vice orators some material to exploit, but soon this would all be forgotten—unless some big new source of pressure could be brought to bear.

William Stead was an obvious man for Scott to approach. Only that morning the ebullient ginger-bearded young editor of the *Pall Mall Gazette* had lashed out in print at the 'loquacity of our legislators', blaming them for the sacrifice of 'the protection of our young girls . . .' 'A House of Commons in which women were represented,' he had declared, 'would not display such indifference to a question which is really one of life or death to an immense number of poor girls.'

There was no doubt where Stead's sympathies lay. Scott had never met him, but he knew that he was friendly with Bramwell Booth and corresponded regularly with Josephine Butler.

Furthermore, Stead was a new phenomenon in British journalism:

a campaigning editor, who had developed original techniques—such as personal interviews that were then quite new to journalism—that had sent his circulation soaring. Two years before, when the government had decided to withdraw British forces from the turbulent Sudan, he had forced them to recall the brilliant but erratic General Gordon to command the area—a decision that had led to his death at Khartoum. The following year, he had attacked the Admiralty in a series of articles on 'The Truth about the Navy', charging that Britain was unprepared for defence. As a result of this exposé, the issue of building warships became one of the main political topics of the day.

Now Benjamin Scott wanted him to apply the same techniques to prostitution, to aim for the objective that Scott and Dyer had failed to achieve with their prosecution of Mrs Jeffries—a public exposé of the facts about the sex-for-sale picture in London that would shock the government into legislation.

All Scott's efforts had been effectively thwarted by the Establishment because it had a strong hold in the only areas hitherto available to the reformers—the courts and parliament. But in the *Pall Mall Gazette*, Stead had a method of communication over which those determined men had no direct control.

In other words, when the old man called that Saturday at the Northumberland Street office of the *Pall Mall Gazette*, he knew that —with the climate that then existed in Britain—the editor had the power to transform the situation. The issue was: what price would Stead have to pay for deploying that power, and would he be prepared to pay it?

For this was not an issue about generals or warships, on which there could be varying viewpoints. It was unfit for public discussion. Even many of Alfred Dyer's Quakers—though committed with him to a staunch policy of destroying the brothels and the trade that supplied them—were completely opposed to the use of publicity to achieve these aims. For they took the view that the exposure of facts about vice to innocent people could be more damaging in their moral repercussions than the evil they were seeking to change.

If reformers could take this attitude, it was obvious that the shocked reaction of the great majority of middle class Victorians to any major newspaper treatment of prostitution would be immense. It could mean ruin for a talented editor. Without question, there could be danger of prosecution for obscenity or libel.

The personal risk was tremendous—but for a campaigning journalist, with a strict non-conformist background, it was a very tempting subject. For all his protestations of horror, it must have thrilled his professional instincts. He must have seen the headlines forming in his mind.

Stead refused to commit himself immediately to taking action on Scott's suggestion, but he did agree to go down with him to Salvation Army Headquarters to discuss it further with Bramwell Booth.

Booth was fully prepared for the visit. Already waiting in the big building in Queen Victoria Street were three of the girls from Florence's shelter—living proof, intended to provide the final argument to convince the young editor how vital it was that he should act. One of them was the fourteen-year-old who had so disturbed Bramwell himself. All of them were under sixteen.

One by one, Stead questioned the girls, who were brought into the office in turn. When the interviews were over and the last girl had left the room, he stayed silent for a moment, staring in front of him. Then, he brought his fist down hard on the desk top with an impact that shook the inkwells. 'Damn,' he snarled.

7
The Campaigning Editor

It was a strange and turbulent mixture of emotions and beliefs that fired Stead with the fierce energy, that motivated him, on that May Saturday in particular, to take the gamble of his life. He planned to attack the morality of a whole society, to rip away the fabric of Victorian respectability, but unlike many moral reformers, he was no cold ascetic.

He was a warm, passionate, excitable man whose main faults—even professional faults as a journalist—stemmed from his emotional overspill. He still bore the marks of his inflexible, God-dominated childhood, of the influence of his grim minister parent with his gaunt warnings of the dangers of Hell. Stead never worked on Sundays if he could help it, and even though he was now thirty-six—and one of the most sophisticated men in London—he had never entered a theatre; for this, as his father had reiterated constantly during his boyhood, was the 'Devil's Chapel'. Like Alfred Dyer's tortured asceticism, the minister's whole theory stemmed from an unwavering belief in the stark doctrine of original sin. The only possibility of salvation lay in the resistance to the often skilful, often concealed temptation of Satan. It demanded a state of constant guard, of rigid avoidance of all the fringe territory where the weakness of the flesh might become vulnerable to insidious pressure—the first stage of total moral downfall.

Yet surprisingly—despite this background—Stead was not repressed. He lived and worked in the strong conviction of the personal guidance of God, but his 'senior partner', as he called Him, permitted him a good deal of leeway in the area of sexual morality.

Perhaps, if there had been no women in his life other than his wife, his campaigning would have lacked edge and feeling. He wrote with shock, but it was not sexual shock. He did not attack the Victorians for having sexual relations with prostitute women, but for supporting a system that enslaved them. He was not concerned, as he was to emphasise in print, with the morality of acts between consenting adults. He was fighting a trade that systematically tricked young teenage girls into a life that they did not seek and, in many cases at least, would later regret.

Truly, he was battling for freedom. It is significant that although Mary Jeffries—and the rather suspect story of the thirteen-year-old girl with which Benjamin Scott had roused his crusading spirit—was one of the main reasons why he took up the cause at all, he did not in practice attack her very fiercely. In fact, he even complimented her in a grudging kind of way on the efficient running of her houses. It was the operators who kept their girls as virtual prisoners and the procurers of unsuspecting teenagers that were his main targets.

Stead grew up in a manse in Northumberland, a beautiful county in the north of England, consisting of miles of hilly moorland, marked by the ugly, grimy towns under their palls of black smoke that signalled the growth of the Industrial Revolution. He went to a special school for congregational ministers' sons and, at fourteen was apprenticed in the counting house of a Newcastle merchant who doubled up as the Russian vice-consul. In his spare time, Stead wrote articles that, as he grew older, were good enough to be published in the local papers. It was because of these freelance articles that, at the age of twenty-two, he was offered the post of editor of the newly-established *Northern Echo* in nearby Darlington.

His editing was personal and vigorous. The *Echo* became a campaigning newspaper that grew into an important political weapon that was staunchly behind the Liberal Party. Also, during his years in the vice-consul's office in Newcastle, Stead had developed Russian sympathies. When, in an outburst of bellicose Jingoism, a nation-wide demand developed to attack Russia in support of the British alliance with Turkey, Stead gave Gladstone strong backing in the Liberal leader's peace campaign. When the Turks crushed a revolt in Bulgaria with great savagery, their attrocities—highlighted in a vivid pamphlet

The Campaigning Editor

by Gladstone—provided the editor with an emotional pitch that he was able to exploit in column after angry column.

Even though the *Echo* was only a provincial newspaper, Stead became well-known. When at last, though still in his mid-twenties, Stead met Gladstone, he found that the politician was a regular reader of his newspaper.

It was inevitable that a man of his talent and energy would move to London, though he did so with some reservations. Nine years after he had taken over command of the *Echo*, he was offered the post of assistant editor—under the famous John Morley—of the *Pall Mall Gazette*.

He dithered rather coyly and scribbled in his diary the arguments for and against. Truly, Stead was a great showoff, even to himself. He had charm and vivacity and he took up his causes with a fierce sincerity, but he lived as though he was watching himself in a distant mirror. His diary was clearly intended for eyes other than his own, even though some of it was extremely intimate—and, for the age in which he lived, extraordinarily indiscreet.

He accepted the *Gazette* appointment, so he told himself, because in London he 'would have more power in driving the machine of state and of reaching the ears of those who with tongue or pen reach others . . .' He might, he mused in a moment of unguarded ambition, become 'one of the half dozen men in London whose advice is listened to by the rulers of the Empire'.

Not that he wanted power for its own sake, of course—at least so he convinced himself. His boyhood training made him frame every decision in a setting of the fight with Satan. 'When I see the Devil so strong and his assailants so timorous and half-hearted, I long to be in a place where I can have a full slap at him.'

The slap, when he delivered it, was to have an enormous impact—meted out by a man with an immense driving energy and a huge capacity for work. When Stead was racing to catch an edition with a leading article, he would dictate his piece to a series of reporters—each man scribbling for one minute before rushing off to write out the copy for the printer while another took his place. By this technique, recorded J. W. Robertson Scott, one of his assistant editors, 'the leader was got out in about twelve minutes and in type in a quarter of an hour'.

He was always on the move, often striding about his office banging his leg with a long-handled clothes brush, talking all the time 'a little through his nose' in his broad north-of-England accent. Proud of his eccentricities, he would boast of the fact that he preferred running to walking. 'I liked the lift that came from running as hard as you can,' he said years later. 'I remember very well telling Morley when I came to London that if I felt cold any day I would not hesitate at running as hard as I could from one end of Pall Mall to the other, and noting with some amusement the expression that came over his face.'

In an age that was formal, Stead was deliberately casual. His dress in the office was often unconventional. He would receive visitors with his feet on the mantelpiece or with a leg dangling over the arm of his chair.

John Morley did his best to curb his assistant editor's volatile enthusiasm. 'Please remember, my dear Stead,' he would comment about his impassioned leading articles, 'not to shout when talking will do.' When eventually Morley became Secretary of State for Ireland, he remarked wryly that 'after keeping Stead in order for three years, I don't see why I shouldn't be able to govern the Irish'.

Stead, with his bushy ginger beard and the ice blue eyes that stabbed from behind his spectacles, was often over-whelming to the people he interviewed. 'When Stead met great personages,' said a contemporary, 'he looked quite steadily right into their eyes . . . It was an almost daunting expression of "nerve force".' In fact, this may not have been deliberate, for he had bad trouble with his eyes. At one stage, in his teens, he almost went blind.

'He was a little turbulent, spectacular and melodramatic,' commented the deeply admiring Robertson Scott gently and it was this tendency towards melodrama that exposed him to the sharp criticism of his enemies. Unquestionably, he was a poseur, and even though he lived in a society which indulged in elaborate and often insincere displays of emotion, Stead frequently overdid it. In fact, if he had not possessed a lot of talent and intelligence and wit and humanity, this aspect would have made him insufferable.

As it was, his heavy self-conscious showmanship earned him the mocking nick-name of 'Barnum'. Almost always, when speaking in public, he would begin dramatically with a prayer. Bernard Shaw has described the occasion when he attended a big meeting in London's Queen's Hall in response to a request for support from Stead who published his book reviews. 'I attended accordingly only to find that he did not know what a public meeting was . . . Treating the assembly as his congregation and nothing else, he rose and said: "Let us utter one great Damn!" Then he burst into hysterical prayer and I left.'

Even his writing, though pungent and vivid, was marred by the same declamatory attitudes. He would urge brevity on aspiring writers, suggesting that—when they had written their articles as well as they could—they should pretend they had to telegraph them to Australia at their own expense before producing their final draft. But, when it suited him, he would ignore his own advice and embark on long allegorical excursions into classical mythology that were in obvious need of sharp pruning.

Stead lived in the confident belief that all his actions were directed by God, who had selected him for a very special role—which may explain his taste for histrionics. Against this background, his deep fascination with the whole area of extrasensory perception was logical, and the fact that a man in close communication with the Deity truly did seem to have a degree of mystical insight is not surprising. 'Why did you bother to wire?' he asked one of his editors who called at his home in Wimbledon. 'You know that you could have made me aware of your coming.'

Six months before Morley resigned as editor of the *Gazette*, Stead told him the date he would be leaving to enter parliament—even though at the time he had not even been offered a seat. With great and ominous clarity, he was to foresee the sinking of one of the great new ocean liners—then a highly modern concept in travel—though his keen sense of occult perception does not appear to have warned him against taking passage in the fatal maiden voyage of the Titanic.

Stead's firm conviction of his partnership with God makes his attitude to his love affairs seem strangely ambivalent. It is an area in his life that strikes a dramatic contrast with his strict upbringing

The Campaigning Editor

and the religious way he lived—family prayers and hymns every morning, chapel twice on Sundays and regular reading of the bible. It carries the taint of Victorian hypocrisy, although there is ample evidence—supported by his diary—that, despite his melodrama and his wordy flamboyance, he did not try to present himself as better than he was. Nor, in his communings with himself, does he appear to explain his feelings about this aspect of his life very satisfactorily.

This would not be relevant in considering the character of Stead as a campaigner purely for issues involving such subjects as warships, but it provides a fascinating extra dimension in the make-up of a man who was attacking a society for its morality.

Stead had married Emma, a local girl from the north whom he had known for years, when he was twenty-four—two years after taking over the editorship of the *Echo*. And, although he was always devoted to the family she gave him, it was clear fairly early that she was not always entirely adequate for his emotional needs.

He wrote often in his diary about his regrets for the hurt he caused her through his relations with other women—which he seems to have made no attempt to conceal—but there is a curious lack of conviction in his concern, a kind of strange unspoken assumption that God would not only forgive these amorous transgressions, but was also partially responsible by permitting them to happen at all.

On one occasion, for example, he conceded just a little breezily that he had 'grieved my wife'—who happened to be expecting another baby—'by a fortnight's flirtation with a Scottish lassie who came over to spend the holidays with us. It was a passing folly. She was a good listener, had good spirits, good complexion . . . I kissed her a good deal more than was wise or right, but I was on my holidays . . . and was more in the mood for any kind of fun than I had been for long. It was driving about in a phaeton that it all happened.'

It was an oddly cheerful admission for a young Victorian husband and it bore the undertone that it was a pity about Emma, but there it was. It came when he was emerging from a long and tempestuous affair with a well-known London hostess that nearly broke his marriage.

Olga Novikoff was a striking Russian woman, with a keen intelligence and a surging patriotism. Thirty-five years old when Stead met her, she was the god-daughter of Tsar Nicholas, but she held no official position in London. Despite this, she promoted the interests of her country with such passion that Benjamin Disraeli leader of the Tories, who tended to be anti-Russian—gave her the mocking tagline 'The MP [Member of Parliament] for Russia.'

Realising early that she would encounter more sympathy among the Liberals, she concentrated her attentions on Gladstone, and they became so friendly that the statesman was accused of allowing himself to be captivated by the proverbial beautiful spy—though the espionage allegation was obvious nonsense, since she made no effort to make a secret of either her motives or her methods.

She first read Stead's pro-Russian articles in the *Northern Echo* very soon after receiving the shattering news of her brother's death in the Balkans. In the emotional aftermath of this personal tragedy, according to Stead's daughter, Estelle, 'she was immensely thrilled by the verve and passion' of the young editor's writing.

She wrote to him and asked him to call on her when he next came to London. It developed into an 'Entente Cordiale,' as the editor described it, that was a lot more than a 'passing folly in a phaeton' and it plunged the Stead home into three years of crisis—of which Emma was fully aware.

'I have treated her cruelly,' Stead confessed to himself, 'not wilfully, but because my whole soul was charged, to the exclusion of everything else, with political subjects with which she sympathised but languidly...'

It was an old story—a simple, small-town wife who was not bound up sufficiently in the working world of a dedicated and progressive husband. They had been married for three years and he was just beginning to feel his power as an editor. The sophisticated **Olga Novikoff**, with her salon at which he met the most important men in London, was able to share fully his intense political interest. In her, he 'met another soul as surcharged with kindred thoughts and we met and our existences mingled'.

The explosion was clearly traumatic. 'Even in the height of the first excitement,' Stead wrote in his diary, 'I never wavered in preferring

Emma as a wife . . . and I have repaid her how? . . . This New Year must see a change. Either it restores my wife to me or it consummates the shipwreck of what I had fondly, passionately hoped would be a christian home . . . It is time to go to chapel . . . Oh God, almighty yet loving God, help me to live without torturing those who love me.'

A year later, he was feeling guilty about Olga and his fading passion. 'I sin no more in relation to her,' he wrote. 'I am still deeply attached to her and would do anything for her, but I no longer love her with that sinful passion the memory of which covers me with loathing, remorse and humiliation. Poor body, she is much shattered, has aged much in the last two trying years . . . She suspects the change that has taken place in me and resents it. But as I am the same in all respects to her cause, all except the fever-blistering passion directed to her, I manage to scrape through without inflicting upon her the pain that I dread. I love her intensely but no longer as a second wife. I am disgusted with myself for having to confess a change, which nevertheless is right. The wrong rises in the passion. And yet who could help? God pardon the weakness of his erring child. My hope that I might be the means of leading her to a trustful faith and hope in God and his Christ is dimmed by the damning memory of my own weakness in having succumbed so far to the temptation of the Devil.'

His marriage survived—not merely in form, at a time when divorce was socially unacceptable, but in a real sense. By 1889, some ten years later, he was wondering in his diary at the fact that 'desire increased with years rather than diminished and the last twelve months I worshipped my wife with my body, as the Prayer Book has it, more than ever before'. All the same, he limited intercourse to twice a week since 'if thrice or four times in the week I got deaf with apparent wax formation in the right ear'.

This, then, was the man who left Bramwell Booth's office after interviewing the three teenagers on that Saturday—disturbed, anxious, pondering what exactly to do. He was no rake, no customer of brothels, but he was a male who was fully familiar with strong sexual need.

For a few hours, Stead considered the alternative courses of action that were available to him. He recalled what he had written in his diary four years ago when, as a young provincial editor, he had been considering the offer from the *Pall Mall Gazette*. Ironically at the time, he had just seen reports of Benjamin Scott's memorial to the Foreign Office, following the continental campaigning of Josephine Butler and Alfred Dyer. 'I have had a curious impulse in the direction of London . . . a sense of the burden imposed upon me to write an Uncle Tom's Cabin on The Slavery of Europe. The burden is greater than I can bear. But, if it is ultimately to be laid on my back, God will strengthen me for it.'

This was Stead showing off to himself again, enjoying his special relationship with his 'Senior Partner'—Stead, too, in one of his clairvoyant moments. But the burden truly was considerable. The exposé he planned was fraught by practical problems that demanded great care. Most important of all was the need to build a strong defence against the inevitable charges that the whole story was an exaggeration. Hard proof to back the statements he made was vital.

The investigation, he decided, would be conducted by a 'Secret Commission'—which in truth was merely a reporting team, though later Josephine Butler claimed to have been a member of it—of which he would be the 'Chief Director'. The commission's evidence would be made available on a confidential basis to a special committee of eminent men who could check out the facts. This should answer the critics.

Time was short. Stead believed it was vital that his series should lever its dramatic pressure on the existing government before the general election. Otherwise the political situation might be quite different, and if the Tories were elected, then the whole campaign would have to be renewed to convince a new administration. This meant that the articles must appear in July at the end of the present parliamentary recess.

Stead went back to Salvation Army Headquarters and told Booth that he had decided to take action. 'I've made up my mind,' he said to him, so he wrote later, 'that if this thing is going on, the only way to stop it is to go right down into the depths myself.'

What he meant by this was that he was not going to rely on hearsay. Like Alfred Dyer, he would pose as a client. He would negotiate for the bodies of young teenagers, drink champagne with brothel owners, pick up girls in the street and even pretend he was a sadist to test just how available was the supply for this kind of taste.

Booth, according to Stead, 'was startled and naturally shocked'—not presumably because the editor was taking up the cause, which he had been urging him to do, but because he was planning to take his researches so far. But he agreed willingly to give him all the personal help he needed.

So, too, he knew, would Josephine Butler. Once the *Gazette* started running the articles, her organisation—working in co-operation with the Salvation Army—would be invaluable. Meanwhile, she was in a strong position to help with the research. For Stead's main immediate problem was to find contacts who could lead him into the sexual underworld to 'get the facts', as he was always telling his reporters. And at Winchester, in a home Josephine maintained for 'fallen' girls, was a woman who, until relatively recently, had actually been running a brothel, who knew the trade and many of the people who were in it.

Rebecca Jarrett—who was to play a key role, epitomising both the success, in terms of practical results, and the failure, from a viewpoint of professional standards, of Stead's sensational campaign—was in her early forties. She wore her black hair in a fringe, and aided by a stick, walked heavily with a limp, due to a diseased hip.

It was a Monday, forty-eight hours after Stead's important decision, that she travelled to London from Winchester to see the editor in the *Gazette*'s dark, untidy offices in Northumberland Street. She had come with extreme reluctance, and only as the result of moral pressure from Josephine Butler who, in effect, was demanding payment for her charitable help.

Gently at first, Stead questioned Rebecca about her experience in the vice trade. She was reluctant to talk about it. She was attempting to fashion a new life for herself, to shake off the past, and it was not easy. But Stead was at the beginning of a crusade that was directed by his 'Senior Partner'. He pressed her relentlessly, peering at her with his pale blue eyes, deploying his considerable persuasive skill as an interviewer.

Haltingly, she told him the story—which conformed with many he had heard before. In fact, it could easily have come out of the confessions of 'Walter'. The daughter of a tradesman who drank, Rebecca had gone into domestic service as a young teenager. One of the guests in the house had seduced her, taken her to live with him for a couple of years and then, presumably when he tired of her, introduced her into a brothel.

She had progressed from being a prostitute employed by others to running her own brothel, assisted by her mother and her brother. Her sisters were co-opted into the family business which supplied young virgins to clients when required. Altogether, she had run three 'gay houses'—in Bristol, Liverpool and Manchester.

There is some evidence that the life troubled her, for she seems to have made an effort from time to time to break away from it. At one stage, she lived with a bricklayer named Sullivan, who may have operated a London brothel with her, and she worked for a while as an ironer in the laundry room of the prestigious Claridges Hotel in London.

Then she had a bad fall—the result, some suggested of being drunk —and suffered the injury that was to develop into a diseased hip that the doctors appeared unable to cure.

She became increasingly lame and found it hard to work. At one period evidently, her circumstances became so bad that she almost had to enter a workhouse—and live on state-sponsored poor relief. She avoided this only because she was helped with money by a woman she had become friendly with in Claridges Hotel, Nancy Broughton, who also was to play an important role in the Stead story, as indeed was the money she loaned Rebecca. Quite why her family did not come to her assistance is not clear, but presumably they objected to her sudden departure to live with Mr Sullivan.

At one stage during 1884, when her damaged hip was causing her a lot of pain—a reason, so she said, why she drank heavily—she lived for a while in Northampton. It was there that she fell ill with bronchitis. Her landlady, who was a member of the Salvation Army, grabbed the opportunity and brought the woman captain of her local corps to see her. At first, Rebecca resisted vehemently all efforts to convert her, cursing the well-meaning hard-bonneted women who

Kate Hamilton's Night House

The Haymarket at Midnight

A Spree in a Railway Carriage

Courtesans in Hyde Park

William Thomas Stead
Josephine Butler

Catherine Booth

William Booth

Bramwell Booth

An Amorous Youth on a Jaunt to London

Prostitute Tipping a Beadle in the Burlington Arcade

'That girl seems to know you, George.'
An Awkward Meeting in Regent Street.

Police Interrupt a Party

Wentworth Street, Whitechapel

A Salvation Army March in East London

The Empire Theatre

talked so incessantly about the Lord, but eventually their message seems to have got through to her. Just before Christmas of 1884—only a few months before she had to endure the ordeal of Stead's interrogation—she arrived at Florence Booth's shelter in East London.

She was not very settled. Within two weeks, she had learned from old associates whom she met in the street that her mother had fallen ill. Rebecca was badly needed to help run the family brothel. Florence found her packing.

To start with, Rebecca rejected all attempts to dissuade her from leaving the shelter. But Florence Booth and her lieutenants were determined women, experienced in handling urges to return to the world of vice. They knelt on the floor around her and prayed aloud through the night for seven hours. At last, at five in the morning, Rebecca broke down, agreed to abandon her plan to go home and 'acknowledged her misery and sin'.

Florence knew that, for Rebecca's salvation to be placed on any permanent basis, she must cut her contacts with her former friends. So she sent her to Winchester to Josephine Butler. There, her hip deteriorated to such an extent that she could barely walk. All the same, she was still a very marginal case. Her persistent underworld contacts traced her south and once more began to lever pressure on her to return. She resisted, promising them not to reveal any information about them—a promise that was to prove vitally important in the story of Stead's campaign—provided they would leave her alone. But, as Josephine Butler reported later, the temptation remained. She still talked of going back—especially as the visits continued from the rather sinister men who clearly did not trust her promises in her reformed state.

Then in April she had some kind of religious vision which she does not appear to have been able to describe very clearly. 'She got a sense,' as Josephine Butler put it, 'that Jesus, whom she had always regarded as far away, was close to her.' More to the point probably, she experienced what seemed like a miracle. After a session of earnest praying for the healing of her hip, 'she recovered the power of walking somewhat suddenly'. She still walked with a bad limp but she was far more mobile than she had been before.

The Campaigning Editor

It changed her dramatically. In a state of surging salvationist zeal, she began to campaign actively in social rescue, 'speaking to her poor lost sisters in the streets and in the public houses on a Saturday night'. According to Josephine Butler, she made a big impact. The girls she 'saved' were housed at 'Hope Cottage', which Josephine acquired for her.

Clearly, Rebecca's conversion from the vice trade to salvationism had made her a formidable influence. Her converts appear to have acquired the same heady enthusiasm for retrieving other 'gay' women that she had. They formed a rescue team and embarked on a crusade in Portsmouth, one of the main home ports of the Navy where, because of the sailors, there was a big demand for women.

Portsmouth had been one of the towns where the CD Act experiment in registered prostitution had been tried out. Now, of course, the acts had been suspended but one of their results had been to consolidate the brothels. For the purpose of the CD legislation had never been to check prostitution but to free it from the dangers of disease.

The port, therefore, was an exceptionally good testing ground for Rebecca and her team. According to Josephine Butler, the mission was a great success. Rebecca, she wrote, 'would stand in the midst of a den full of men and women of the worst type, get them down on their knees, pray with them and for them . . . and, when other persuasion failed, she related to them what she herself had been . . .' In particular, Josephine claimed, she had a high success rate with men who were living on the earnings of prostitutes. In fact, one of them called on Rebecca in Winchester to express his gratitude to her for revealing to him the evil of his life.

An even more spectacular triumph, though, were the man-and-wife team who actually ran a notorious Porstmouth brothel. For they, so Josephine asserted, abandoned the business as the result of Rebecca's prayers and exhortations, and did their best to reform the girls they employed. The story is barely credible—though it just possibly might have been true—but the point is that Rebecca, having at last forged this new role for herself, had only just returned from her Portsmouth crusade when she was faced with the demand to help Stead. Josephine was anxious that the editor's need for a lead to Rebecca's former friends might set up temptations for her that could undo all the good that had been achieved over the past few weeks—and her concern was well grounded.

In fact, the deliberate sacrifice of Rebecca Jarrett—which is what it turned out to be—by both Josephine Butler and Stead, to what they saw as a greater cause, was appalling. From the start, they treated her as though she was expendable—and she was certainly expended.

In answer to Stead's persistent questioning, as he reported later in his articles, Rebecca told him how the trade in girls was operated—especially the trade in virgins which, as Stead saw it, was the aspect most in need of government action. It also provided the best and most stirring dramatic copy.

The editor jabbed question after question at her. She assured him that there was no shortage of these young girls, that—if she returned to the trade—she would have no difficulty in acquiring as many as she needed.

But would these children be virgins literally, Stead wanted to know. 'Or will it merely be a plant to get off damaged articles under that guise?'*

Despite her Salvationist campaigning, Rebecca slipped back easily into her old professional role. 'You can soon find out, if you're in the business, if a child is fresh or not,' she told him with the confident assurance that made him describe her later as 'an old hand at the game'.

He was not satisfied. 'Does the girl know why you're taking her away?' he asked.

'Very seldom,' she answered. 'She thinks she's going to a situation. When she finds out it's too late. If she knew what it meant, she either wouldn't come or her readiness would give rise to a suspicion that she wasn't the article you wanted...'

Horrified though he was, Stead was intrigued by the whole background to the situation she was describing. For where was the source for traders such as Rebecca had been? 'Who are these girls?' he asked.

'Orphans, daughters of drunken parents, children of prostitutes, girls whose friends are far away.'

* The dialogue on this and following pages is taken either directly from Stead's articles or from court testimony.

Rebecca must have been waiting for the inevitable question. Stead was a Victorian in character and mood but, as a professional journalist—aside from the one area of sex where he did not question his facts closely enough—he was years ahead of his time. And now his reaction to the subject was the same as that of the editor of any modern city newspaper. If people were buying and selling young teenage girls, the obvious way of handling the story was to go out and purchase one.

But when he asked Rebecca if she would go back among her old vice contacts and do this for him, she reacted violently. 'She pleaded to be spared this burden,' Stead said later. 'I was inexorable: "You have told me that you have procured and ruined in terrible earnest scores of innocent girls. If you are really penitent, make amends for your crime by procuring one, not for ruin but for rescue . . ."'

Poor Rebecca did not stand a chance. This campaigning moralist, with his beard shaking, his eyes shining, was employing the technique that reporters were often to use as sensational journalism developed. He was jamming his foot in the door so that it could not be slammed shut: he was applying emotional blackmail.

In response to this pressure, Rebecca conceded reluctantly that she knew a brothel in the East End of London where she could probably get a virgin. She agreed to make enquiries about the girls 'then in stock or procurable at short notice'—and limped sadly out of Stead's office.

That day, he had another visitor, sent to him on the recommendation of Benjamin Scott—a tall, burly Greek in his sixties, whose real name was Mussabini but who was currently using the pseudonym of Sampson Jacques. Like Stead four years before, he had been fired by the stories of the white slave trade to the continent and was keen to campaign against it. Already, he had approached the editors of several newspapers with the proposition that he should tour the Continental brothels, as Dyer had, and expose them in a series of articles.

Inevitably, in view of the subject, his offer had been declined but Stead, studying him that day in his office thought he might be useful for research. 'I liked the spirit of the man,' he said later. 'He was an old warrior who had faced death on many battlefields . . . He was not animated by the high enthusiasm and religious feelings which animated my other colleagues . . . but he was a man of the world . . .' So Jacques became a member of the Secret Commission.

At this early stage—when the project had only been under serious consideration for a weekend—Stead had not yet formulated in his mind any exact plan of campaign. He had urged Rebecca to buy him a virgin because that had emerged from his interview with her as an obvious thing to do, but he had not thought it through to the carefully calculated, though wildly misconceived, plan that eventually developed from it. Furthermore, overbrimming with enthusiasm though he was after all his soul-searching on Saturday, he still had some reservations. There must be no mistakes with a project of this nature. Did the trade in girls truly exist on the scale that Rebecca and the Booths—and even the House of Lords Committee—suggested that it did?

For this reason, for a few days, Stead made his enquiries at an official level. He called on Police Superintendant Joseph Dunlap of the West End 'T' Division who had testified four years ago to the House of Lords Committee about the house he raided near Piccadilly to find, in room after room, an elderly man in bed with two children. But Dunlap would give him no information without permission from Scotland Yard. When this was refused, Stead approached the Home Secretary, Sir William Harcourt, 'as the minister interested in the passing of the Criminal Law Amendment Bill'. But Harcourt declined to allow the police to be interviewed by 'newspaper people'—for which, so Stead announced in print, he was grateful later. For, owing to the bribed tie-up between the police and vice interests, he alleged, 'the brothel keepers would have been put on their guard'.

Faced with this blank refusal of official co-operation, 'I had to fall back on ex-officials, jail chaplains, rescue workers . . . Their evidence was unanimous. Young girls . . . were constantly procured for dissolute men, inveigled into brothels, outraged with impunity and then spirited from brothel to brothel, or taken out of the country to feed the slave markets of regulated prostitution of the Continent . . .'

'The evil, instead of being abated, had rather increased during the last two years.'

The Campaigning Editor

A prison chaplain told him that, in a home near Newport, there were fifty children under ten, all of whom had been victims of sexual assault. In an establishment in Farnham, in Surrey, just south of London, were forty girls under twelve who had been violated. Cases like these would not be affected by any change of law, for they were illegal already—and, as he admitted in his series, they were rare—but they fanned Stead's sense of indignation because official attitudes to them were so apathetic.

He found apathy in other places—places where he did not expect it. When he called on the president of the Society for the Protection of Women and Children, he was astonished to discover that the official was only concerned with protecting fortunate women. Those who had 'fallen' merited no consideration from his organisation. Coolly, he ridiculed the idea that any woman 'ever became a harlot except of her own free choice'.

'The society of which I am President,' he told Stead unctuously, 'has almost always found that women were in the wrong.' Women, he pointed out, were truly the aggressive sex.

Angrily, Stead told him about a girl he had learned about who had been tied up naked in a house in Trevor Square, near Hyde Park, and flogged by a pervert until the blood flowed. 'What would your society do if I placed the case in your hands?' he demanded.

'Nothing,' answered the other, 'The girl consented to be tied up to receive a birching. If she got more than she bargained for that is not our affair.'

However, despite this display of cold disinterest, Stead found plenty of sympathetic evidence in other quarters. Officials of The Girls Friendly Society explained to him that whenever one of their members travelled into London, they had to send someone to meet her. Otherwise, they had found by bitter experience, they were in great danger of being waylaid and tricked into prostitution.

Cardinal Manning, head of the Roman Catholic Church in Britain, drew a grim picture of the dangers that faced Irish girls arriving at London docks. Procuresses, disguised as Sisters of Mercy, would accost the girls, explaining that they had been sent by the mother superior to take them to suitable lodgings. One notorious woman, the Cardinal told him indignantly, boasted of having rounded up no less than 1600 girls by this technique.

Although Stead could get no official help from the police, he was pleased and surprised to find that Howard Vincent—Josephine Butler's old adversary who had now retired as the head of the CID—was prepared to talk. During an interview in the *Gazette* offices, Stead asked him bluntly: 'Is it or is it not a fact that, at this moment, if I were to go to the proper houses, well introduced, the keeper would, in return for money down, supply me with ... a girl who had never been seduced?'

'Certainly,' Vincent replied.

'At what price?'

'That's a difficult question. I remember one case which came under my official cognizance at Scotland Yard in which the price agreed was stated to be £20.'

'But,' asked Stead who well knew the answer to the question, though he had a special purpose for asking, 'are these "maids" willing or unwilling partners to the transaction ... ?'

Vincent looked surprised by the question. 'Of course they're rarely willing,' he said.

'Then do you mean to tell me,' demanded Stead warming to his point, 'that in very truth actual rapes, in the legal sense of the word, are constantly being perpetrated in London on unwilling virgins, purveyed and procured at so much a head by keepers of brothels?'

'Certainly.'

'But do the girls cry out?'

'Of course they do. But what avails screaming in a quiet bedroom? Remember the utmost limit of howling or excessively violent screaming, such as a man or woman would make if actual murder was being attempted, is only two minutes and the limit of screaming of any kind is only five.'

'But the policeman on the beat?'

'He has no right to interfere, even if he heard anything.'

'But surely rape is a felony ... Can she not prosecute?'

'Whom is she to prosecute? She does not know her assailant's

The Campaigning Editor

name . . . Even if she did, who would believe her? A woman who has lost her chastity is always a discredited witness. The fact of her being in a house of ill fame would possibly be held to be evidence of her consent . . . and the woman would be condemned as an adventuress who wished to levy blackmail.'

Before he left the office, Vincent urged Stead to give up his investigation, stressing how dangerous it was. Adamantly—no doubt with his chin held high in his new role as a crusader in the cause of British womanhood—Stead insisted that he must continue. 'In that case,' remarked Vincent lightly, 'I have no doubt that the next time I shall see you will be in the dock.'

It was to prove an accurate forecast. However, any remaining doubts Stead might have had that the picture had been exaggerated were now dispelled. It truly would be hard to find a more reliable authority than the man who, for years, had run the CID.

Meanwhile, Rebecca Jarrett had tried to buy a girl from the East End brothel she had mentioned—and she made such a mess of it that it is very surprising that Stead did not question either his own assessment of the vice trade or Rebecca's background.

Admittedly, he had insisted that she take a woman observer—loaned to him by Booth from the Salvation Army—and this caused problems. For the procurer was nervous of negotiating with Rebecca in front of a stranger. Perhaps she sensed that the transaction was artificial, which would explain why the two girls she promised to deliver to her, at Waterloo Station, the following Saturday, never turned up. Waterloo had been chosen because it was the main line station for Winchester, for temporarily Stead planned to put his purchases in the care of Josephine Butler.

At any rate, with an apparent determination to execute the commission, which contrasted strangely with her earlier reluctance, Rebecca went back to the East End with her Salvation Army escort to see her contact. This time, after making excuses for the non-delivery, the procuress sent for a local girl who had been offered to her. The terms were to be £2 down and £1 when her virginity was certified. The girl had been brought up in the London suburb of Streatham, had already worked as a domestic servant, but was now out of a job.

She left the brothel with the two women, but clearly she was not as unsophisticated as she seemed. Rebecca's questions had alerted her suspicions, and choosing a moment when the cab slowed down, she leaped suddenly into the street and escaped.

Despite the rampant market in virgins for sale—that was confirmed by men who were far less emotionally involved than Stead—he still had not succeeded in buying one. Once again, Rebecca made her plans. This time, for reasons that were never explained, she decided to avoid the brothels and to try to effect a purchase direct from a mother.

Meanwhile, Stead set up his research programme on a systematic basis. The Secret Commission went out in search of the facts at a personal level. Stead himself adopted the alias of Charles Kennedy and rouged his pallid skin to the bucolic hue that was in keeping with his new character as a letcher. Like 'Walter', he strolled through the Quadrant in Regent Street, a fat cigar clamped between his teeth, picked up young girls and went back with them to accommodation houses—though presumably he did not sample the merchandise. He called on the fashionable brothels and drank champagne with the madames, while pretending to cast a keen eye over the girls they offered him.

He was in his element, playing a flamboyant part, and—as in the case of Alfred Dyer—it is hard to believe that he fooled the professionals for a moment; though he was undoubtedly a far better actor than Dyer. Maybe, however, he *did* deceive the very young freelance girls whom he met in the 'foreign' cafes near Leicester Square, which were regular pick-up places. Certainly, they gave him a new perspective. To his surprise, he found that the men and women, waiting at the docks and railway stations scanning the arriving teenagers for likely 'marks', were not the only dangers. Young girls collaborated willingly in the seduction of their friends.

In one cafe, Stead got talking to two youngsters—Annie, aged fifteen, and a thirteen-year-old named Lizzie. Annie had been enticed into the cafe in which Stead was interviewing her by a friend who had suggested that she should come with her to meet her 'uncle'. He would buy them both ice creams, she had said. The 'uncle' did buy them ice creams—and wine. Annie had become quite drunk by the time her friend stood up and said: 'You must come upstairs now.'

'What for?' queried Annie.

'Never mind what for,' insisted her friend. 'You'll get lots of money.'

Upstairs, her friend took the initiative. She undressed the bewildered girl for her 'uncle', and took the £4 he paid, handing over half to Annie as her share.

Lizzie's experience, so Stead learned, had been fairly similar. 'Now,' he was to write, 'the two girls went on the streets occasionally . . . to add to their scanty earnings . . . it's the first step that counts . . .'

The brothels, he discovered, frequently used their own girls to attract new recruits to the 'Black Army', approaching likely prospects in the streets or in the cafes, describing their lives in glowing terms of champagne and beautiful clothes.

By now, Sampson Jacques, Stead's new Greek investigator, had called on Mrs Jeffries in Church Street. Although the Secret Commission were mainly operating incognito, it would seem that Jacques declared his real purpose to her, for Stead acknowledged her co-operation in print. Presumably that experienced lady felt that, following her trial—and the resultant howls of the purity movement—she had little to lose by winning the goodwill of the investigators. By now she no doubt also realised that the main weight of the attack would be pitched on the trade in very young girls in which there is very little evidence that she took part. At any rate, she gave the Greek a detailed rundown on the operations and techniques of her competitors and conceded, as Stead wrote, that she had 'supplied at least one English girl to the King of the Belgians'.

By following up a tip from a prostitute, Jacques had also ferreted out a new aspect of the trade. He had discovered a woman named Madame Louise Mourey, seemingly a completely respectable accoucheuse but, beneath the cover, a specialist in virgins. Not only was she used by all the top brothels to certify that maidenheads were intact, but she also had an unrivalled reputation for 'repairing the laceration caused by the subsequent outrage' in the more brutal cases.

Madame Mourey was remarkably frank with Jacques, who represented himself as an agent for a man with a taste for virgins. She had many regular clients with similar inclinations, she told him. There was one man, in particular, who took frequent trips to the East End to watch the girls coming out of offices and shops, befriending those who appealed to him, ravishing them and handing them over to Madame Mourey for repair. She enlarged about a regular customer who only had one arm, but evidently Stead felt that this was too grisly a detail to add to his horror story. For, although he wrote of it elsewhere, he did not mention it in his articles.

What incensed Stead—for it underlined the whole point of his series—was that Madame Mourey's house, no 3 Milton Street, Dorset Square, was 'imperturbably respectable in its outward appearance'. This was the truth that lay beneath the pious face of middle and upper-class Victorian society. 'It's a sham,' he cried out to Josephine Butler one night, 'a horrible sham—the whole of our professed christianity and civilization.'

By this time, he himself was onto a new line—two young, pretty and clearly intelligent girls who had set up in full time business as procuresses. One of them was only twenty. Four years before, at sixteen, she had been seduced, through the connivance of one of her friends. But evidently the biggest impression that this had made on her was not the loss of her virtue so much as the ease with which her friend had earned her money. She was fascinated by the big commercial scope that clearly existed in the provision of virgins, and she set up a business supplying them on systematic lines. Within two years, her operation had grown to such a size that she could no longer handle it herself. She took in a twenty-two-year-old friend as a partner.

Even Stead was impressed by their business-like approach. The girls they supplied were mainly governesses and nursemaids they picked up in the Parks or servants they encountered running errands. They were specialists, concerned only with virgins—who usually returned to their home or employers after the rape. They did not supply brothels, though they conceded that many of the girls ended up on the streets eventually. They concentrated on the fourteen to fifteen year old group because they had found that the girls were most malleable at this age. However, they did have one client who took seventy virgins a year from them—but insisted that they should be over sixteen because, regardless of the issue of sexual consent, the abduction laws were strict up to this age.

These two tough and pretty operators had developed their procuration techniques to a fine point. 'It takes time, patience and experience,' said one of the partners, explaining how they got friendly with the girls and matured them carefully for the day of their call. 'Many girls need months before they can be brought in. You need to proceed very cautiously at first . . . week after week, we see her as often as possible . . .'

Sometimes, they admitted, they had trouble with the 'little fools' when they were confronted with a man. 'The right way to deal with these silly girls,' said Miss X, as Stead called her, 'is to convince them that, now that they have come, they have got to be seduced, willing or unwilling . . . Do you remember Janie?' she asked her friend.

'Don't I just!' answered Miss Y.

'We had fearful trouble with that girl,' Miss X explained. 'She wrapped herself up in the bed curtains and screamed and fought and made such a rumpus that I and my friend had to hold her down by main force in bed while she was being seduced.'

'Nonsense,' said Stead with feigned surprise that the girl should prove so unresponsive, 'you didn't really!'

'It gave me such a sickening,' Miss Y commented, 'that I was almost going to chuck up the business, but I got into it again.'

'It pays, I suppose,' remarked Stead sympathetically.

This interview, in which the dialogue is quoted directly from Stead's articles, shows clearly that the allegations of professional irresponsibility that were thrown at him were well grounded. It also provides a fascinating glimpse of his character. He was not just reporting a social evil. He was playing it up flippantly, dramatising it to suit his own ends.

In fact, he ordered five virgins from the firm at £5 a head, although eventually, because they were not all declared *virgo intacta* by Stead's doctor, nine were delivered. All signed a document agreeing to their seduction on payment of £4, the remaining pound being agency commission. Significantly, in view of his colourful evocation of the screaming rape scene, none of them, it seemed, would need to be held down.

The Campaigning Editor

In the case of one girl, Stead offered her a choice: she could have the whole fee and submit to seduction, as she had contracted, *or* she could have half the fee and leave the house as pure as she had entered it. To Stead's concern—partly because he realised the background of poverty that dictated the decision—she opted for the bigger money.

Most of these girls were relatively mature, and Stead's main target remained the exploiters of the very young—like the baby-faced girl in a house in St John's Wood, with 'features, not much larger than those of a doll' who 'came into the room, with her fur mantle wrapped closely round her and timidly asked me if I would take some wine.'

'She is too good for her trade,' Stead told the brothel keeper.

'Wait a bit,' advised the Madame, Stead reported with horror, 'She is very young . . . has just come out you know. Come again in a couple of months and you will see a great change.'

At a Park Lane accommodation house, when he asked if they had any objection to the introduction of very young girls, they almost laughed at him. 'Do you think we insist on the production of the baptismal register of all the ladies who visit us?' they asked.

Grimly, he studied the practice of parents who sold their daughters. One of his friends, he wrote later, was even prosecuted for the assault of a woman who had consented 'to her paramour "cleansing himself" on the person of her innocent eleven year old daughter'. No less than three mothers offered to sell him their virgin children—although by that time he was no longer in the market. One apparently respectable mother appalled him when, after she had been praising her young daughter's 'graces and accomplishments,' Stead commented that he was sure she would take care that no one was allowed to seduce her. 'It depends on the price,' she responded drily.

The burden of the investigation, added to the work of editing his newspaper, was heavy on Stead. Quite apart from the distressing nature of the encounters, he was having to drink champagne after a lifetime as a teetotaller. Nor had he ever smoked before, though the big cigars would not seem to have been entirely essential to the character he was trying to portray. But Stead never did things by half.

For several weeks, since it was usually too late for him to travel home after his evenings of research, he slept in the office. He met frequently with Bramwell Booth and Josephine Butler, and indulged with them in histrionic orgies of pious shock. Both of them feared that the editor would crack under the strain of exposure to so much sin.

'We stumbled up the narrow dark stairs,' said Josephine, recalling a night she had gone back to the *Gazette* office with him after he had been investigating all evening, 'the lights were out, not a soul was there, it was midnight. I scarcely recognised the haggard face before me as that of Mr Stead. He threw himself across his desk with a cry like that of a bereaved or outraged mother, rather than that of an indignant man, and sobbed out the words: "Oh Mrs Butler, let me weep, let me weep or my heart will break." He then told me in broken sentences of the little tender girls he had seen that day sold in the fashionable West End brothels, whom he (father-like) had taken on his knee...'

Bramwell Booth recorded a similar scene in similar terms. 'I have seen him on my office floor sobbing, partly no doubt owing to the extreme tension and horror of the enquiry, but in a large measure also because of the human grief of his fervent spirit at the heart-rending cruelty which stood disclosed.'

'Oh Bramwell, it is killing me—the Devil's work,' Stead cried out to his partner in one letter. 'But courage! I must now hasten to the cafe in . . . Street to eat Supper, infernal sacrament of the Devil, with one of the worst procuresses in London. Good Lord, help me.'

Stead was such a 'ham' and some of his facts were to prove so distorted that, even though a lot of the material he was probing was clearly appalling, these emotional outbursts provoke suspicion. Was his dinner date, perhaps, with one of those pretty young procuresses about whom later he was to write so lightly?

Booth had been a great help to Stead and, in one particular respect, his co-operation had been vitally important. The Salvation Army had provided him with a decoy—a girl, never named, who had wandered in the park, deliberately allowed herself to be picked up and introduced into a brothel in Wanstead where she lived for ten days. The Army claimed that, because they gave her plenty of money to hand over to her procurer, she had avoided seduction. Stead visited her regularly, posing as a client, to get her first hand accounts of a girl's eye-view of life in a brothel.

For the girl, it was a highly dangerous mission. Just how dangerous became apparent when she warned Stead, on one of his night visits to her, that she was being sent to the Continent. Stead planned to rescue her from Charing Cross Station on her way to the coast, but a sudden crisis caused a drastic change in plan: the brothel keeper discovered her true identity—through a Salvation Army badge that, as a talisman, she had inserted into the lining of her coat. She was placed under close confinement. Presumably, though the editor made little reference to this incident, that is featured in Salvation Army records, Stead found that she was not available to him when he called.

Her anxious fiancé, the Army's Captain Frank Carpenter, decided that drastic measures were necessary. With a Salvation Army unit, he stormed the brothel. The girl was found lying in the garden with a broken ankle—the result of leaping from the window of her room in an attempt to escape.

Once again, it seems probable that the brothel-keeper must sooner or later have suspected that the girl was a plant—or, at least, that something was not quite what it should be. These were professional people as accustomed to handling young girls as any school teacher. Under their keen and experienced eyes, it is unlikely that a fervent Hallelujah Lassie could conceivably have made a convincing whore—any more than Stead himself, with his heavy disguises, could have convinced them he was an old roué. Why, for example, did the brothel keeper explore the lining of the Salvation Army girl's coat, unless his suspicions were already aroused?

Meanwhile, Stead—disguised, horrified, even elated by his crusading, fever—plunged on with his investigation. Having scoured London for the truth about the city's underworld sexual life, he now placed the foreign trade under his impassioned scrutiny.

There was not quite the same scope here, since Alfred Dyer and Josephine Butler had been campaigning over this ground before him. However, apart from tightening up the existing systems, the government had been very apathetic. The publicity about the white slave traffic—followed by the Brussels trials—had eventually inspired the Criminal Law Amendment Act, but that had now been killed by Cavendish Bentinck and the brothels lobby. So, although white slavery was not a new issue—in the same journalistic sense as the trading in young teenagers—it presented some opportunity as a secondary feature of his series. Stead planned to demonstrate that the official attitude —that the excesses had now been dealt with—was far short of the truth.

Thomas Snagge, the lawyer the Government had sent to the Continent after Alfred Dyer's revelations, had insisted in his testimony before the House of Lords committee that the trade was at an end. There were, he said, no English girls remaining in the Brussels brothels—and certainly there should not have been for, under the new rules, they had to be questioned in the British Consul's office before admission into the houses.

Stead did not mention this, did not even suggest that the system was being abused, as it probably was. He asserted that all that had happened was that the emphasis of the trade had switched from London—where the publicity had alerted many girls to the dangers of accepting jobs abroad—to the provinces, where teenagers were more naïve.

What is more, the editor had found a good source—none other than Jean Sallecartes, the 'placeur' who had shipped so many girls to France and Belgium. Now, deterred by his spell in jail, he claimed to have given up the profession—although, since he accused his estranged wife of still operating from the provincial towns, it is possible that much of his story was motivated by spite. At any rate, Sallecartes had a keen listener when Stead took him to lunch in a restaurant in the Strand. And the editor did not question his assessment that some 250 girls a year were still being shipped from Britain to the Continental brothels—although the basis of his calculation was not disclosed.

By now, after weeks of gruelling research, Stead and his Secret Commission had built up a substantial mass of evidence. He had also executed the human purchase that he planned as the dramatic central feature of his series.

Since first asking Rebecca Jarrett to buy a girl for him, he had improved on his original idea. He wanted to do more than merely illustrate that girls could be bought and sold like slaves: he sought to demonstrate it in the most emotive way he could, to expose the London prostitution scene.

His planning was carefully calculated. The girl must be thirteen. She would be examined professionally to certify she was a virgin—as in fact was customary in the trade. She would then be introduced into a London brothel—to show how easily this could be done—before being shipped abroad, just as a 'placeur' like Jean Sallecartes would export a 'parcel' to a house in France or Belgium.

The only difference, in the case of Stead's purchase, would be that she would come to no harm in London, and her destination on the Continent would not be a brothel but the Salvation Army headquarters in Paris.

Stead realised fully that this purchase and transportation would be the most shocking aspect of a shocking series of articles, and he took trouble to cover himself. He consulted a lawyer, William Shaen of Shaen, Roscoe & Co, on his legal position. Could he be prosecuted? Shaen advised him that, so long as he could prove that his intent was not criminal, the authorities would have no grounds for action against him—especially since he would be able to show that no harm had come to the girl. As an extra precaution, Shaen suggested that he should have with him a man of some standing—such as a member of Parliament—who would then be able to vouch for the purity of his intent.

Stead intended to do better than that. He called on the two most eminent churchmen in Britain—the Archbishop of Canterbury and Cardinal Manning—to explain his plan. Both of them agreed to confirm his motive should it ever be called in question.

The campaigning editor devoted a great deal of thought and trouble to this aspect of his protection. Quite rightly, he realised that the buying of the girl was the most dangerous aspect of his whole project—the one area in which, unless he was scrupulously careful, he would expose himself to the enemies he would inevitably create with the series. However, as it turned out, in concentrating on the technicalities, he neglected a more important aspect which he was

The Campaigning Editor

always urging on his staff : he did not check the facts of the story he reported.

In the first week of June, following her two earlier attempts that proved abortive, Rebecca Jarrett bought Stead a virgin—at least Stead thought she did.

8

*The Sensational Exposé**

It was nearly noon on Tuesday, 2 June, when Rebecca Jarrett arrived at 37, Charles Street—a little road of tightly packed, drab, terraced houses in the slum section of Marylebone. She had known Nancy Broughton, who lived with her husband John in one room of the house, for two years, since the time that they had worked together in the laundry of the luxury Claridges Hotel.

The Broughtons were a friendly and gregarious couple and, during those weeks in 1883, Rebecca had often visited them in their room in Charles Street—that was 'hung round', according to one reporter, 'with scenes illustrating the station of the Cross and the walls decorated with crucifixes and portraits of popes and Cardinals'.

Rebecca got along well with John, whom she knew as 'Bash'. Sometimes, so she was to testify, she told the Broughtons about her previous life when she had run 'gay houses'. Later, when she was out of work and ill, Nancy Broughton had helped to support her—a demonstration of friendship that Rebecca, working for a larger cause, was shortly to reward by reflecting on her the spotlight of public criticism.

The two women had kept in touch by correspondence, the Broughton's letters—since they were both illiterate—being written and read for them by a young girl named Jane Farrer who lived nearby in the street.

Rebecca's selection of Nancy Broughton as the means of purchasing

---

* The material in the earlier part of this chapter is based mainly on the testimony of Rebecca Jarrett. It is, in effect, her version of the story, though I make clear the more important aspects that were challenged. But the truth about the abduction of Eliza Armstrong has never been satisfactorily established, not even in Court.

The Sensational Exposé

a child is curious, in view of her own underworld contacts. Stead was to write about the roaring traffic in young girls but he had a lot of trouble in tapping it. Clearly, after Rebecca's attempts to make the purchase through the East End brothel had failed, she had now decided to go onto the open market and buy a girl directly from a family.

The Broughtons lived in a poor area where no doubt there were parents who were willing sellers. For her visit on that June morning, Rebecca—so she said in court—deliberately put on her silk 'gay clothes', although there was never any evidence to suggest that the Broughtons were associated with prostitution or its related traffic. It is possible that Rebecca had been caught up in Stead's melodramatic approach to the whole subject. Wearing 'gay clothes' to visit her old friend conformed perhaps with the whole plan of taking a young girl into a brothel and on to Paris to demonstrate the easy and well-worn route in human traffic. Perhaps, too, she saw it as a kind of uniform, making her purpose quite obvious—a purpose that was to be vehemently challenged.

When she told Nancy Broughton that she was looking for a girl, her friend suggested nineteen-year-old Jane Farrer who was in the room when she arrived. But Rebecca rejected her at once as being too old. A sixteen-year-old, whom Mrs Broughton called in to the house from the street, was declined for the same reason. Also, she was too plain for Rebecca's plan. 'I want something more interesting and pretty—about thirteen or fourteen.'

Mrs Broughton thought she knew the ideal child. She left the house and returned with a pretty young girl whom Rebecca would have been glad to take. But her elder married sister, whom she lived with, refused to let her go.

By then, thirteen-year-old Eliza Armstrong, who had heard in the street that there was a domestic vacancy on offer, had come into the room and asked Rebecca if it was true that she was looking for a girl. Eliza was an attractive child, with long black hair and a pleasant easy manner. But when she fetched her mother, Mrs Armstrong was unwilling to allow her to leave home. 'She's earning a shilling or two for herself close by,' she said.

The Sensational Exposé

When Eliza and her mother had left the room, Rebecca told Nancy that she was just the sort of girl she was looking for. 'Is she pure?' she asked.

'I think she's all right,' answered Nancy.

John Broughton returned home for his dinner and Rebecca shared the meal with them. They reminisced enjoyably and she told them, so she testified later, that she was now living with a man named Sullivan.

When she left, Nancy said to her: 'I'll do what I can to find you a girl.' She suggested she came back the next morning to find out what success she had had.

The following day was the first Wednesday in June when, by tradition, the Derby is run at Epsom racecourse—important as a detail in the story only because it pinpointed the date. As her friend had suggested, Rebecca returned to Charles Street before midday. By then, Mrs Armstrong appeared to have changed her mind about Eliza and strongly advised Rebecca not to take the daughter of one of their neighbours whom Nancy Broughton had been to see—Mrs Woodward. 'She's full of vermin,' she said disparagingly of the competition.

Rebecca—according to her testimony—made it quite clear why she wanted Eliza. 'I keep a gay house,' she said. 'I want a little girl about Eliza's age, but she must be pure. Is Eliza pure?'

Mrs Armstrong assured her categorically that she was.

'I want her for a gentleman,' Rebecca continued, 'and if you'll let her go, I'll give you some money.'

According to Rebecca, Mrs Armstrong hesitated and then agreed with some evident reluctance. 'Are you quite willing?' queried Rebecca.

'Yes,' answered Mrs Armstrong more firmly, 'Yes, I'll let her go.'

Rebecca arranged to take Eliza out that afternoon to buy her some clothes for her new life and, after Mrs Armstrong had left, she gave Nancy Broughton two sovereigns. 'This is for your trouble in getting me the girl,' she said. 'If she proves what I want her to be, you'll be sent some more.'

After the shopping expedition, Eliza was changing into her new dress when her mother arrived at the Broughton's home with blood streaming down her face.

'What's the matter with you?' asked Rebecca.

The Sensational Exposé

Mrs Armstrong explained that her husband had struck her because she had insisted on going to a funeral that he did not want her to attend. Evidently, the blow had only made her more determined to go—but she did not have enough money to get there. 'Lend me a tanner,' she said to Nancy Broughton, but she, too, was a bit short of cash.

Rebecca reached into her purse and, since she did not have a sixpence (a 'tanner') handed her a shilling. Then, deciding, presumably that this was a suitable time, she followed her to the door and gave her a sovereign. 'This is according to my promise,' she said, so she told Stead later and testified in court.

No one ever contested the fact that Mr Armstrong struck his wife that afternoon—which provided Stead with good background copy because it placed Eliza in a setting of violence—but both Nancy Broughton and Mrs Armstrong were to deny that they handed over Eliza for anything more immoral than domestic service. It was to prove a moot point because even Rebecca agreed that, in the presence of the child, she preserved the fiction that she was required as a servant.

At any rate, when Eliza was dressed, Rebecca sent her to say goodbye to her parents, but they had both left home—her father to return to work and her mother to attend the controversial funeral. It struck Rebecca as a little callous for a mother who had just sold her daughter into sin. 'You'd think she'd come to see her off wouldn't you?' she commented to her friend. At least, that was *her* story, and nobody challenged the remark, though it was almost as callous not to see off a daughter who was going to take her first job in domestic service.

So they walked up Charles Street to the bus stop in Lisson Grove —this big rather sinister looking woman, wearing a dark gown and a straw hat turned up at the side, limping with the aid of a black stick with a silver knob; and the girl delighted with her new purple dress, sidespring boots and a reddish straw hat with a yellow feather in the front.

They certainly looked what they were later purported to be—a procuress and her victim. Their clothes were important, too, for it was by these that they were later identified.

The Sensational Exposé

Rebecca took Eliza by one of London's two-horse omnibuses to an apartment in Albany Street, about two miles away, that Stead had rented temporarily. Inevitably, since the editor let no opportunity pass to prove his point, it was a house that, like the district in which it stood, was often used for sexual assignments.

When they arrived there, Stead was waiting for them together with Mrs Reynolds of the Salvation Army. Over cups of tea, he chatted to Eliza and asked her a few questions about her life. She told him that she had only been in the country twice—on two school trips to Epping Forest and Richmond. Although she had been brought up in London, she had never seen the Thames, except on the visit to the river town of Richmond.

Stead was deeply impressed with her. She was exactly what he wanted to point up the tragedy of the situation he was campaigning against—'a warm hearted little thing . . . with dark black eyes,' as he was to describe her, 'who was full of delight at going to her new situation and clung affectionately to her keeper who was taking her away—where she knew not'. He was moved by her 'kindly feeling for the drunken mother who had sold her into nameless infamy'.

Taking Rebecca aside, he asked her if there could be any possible question as to whether Mrs Armstrong knew the purpose for which Eliza had been acquired. Rebecca assured him that there could be no doubt at all.

Carefully, Stead directed the mock sequence of seduction and export of his purchase. Rebecca took Eliza to Milton Street—to Madame Louise Mourey, the expert on virgins whom Sampson Jacques had traced. Jacques went with them, posing again as an agent for the prospective seducer.

The accoucheuse examined Eliza and confirmed that she was a virgin. 'The poor little thing,' she told Jacques. 'She is so small her pain will be extreme. I hope he will not be too cruel with her.'

'Can you supply anything to dull the pain?' he asked.

Madame Mourey sold him a phial of chloroform and agreed, so Stead was to write, that if the child was badly injured in the rape she 'would patch it up to the best of her ability'.

From Milton Street, Rebecca and Eliza travelled by hansom to a

The Sensational Exposé

notorious accommodation house over a ham and beef shop in Poland Street, which was a notorious road. Stead and Jacques followed in a second hansom—a fact that did not escape the notice of the driver of the first cab, already suspicious about the purpose of taking a pretty little girl to so immoral a neighbourhood.

In fact, Stead had selected the house deliberately, for one of the young girls he had picked up in the street during his researches had, in truth, been taken there as a virgin and raped—and he wanted his reconstruction to be as close as possible to real life situations.

While Rebecca undressed Eliza and prepared her for bed, Stead and Jacques in a neighbouring room ordered whisky. Also, they asked for some lemonade—to demonstrate that the management must have suspected that a child was involved and yet were completely unconcerned.

On instructions, Rebecca tried to help Eliza to sleep with the chloroform, but the girl objected to the smell and waved it away, She was not asleep, therefore, when Stead, playing the role of lecher, entered and locked the door behind him. 'There was a brief silence,' he wrote. 'And then there rose a wild and piteous cry . . . "There's a man in the room! Take me home, oh take me home!"'

Eliza retained her virtue during this charade, but she had an eventful night. She was taken from the brothel to a reputable Harley Street doctor who—unlike Madame Mourey—would be an acceptable expert witness in a lawcourt. Once more, the child was examined—this time unconscious under chloroform—and then taken at last to a private hotel for the rest of the night.

The next morning, Rebecca and Eliza went to Charing Cross to catch a train to Paris. Stead—now playing the part of a white slaver shipping his 'parcel' across the Channel—met them on the platform with Madame Coombe, a Salvation Army officer who would be looking after the child in France. Then all except Stead boarded the train.

Rebecca stayed in Paris for a few days. While she was there, so she testified, she mailed two £1 postal orders to Mrs Broughton in Charles Street—the final payment which she was to share with Mrs Armstrong, making the price of Eliza a total of £5.

The evening before Rebecca left Paris, she said goodbye to Eliza.

By this time they had grown fond of each other, and the child was sorry to see her go. 'Now Eliza,' Rebecca told her, 'I want you to be a very good girl. You were handed over to me for something worse by Mrs Broughton'—an unnecessary comment, it would seem, but several people heard her make it.

And she returned to Josephine Butler's cottage for fallen girls in Winchester. Three weeks after her return to England, she had a note from Eliza with a tender little rhyme that was to prove of the greatest importance:

As I was in bed
some little forths [thoughts] gave [came] in my head
I forth of one, I forth of two;
but first of all I forth of you.

It was a nice touch—a spontaneous demonstration of the young girl's innocence that, if she had been sold to anyone but Stead, would by now have been stripped from her in brutal violation. The Editor was at last almost ready to spring his sensational revelations on the people of London.

The news in the first week in July was dominated by the fall of the Gladstone Liberal administration, which was outvoted in parliament. The Conservatives, under the leadership of Lord Salisbury, took office. They could not rule for long, for the time for a general election would soon be due. On Monday, 6 July, however, the new ministers assembled at no 10, Downing Street for their first cabinet meeting—and there is little doubt, though no record, that one of the main items of discussion was William Thomas Stead.

The previous Saturday, the *Pall Mall Gazette* had run a warning to squeamish readers about the nature of the series that the paper would be starting on Monday. Even so, it is doubtful if anyone had foreseen the frank and explicit extent to which Stead was to go even in the opening article.

In six whole pages, under the title *The Maiden Tribute of Modern Babylon*, the impassioned editor lashed out at Victorian society and lifted the lid—comparing it dramatically with the raising of the Campo Stone of Naples that covered a mass grave of festering corpses—off the city's seamy sex life.

The Sensational Exposé

Systematically, one by one, he attacked 'the forces upon which we usually rely when dealing with other evils'. He charged parents with neglecting 'even to warn their children of the existence of dangers of which many learn the first time when they become their prey'. He taunted the press which, though it printed verbatim the full scabrous details of divorce cases, 'recoils in pious horror from the duty of shedding a light upon these dark places'. He castigated the Church whose failure to take action was 'the most conspicuous and complete'.

But his main target was the rich. 'In all the annals of crime can there be found a more shameful abuse of the power of wealth than that by which in this nineteenth century of Christian civilisation, princes and dukes and ministers and judges and the rich of all classes are purchasing for damnation . . . the as yet uncorrupted daughters of the poor?'

Vividly, he compared the nightly sacrifice of virgins in London to the mythological Athenian tribute—the selection by ballot once every nine years of seven youths and seven maidens who were sent to Crete in a black-sailed ship to become victims to the Minotaur, the monster who was half-bull and half-man.

'I am no vain dreamer of Utopias peopled solely by Sir Galahads and vestal virgins . . . ,' wrote Stead. 'London's lust annually uses up many thousands of women . . . That may be inevitable . . . but I do ask that those doomed to the house of evil fame shall not be trapped into it unwillingly . . . If the daughters of the people must be served up as dainty morsels to minister to the passions of the rich, let them at least attain an age when they can understand the nature of the sacrifice which they are asked to make. And if we must cast maidens . . . nightly into the jaws of vice, let us at least see to it that they consent to their own immolation, and are not unwilling sacrifices procured by force or fraud. That is surely not too much to ask from the dissolute rich.'

Relentlessly, he exposed the system—the decoying of the girls, the traffic, the cries that nobody answered, the strapping down of those who resisted, the indifference of the authorities.

Dramatically, he related the story of Eliza—naming her as Lily—in terms so distorted that it seemed barely credible that they came from the pen of a journalist who was normally so professional. He described the Broughton's one-room house in Charles Street as a brothel—which was patently absurd. He portrayed Mrs Armstrong as a woman 'indifferent to anything but drink' who pressed her daughter on the procuress, slobbering to Nancy Broughton the words: 'Don't you think she'd take our Lily?', whereas even Rebecca indicated that she had refused to let her go for twenty-four hours.

He wrote that the father was at home 'drunk and indifferent' when 'Lily' went to say goodbye, while in fact he had already returned to work—and, since Mr Armstrong was to hit his wife again for permitting their daughter to leave home without consulting him, it is highly unlikely he was indifferent.

Carefully, since it did not suit his angle, he omitted the fact that 'Lily' had told him she attended Sunday School. More important perhaps, he did not disclose the fact that he was the purchaser—although he admitted his role in other transactions featured in the series—nor that he was employing the procuress. Furthermore, he depicted Rebecca—without any reference to the fact that she was now reformed—as 'an old hand at the game'. To compound his felony, he went further in his claims, that the story was factually true, than he did in any other incident in the series. 'I can personally vouch for the absolute accuracy of every fact in the narrative,' he declared.

From any professional standpoint, his exaggerated treatment of the 'Lily' story, to the deception of his readers, was disgraceful. Unfortunately, as it was to turn out, he left enough accurate details in the story to make 'Lily' completely recognisable, in the tight gossipy neighbourhood of Charles Street, as Eliza Armstrong.

To counter charges that the whole sensational series was an exaggeration (which, in the case of 'Lily' would have been well grounded) Stead offered to reveal his evidence—including identities of brothel keepers and procurers—to any of six men, whom he named, in return for an undertaking that the information would not be used to bring charges against them. The six included the Archbishop of Canterbury, Cardinal Manning, and the Earl of Shaftesbury.

The public reaction to the opening article was all that Stead could have wished. It shook, to the foundations, a London that had never read in print such details as Stead now remorselessly exposed. Demand for the paper was so great that, by the end of the day, it was selling on the black market at a 1/- a copy—twelve times the usual price.

W. H. Smith, the biggest chain of newsagents in the country, refused to handle it—so distribution was channelled through newsboys, the Salvation Army and volunteers who saw the ban as an attempt at censorship. Such a big crowd crammed Northumberland Street, that Stead and his staff had to barricade the doors. Allegedly among the sellers was Bernard Shaw, one of the *Gazette*'s reviewers, who reputedly set up a post in the Strand, vending the paper to passers-by. Later, the series may well have given him some of the source material for his 'shocker' play *Mrs Warren's Profession*.

Although most newspapers refrained from comment in what Stead called 'a conspiracy of silence', the *St James Gazette* a direct competitor edited by an ex-*Pall Mall* staffman—lashed into him in an assault that must have satisfied even Stead. 'Newspaper sensationalism had been carried very far before this present week of grace,' it declared, 'but yesterday it reached its utmost possible point in the production ... of the vilest parcel of obscenity that has ever yet issued from the public press ...'

Sneering that the motive 'of imperative public duty' was 'the excuse of every literary gentleman who ever sought to make a little money in the same way', the *St James* asserted.

> Of revelation, there is not one word; of mere gross concoction, there are signs innumerable ... The man who invented the 'sensation' might have worked it out with some little regard to public decency. This shameless creature has flung all decency aside, openly dealing with the worst abominations in the plainest and foulest language.

If the *St James*' leader writer thought he had read the 'worst abominations' on Monday, he must have had convulsions on Tuesday. This article focussed almost entirely on the actual seduction system—with elaborate descriptions of decoying techniques, a vivid personal interview with the girl who escaped from the Pimlico brothel to the Salvation Army HQ, lurid stories of the young girls who inveigled their friends to their ruin and, in particular, a sensational, highly dramatised account of the two young procuresses who had impressed Stead so much. Finally, he told the story of how nine girls had been brought to him with signed certificates agreeing to sell themselves. Stead declared:

> The report of our Secret Commission . . . has produced an effect unparalleled in the history of journalism. The excitement yesterday in London was intense. The ministerial statements (of the new Government) were comparatively overlooked in the fierce dispute that went on everywhere over the revelations of our commission. We knew that we had forged a thunderbolt; but even we were hardly prepared for the overwhelming impression which it has produced on the public mind.

In the House of Commons, Cavendish Bentinck asked the Home Secretary if there was any way of submitting the authors and publishers of the articles to criminal prosecution. Another indignant member wanted to know if the minister was aware that, owing to the prurient content of the series, the *Pall Mall Gazette* had raised its wholesale price by 25 per cent—an accusation that Stead denied angrily in the paper the next day.

By Tuesday evening, the new administration had had enough. Sir Ralph Assheton Cross, the Home Secretary who had only just taken office, sent for Stead and asked him to stop publishing the articles. Indignantly, Stead refused and urged Cross to climb on the bandwaggon he had created. 'Say in the House of Commons that the *Pall Mall Gazette* has covered itself with everlasting glory,' he suggested.

'Of course I can't say that,' snapped the politician.

'Then . . . ,' Stead countered mischievously, 'say that the *Pall Mall Gazette* has committed an abominable outrage on the public morals and that you have instructed the Law Officers of the Crown to prosecute me at once.'

The Home Secretary would not do that either. In fact, a letter from the Lord Chancellor in the closed Home Office files reveals that the government considered prosecution, but decided against it because it would have the appearance of 'H.M. Government shielding the depravity of the rich at the expense of the poor'. However, the minister

The Sensational Exposé

did announce that night that the new administration—with the promised support of the opposition—would promote the Criminal Law Amendment Bill.

'This,' he asserted from the floor of the House, 'is a question that has stirred England from one end to the other . . . There is nothing the English are so determined to maintain as the purity of their households.' This time, with the full weight of the government behind the bill, there would be no scope for filibustering.

In two explosive days, Stead had achieved his declared objective but he was not weakening his pressure, now that he had the country roused. Perhaps he feared that the administration could still back down. Maybe he was afraid that his competitors would accuse him of yielding if he did not run the series to its conclusion. On Wesdnesday, piling horror upon horror, he exposed the trade in juveniles—though he conceded this was small, and even that no one had offered him a child under thirteen. He elaborated on the vice networks that preyed on young girls arriving at the stations and the docks. He described 'a London Minotaur' who was 'here in London, moving about clad as respectably in broad cloth and fine linen as any bishop . . . whose quantum of virgins from his procuresses is three per fortnight . . .' He depicted another who, so he reported, boasted of having ruined 2,000 women.

Defiantly, following up his private suggestion to the Home Secretary, he front-paged a challenge to the government to prosecute him. 'Mrs Jeffries,' he taunted, 'pleaded guilty in order to save her noble and Royal patrons from exposure. There would be no such abrupt termination to any proceedings that might be commenced against us . . . We await the commencement of those talked-of proceedings with a composure that most certainly is not shared by those whom in such an extremity we should be compelled to expose in the witness box.'

Sarcastically, he pointed out that, in the enormous mail the *Gazette* had received since it had started running the series, the supporters of his campaign had all signed their names. Most of the letters from critics had been anonymous.

Quite a lot, however, wrote openly cancelling their subscriptions on

The Sensational Exposé

the grounds, as one reader put it, 'of the mass of disgusting detail which pollute your pages and render your journal unfit to be received in any respectable or decently conducted family ...'

'I have taken care that my girls do not read such filth,' wrote another, 'and I hope every other parent has done the same.' It seems a pity,' chided a subscriber from an address in Cavendish Square, 'that innocent people who know nothing of these crimes should have them brought prominently before them.'

Certainly, some of the correspondents to the *St James Gazette* did not sign their names, though their letters were hardly admissions that they were among the men of vice that Stead was attacking. 'They [*Pall Mall Gazette*] are, in fact, burning with indignation at the debauchery of the poor man's children,' wrote one, 'and yet they do not scruple to put their unutterably obscene "revelations" into the hands of these helpless boys [newsvendors] not only to read, but to make a profit by selling it.'

Ironically, in view of all the talk of sinful exposure, the Church of England gave the *Gazette* its strong support—without actually mentioning the paper. The Upper House of the Convocation of bishops formally informed the government of its 'deep conviction that there should be no delay' in getting the Criminal Law Amendment Bill through the Commons.

On Wednesday, the crowd in Northumberland Street erupted into a riot. 'For three days, the crowds have surged down upon us,' Stead trumpeted triumphantly. 'Gaunt, hollow-faced men and women, with trailing dress and ragged coats ... they fought for profit, buying the paper in a cheap market to sell in a dear one ... London is raging for news and sends its regiments for the supply. And so the crowd raged at the door under the summer sky—raged and wrestled, fought with fist and feet, with tooth and nail, clamouring for the sheets wet from the press, a sea of human faces ... And the surging force grew in numbers and battled at the doors like troops of devils.'

Purity movement sources have since suggested that the brothels put thugs among the crowd to break up the *Pall Mall* presses, but Stead made no mention of this in his columns. The crowd, he suggested, consisted of people who wanted to make money by selling his sensa-

The Sensational Exposé

tional paper, the violence resulting only from frustration because they could not obtain enough copies of it. 'At one window the smashing began,' he reported. 'The windows of machine room, the windows of publishing office, fell.' The angry crowd was so large that the traffic in the Strand came to a halt.

Whoever caused the riot, the police were called out in force to control it. In his columns, Stead complimented them but in a blistering private letter to the Home Secretary he charged them with failing to provide adequate protection, alleging that their apathy was due to politically-motivated orders.

From Queen Victoria Street, Bramwell Booth sent Stead his encouragement. 'Go on!' he wrote to him. 'Every blow tells . . . multitudes are filled with horror and . . . cry out with agonising entreaty for the bill.'

Josephine Butler, in London for the fight, also gave him her strong support and, as she said in public the following week, thanked him many times on behalf of 'the women of England'. He published a letter from her which revealed that a peer had written to her, warning her against divulging the name of any of his class who might have 'been discovered haunting the London inferno'. 'Vengeance is mine,' she quoted with some relish from the Bible, 'I will repay, saith the Lord.'

By Wednesday night, the City of London authorities had provided Stead ingenuously with yet another angle to exploit. The City Solicitor had ordered the police to arrest newsboys selling the *Gazette*, and had charged them before the Lord Mayor of London with vending obscenity.

Happily, Stead accused the city authorities with out-raging the liberty of the press, alleging that they rushed the hearing deliberately so that the *Gazette* could not arrange a defence of the boys.

'If we are guilty, it is we (not newsboys) who deserve to be punished,' he declared, adding 'We challenge prosecution. We court enquiry.'

Stead was yearning to find some way of attacking the Prince of Wales, following his alleged inclusion in the list of guilty men who patronised Mrs Jeffries in ex-inspector Minahan's dossier. Artfully, he used the arrest of the newsboys as an excuse to announce: 'We are prepared, if we are driven to it, to prove our statements . . . to subpoena as witnesses all those who are alluded to in our enquiries . . . from the Archbishop of Canterbury to Mrs Jeffries and from the Prince of Wales down to the Minotaur of London.'

On Thursday, in the House of Commons, the Home Secretary moved the Criminal Law Amendment Bill, claiming a bit speciously that 'no one can say that the question has been approached in a hurried manner', since similar bills had been discussed in parliament for so long. He was strongly supported by the Attorney General, Sir Richard Webster.

There were a few voices of caution. 'It was a measure,' said one MP, 'that would open the door to unlimited extortion and which took the false step of confusing the distinction between vice and crime.' But the opposition was relatively mute. Even Cavendish Bentinck barely said a word and the bill was passed by a big majority to the committee stage, when the details would be hammered out.

One ominous sign that the moral pendulum might swing too far was a question in the Commons about the 'fixing' of the Jeffries trial. Was it true that there was an agreement of a low penalty for a guilty plea? Mrs Jeffries' case was over but, in the new climate, she was by no means safe. It was not the best time to be a famous procuress.

That night, Stead was dictating his final article to the reporters until well past midnight. He wrote later:

> It was three o'clock in the morning, when we went down the [Thames] Embankment in the early summer dawn. A faint flickering smoke arose from the housetop in a street close to a house of ill-fame and within a very few minutes . . . from the north and west and east came clattering in fierce haste the fire engines anxious by any and every means to save one person who might be in danger . . .

Characteristically, elated as he was by his long spate of dictation, Stead speculated on the difference between the occupants of the house in flames and those of the nearby brothel. 'Where,' he was to demand later in Court, 'were the organised appliances to rescue *them*?'

A few hours later, yet another sensational exposé was running off the presses in Northumberland Street. It followed a quiet twenty-four hours, for Stead had spared his readers any revelations on Thursday

The Sensational Exposé

—feeling presumably that they needed a respite to digest the facts with which he had already horrified them—but Friday's article moved into the attack again.

This time, apart from a vivid treatment of international white slaving with interviews with Jean Sallecartes and some girls who had been sold to foreign brothels, Stead charged the police with 'an unnatural alliance' with vice, alleging that they were paid off liberally by the brothel keepers for protection from prosecution.

After a week of scandal, the public's capacity for shock was diminishing. In the Home Office, the Permanent Under-Secretary, Sir Godfrey Lushington, ordered an enquiry into Stead's allegations against the Police, to be carried out, under the quaint system that still exists today, by the police themselves.

The newspaper campaign was over—in Britain that is, for already it was making an enormous impact overseas. On Thursday, the Central News Agency had started telegraphing the articles across the Atlantic for syndication through America. Before the end of the month, more than 100,000 copies of the series, printed in book form, had been sold in Paris. It had been translated into Danish, German, Russian and Polish.

By then, following Stead's offer in his opening article, a five-man committee of investigation—that included the Archbishop of Canterbury, the Bishop of London and Cardinal Manning—had been formed to examine Stead's source material in response to allegations that the articles were made up of sensational invention.

Meanwhile, now that the series had stopped, the purity movement took over the campaign throughout the country to ensure that the Criminal Law Amendment Bill was not dropped, on its tortuous way through parliament, before it became law. Big meetings were staged in London through the first three days of the following week. Josephine Butler gave public thanks to Stead and Bramwell Booth, and read out a petition to parliament in support of the bill that was to be promoted through the branch offices of the Salvation Army. Catherine Booth knelt on the stage and prayed emotionally that 'illumination might be given to those who govern'. She announced that Salvation Army Units would patrol Oxford Street every day between the hours of 12.0 and

3.0 on a continuous mission to rescue 'fallen girls' and revealed that their cause had the implicit support of the Queen, to whom she had been addressing letters.

Never, Catherine asserted to a long burst of applause, would she recognise two codes of morality, one for men and another for women. General Booth gave a resounding rebuke to those critics who argued that Stead's series did more harm than good because of its revelations of sin before the eyes of the innocent, and, in consequence, had withdrawn their financial support from the Salvation Army. This, he declared, was like complaining of the dogs that barked rather than the wolves that bit. 'What matters it,' he demanded, 'that the alarm bell has a harsh and grating sound? It is not the bell that we are concerned about—it is the fire.'

At another meeting in London, Catherine Booth, shocked her audience with what she claimed was a true story from Salvation Army records of a man who paid a brothel-keeper to provide him with a young girl. Cleverly, the procurer enticed her away from a Sunday School—but his skill backlashed. His client was shocked to find that the girl who was confined, awaiting seduction, was his own daughter.

For seventeen days, the Salvation Army held protest meetings throughout the country, demanding that parliament should raise the age of consent—which it was, of course, in the process of doing anyway, although the Purity Movement did not trust it. William Booth stomped the country leading mass meetings at Manchester, Leeds and Sheffield.

Other purity organisations joined the campaigning. From all over Britain, memorials were streaming into the Home Office, demanding action—among others from 3,000 people in Newcastle, from the Wesleyan Congregations in North Devon, from the White Ribbon Movement in Plymouth.

The petition to parliament, which Josephine Butler had read out in the Princess Hall in London, was signed by 393,000 people and, when it was unrolled, stretched for two and a half miles. On Thursday, 29 July, it was conducted to the Houses of Parliament by a corps of hundreds of Salvation Army soldiers who marched, to the thumping

The Sensational Exposé

of a blaring band, from Clapton in East London to Trafalgar Square. The monster petition, itself, was carried in a carriage drawn by four white horses under the escort of a special detachment—'the Lifeguards' of the Army, wearing white hats. On the sides of the carriage, massive banners demanded that 'this iniquity shall cease' and warned: 'Beware'.

In Trafalgar Square—since processions were banned from the precincts of Parliament—the petition was transferred from the carriage to the shoulders of eight 'Lifeguards' who bore it formally down Whitehall on the last leg of its journey to the legislators, elected by the people of Britain.

On the same day—29 July—the committee of investigation, that had been examining Stead's source material and interviewing witnesses in formal hearings in the Mansion House, pronounced its findings. 'After carefully sifting the evidence . . .' the committee declared, 'and without guaranteeing the accuracy of every particular, we are satisfied that, taken as a whole, the statements in the *Pall Mall Gazette* on this question are substantially true.'

Triumphantly, on the front page of the *Gazette*, Stead shrugged off the committee's reference to inaccuracies—'In a report covering so much ground . . . trivial errors in points of detail were unavoidable'—and trumpeted this confirmation of his disclosures by 'the most influential Grand Jury that could be empanelled'.

Referring to the enormous foreign response to the series, he asserted: 'We stand here in the belfry of the world, ringing a tocsin whose peal clashes discordant upon the ear of civilised mankind.'

Meanwhile, in parliament, the Criminal Law Amendment Bill was being thrashed out in committee. Both Stead and Bramwell Booth were consulted by the Home Secretary 'to suggest', as Booth wrote, 'how the measures could be strengthened'.

On Friday August 14th, the bill in its final form was moved by the Home Secretary and passed into law with a majority of 179 votes to 71. The age of consent was now sixteen. Brothels could be raided by the police. There were new penalties for whiteslaving, stricter regulations about soliciting. Children could be taken from the care of parents who exploited them.

The Sensational Exposé

Even this victory—total though it was—did not stop the purity campaigning. A week later, on Saturday 22 August, an enormous demonstration was staged in London 'to denounce criminal vice'. At 2 o'clock in the afternoon, nine processions started towards Hyde Park from different parts of London, to the music of thirty-four brass bands.

More than a hundred-thousand men, women and children were in the marching columns, representing organisations with a wide range of religious and political aims that now centred on the issue of child prostitution.

The slogans were heavy with dramatic symbolism. A large waggonette filled with pretty little girls carried a large message worded: 'Shall the innocents be slaughtered?' A hundred and fifty banners made such demands as 'Men, protect England's Girlhood' and 'Equal rights for men and women'. Many of the marchers wore white armbands urging 'Mourning, lamentation and woe', on behalf—as one paper assumed—of 'children worse than dead'.

Later in the afternoon, the processions of marchers began to merge as they arrived from their various starting points at Hyde Park Corner and streamed into the park, where twelve wagons had been set up as speaking platforms. One was a specifically feminist area—with female speakers adressing a female audience—though there were many women in the crowd listening to every orator. It was, after all, a woman's success. Without Josephine Butler and Catherine Booth, and the women they directed, Stead would probably never have taken up the issue at all. And, without question, but for them, he would not have obtained the enormous response.

For many of the speakers, the vice issue was a vivid proof of the need for radical policies. 'Let the rich and upper classes understand,' declared Lord Lymington 'that they cannot with impunity take advantage of the destitution and extraordinary temptations of the daughters of the poor'.

'The truth must be spoken,' asserted another speaker from a different platform, 'no matter what interests or class are affected. The chief cause of criminal vice is to be found in our economic system . . . The same system that cleared the countryside of its labourers filled the brothels with girls . . . and the cause is the possession of the land

The Sensational Exposé

by a few good-for-nothing aristocrats.' It was a new viewpoint on the Industrial Revolution.

Others campaigned purely on a basis of public morals. The least that the people of Britain could demand of the people 'who filled high positions in the state,' insisted one speaker, was that 'they should be decent men and should not visit immoral houses'.

The editor of the *Methodist Times* gave public credit to the early role played by Alfred Dyer, who had been rather forgotten in the furore surrounding Stead. 'The great movement which was now being carried on,' he declared, 'was begun in 1880 by Mr Alfred Dyer, a Quaker . . . The facts were denied by the Police and the *Standard Newspaper* charged him with telling lies. But Mr Dyer was a Quaker and it is no use bullying a Quaker. A Quaker is like a bulldog . . .'

No wonder Dyer commented brightly in *The Sentinel*: 'We never expect to witness a grander sight than we beheld . . . In Hyde Park on Saturday afternoon.'

From one platform, Stead himself addressed an enormous crowd who gave him a long, roaring ovation. He, too, saw the prime cause as economic. 'The wages of working girls must be raised,' he told his audience but chivalrously, he assured them that it would be quite wrong for them to assume that the majority of girls earning low wages were immoral.

At half past six, a fanfare of trumpets signalled every platform that the resolutions, that were the purpose of the rally, should be put to the audience. The crowd resolved noisily that 'the people of London hereby express their shame and indignation at the prevalence of criminal vice in their midst' and pledged that it would assist in the 'vigorous enforcement of the Criminal Law Amendment Act'. And throughout Hyde Park the great mass of people cheered and waved their banners. The men flourished their hats. It was the climax of the campaign that Josephine Butler had started twenty-five years before.

Stead—elated though he was by a great sense of achievement—was exhausted. He planned a vacation in Switzerland. By then, he knew that the reaction was setting in. Two newspapers were campaigning aggressively against him. The questions in parliament were becoming more pointed.

However, there was one fact that he did not know: a week earlier, on the very day that the Criminal Law Amendment Bill had passed into law, an official in the Treasury had been ordered to organise the editor's prosecution.

9
The Reaction

In Britain, the main immediate impact of Stead's articles had struck only one small segment of society—namely, the middle and upper classes who formed the readership of the *Gazette* and its competitors. While parliament and the Home Office and Scotland Yard and fashionable London were being shaken by the repercussions, two or three days were to pass, before the news of the sensational series percolated down to the great mass of the population, whose daughters were the subject of the articles.

It was not until Thursday of the week of publication that Monday's copy of the *Pall Mall Gazette* was being read in Charles Street, where it caused reactions of a different kind—reactions that were more personal and less dramatic, but that were, nevertheless, to become extremely significant. Stead's attention, of course, was fixed firmly on the corridors of power, where the response to his articles was proving so rewarding. But, in that little slum street in which Eliza Armstrong had spent her childhood, events were happening that, in time, would affect him very closely.

From early in June, the sudden disappearance of Eliza had provoked some comment in the street. One reason for this was that it had caused a quarrel between her parents of which, since there was little privacy in those crowded tenement buildings, the neighbours were all aware. When Charles Armstrong, who was a chimney sweep, had returned that night to the one-room home he shared with his family, he had asked where Eliza was. On hearing that she had left home to take a position in service, he was angry because he had not been consulted, and with some reason, for Eliza had a baby sister that she had helped to look after. Her departure from home meant that her mother would

The Reaction

not have so much time to go out to work, to earn the extra money the Armstrongs badly needed.

When he discovered that his wife did not even know the address where she had gone to work or anything much about the woman she had gone with, he was so furious that he hit her—for the second time that day. At least, that is the story the Armstrongs told.

What is not in dispute is that, following the row, Mrs Armstrong stamped out of the house, stalked to the 'Marquis of Anglesey', the local pub, and got so drunk that the police arrested her—though, where she acquired the money was to be an important point of speculation.

If Charles Armstrong was uneasy about his daughter, it was not strange that this concern was shared by some of the other people who lived in Charles Street, especially by those who had seen the sinister figure of Rebecca Jarrett limping up the road with Eliza, decked out in her new clothes.

To Mrs Armstrong, the enquiries about Eliza from the neighbours seemed pointed and she resented them. Although there is no doubt that there was a trade in teenagers—confirmed by such men as Howard Vincent as well as by Stead—clearly it was not a custom that was socially acceptable, even in such poverty-marked roads as Charles Street. It was the kind of practice that mothers kept to themselves or concealed with some kind of cover story. Mrs Armstrong always denied vehemently that she had sold Eliza for an immoral purpose—denied, too, that she had ever received any money for her from Rebecca Jarrett. The story she stuck to rigidly was that she had gone into service with an old friend of her neighbour, Nancy Broughton.

Whatever the true facts may have been—for these have never been proved satisfactorily—the complete lack of news about Eliza was an increasing embarrassment. In fact, Eliza *had* written to her mother but, when the letter arrived at Salvation Army Headquarters in London, five days after she had left Charles Street, Stead urged Booth not to send it on to the Armstrongs. He had, he thought, saved Eliza from a life of vice, and he believed it was in her interest to sever her contacts with her background as completely as possible.

However, news did arrive in Charles Street about a week after Eliza

The Reaction

had left—and it was the source of some relief to Mrs Armstrong. Rebecca Jarrett wrote to Nancy Broughton from Winchester, where she was staying. She said that Eliza was with her—which, of course, she was not, since she was still in France—and was well and happy. The letter was public enough. Young Jane Farrer, who helped Nancy Broughton with her correspondence on the rare occasions that this was necessary, read it to her. And the hinted criticism of the two women by the neighbours ceased for a time—ceased, at least, until the second week of July when the first of the 'Maiden Tribute' articles in the *Pall Mall Gazette* exploded in Charles Street.

For in this atmosphere of suspicion and mistrust, the similarity between Stead's Lily and Eliza Armstrong seemed too striking to be mere coincidence.

The sale of Lily happened on the same day that Eliza left Charles Street with Rebecca Jarrett—3 June, Derby Day. Both girls were the same age. Both had been taken on school outings to Epping Forest and Richmond. Lily's mother was characterised as a drunken woman —a description that, since she had been formally charged with drunkenness by the police on the very night that Eliza had left home, could obviously be applied to Mrs Armstrong.

Furthermore, the article stated clearly that the 'brothel-keeper', who had introduced the procuress to the girl's mother, had been paid two sovereigns. Nancy Broughton admitted receiving money from Rebecca in the presence of Jane Farrer—though she alleged that it was only one sovereign—but insisted indignantly that it was nothing to do with Eliza. It was, she said, repayment of past debts.

Of the two women most closely concerned, Mrs Armstrong learned about the article first—then took it along to the Broughtons. 'I'm all of a tremble,' she said, according to her testimony.

Stead's baring of life in Charles Street—or, at least, a street that was remarkably like it—shamed its residents into indignant anger. The criticism of Eliza's mother that had previously been muted, was now renewed in the form of open and contemptuous accusations. Mrs Armstrong, so the neighbours charged, had sold her daughter for rape and Mrs Broughton had pocketed a big commission for the introduction.

The men of the street did not leave it all to their wives. Charles

Armstrong was a big man of few words, easily roused to anger. But there was little he could do when his neighbours passed by outside the house chanting: *'Gazette! Gazette!'*

Under the accusations, Mrs Armstrong angrily denied the charges of her neighbours—then, operating on the principle that attack would provide the best defence, launched into a furious onslaught on Mrs Broughton. After all, Rebecca Jarrett was *her* friend. Before a crowd of neighbours, she accused her of being 'a drunken brothel-keeper'—which was a bit steep from someone who had been prosecuted for drunkenness on Derby night—and charged her with selling her child for £5.

Poor Nancy Broughton, dazed by the suggestions that she ran a brothel, insisted that she could not believe that Rebecca had done this and, with the help of Jane Farrer, sent off a telegram asking her to return the child to prove that the whole story—or at least the implication concerning Eliza—was nonsense.

Meanwhile, Mrs Armstrong had to do something to answer the taunting criticism. The day after she had read Stead's article in the *Gazette*, she applied to the local magistrate in Marylebone for help. Crying bitterly, she told him how Eliza had left home with an old friend of one of her neighbours to go into service. The child's employer had said that she would write regularly, but she had not heard from her since the day she left. 'The dear girl's only thirteen,' she sobbed in a display of emotion that, when she repeated it on another occasion, Stead was to mock as 'maudlin,' 'and I'm afraid some harm might have happened to her.'

'Do you mean to say you let the girl go away with strangers,' said the incredulous magistrate, 'without making further enquiries than you have just explained?'

'Well, sir,' answered Mrs Armstrong, according to a press reporter, 'she said I'd hear from her every week.'

'Then I consider it a very great negligence on your part,' he asserted.

A court official was ordered to make immediate enquiries but, when he reported that even the neighbour—whose friend had employed Eliza—could not give a more detailed address than Croydon, the magistrate instructed the police to investigate.

The Reaction

The next day, Police Inspector Borner questioned Mrs Armstrong and Mrs Broughton—then took a train to Winchester to the address on Rebecca Jarrett's letter. He found Hope Cottage locked up and empty, for Rebecca had gone to Jersey for a holiday—mainly to get away from her underworld friends who were still pestering her. Neighbours, however, directed the inspector to Josephine Butler.

He did not get much in the way of co-operation from her, because she distrusted the police on principle. 'I am a member of the Secret Commission,' she told him coldly, 'and my instructions are to reveal what I know to nobody.' However, with a great deal of reluctance, she did refer him to Bramwell Booth.

This made the whole affair seem far less serious. For although Booth's association with Eliza seemed rather strange, he was a man of such stature that none of the inferences of immorality that lay behind the investigation could possibly apply to him. When the inspector saw him, the following week in Salvation Army Headquarters, he admitted he knew something about the case of Eliza. 'I can't tell you exactly where the child is now,' he said, 'but she's in service with a lady and being properly educated and brought up as a Christian. If you like I'll make enquiries during the day about the child's address and let Mr Munro have it.'

Mr Munro was the commissioner of police whom Booth knew personally. Because of his constant contact with the fringes of crime, Booth knew a lot of police officers. From Inspector Borner's point of view, his investigation was virtually at an end, which was a relief, for he was soon to go on vacation. He thanked Booth and left.

Booth, of course, was playing for time. For one thing on which both he and Stead were determined was that Eliza must not return to Charles Street. For, if she did, she would obviously be in immediate danger of being sold again—this time truly to become a victim of vice. Both men believed that there was absolutely no doubt that Eliza had been sold for rape. Nor, did they yet question the fact that Nancy Broughton ran a brothel.

By now, two distinct versions of what had happened on Derby Day and the previous morning were emerging. While Mrs Armstrong and Mrs Broughton stuck to their story that they had handed over Eliza to take a job as a servant, Rebecca was adamant that she made it quite clear that she was taking the girl for sexual purposes.

As the pressure on them all was stepped up, they retreated further into their stated positions. Rebecca said she had paid them both and sent additional money to them from France. They insisted that they had no money—except for the £1 that Mrs Broughton admitted receiving for Rebecca's past debts to her. Already, therefore, the issue that was to face a court was being posed: who was lying—Rebecca or the other two?

In any event, of course, if her testimony of what she told the editor can be believed, Stead had dramatised even what Rebecca had told him to an extent that was both ridiculous and culpable—the result of trying to make the facts fit his angle.

Strangely, despite Booth's admitted involvement, Mrs Armstrong had made no official claim that the departure of Eliza had any connection with Stead's story of Lily. To start with, she had been nervous of mentioning the *Gazette* article to her husband, since he was so free with his fists. Also, Stead had drawn such an unsympathetic picture of her—a vile, drunken mother who had sold her daughter into 'nameless infamy'—that she did not want to suggest that any part of it could be true.

The two cockney working-class families—the Armstrongs and the Broughtons—who were now at the centre of the new issue that was emerging were in an unhappy position. Suddenly, they had found themselves ranged against highly respected campaigning men of considerable power who, until now had been riding high on a surge of public moral enthusiasm.

Whether or not Eliza was sold for immoral purposes can never be known for certain, but Stead's gross distortion of other facts in the story—and Rebecca's new Salvationist fervency—make it, at least, dubious. If so, the Armstrongs and the Broughtons were the innocents, caught up in a situation that they found hard to comprehend. For who was going to believe them, branded as they had been as child-sellers, against the word of such prestigious men as the celebrated editor of the *Pall Mall Gazette* and the famous Bramwell Booth of the Salvation Army?

The Reaction

What made their position worse was that they were truly incapable of defending themselves. Three out of the four were completely illiterate. All experienced great difficulty in self-expression, and what little capacity Mrs Armstrong possessed for communication was greatly weakened by the fact that, every time she tried to explain her case, she collapsed into floods of tears.

At no stage—not even after he discovered that Mrs Broughton did not run a brothel—did Stead ever concede that his story might have been wrong. And his attitude to the people from Charles Street who, without question, could have won swingeing damages in libel actions, had they had the resources to sue, was that they were being used as pawns by his enemies.

Certainly, Mrs Armstrong acquired some supporters—and she was badly in need of them, though their alleged links to Cavendish Bentinck and the brothels lobby in Parliament seem tenuous.

The Editor of *Lloyds Newspaper*, which specialised in scandal, was the first friend that Mrs Armstrong acquired. Picking up the story at the Magistrate's hearing, he clearly suspected that there was more to her complaint than appeared on the surface. Within twenty-four hours, a *Lloyds* reporter arrived in Charles Street and interviewed both Mrs Armstrong and Mrs Broughton but, although he must have discovered the possible links between Eliza and Stead's Lily very soon, he made no reference in his article on Sunday to the series in the *Pall Mall Gazette*, that had been causing such a furore all week.

However, the paper gave it surprisingly good coverage for a story of a missing teenager—an incident that was not particularly novel in London. In three quarters of a column, the reporter described in precise and vivid detail exactly what happened in Charles Street on those two days in June. Although there was an inference throughout that Eliza had been taken for sexual purposes, the reporting portrayed a picture of a woman seeking a girl for domestic service—a picture of course, that put Mrs Armstrong and Mrs Broughton in the most favourable light.

The story bore all the signs of a stimulating campaigning piece that would run on in several circulation-promoting issues, but the following week nothing further was printed. Later, the paper explained why. The police had told Mrs Armstrong that Eliza was quite well 'and that she had better let the matter drop'—which, with a surprising lack of vigour, *Lloyds* did too.

If there had been any doubt previously about the connection between Eliza and Lily, there was none now. The magistrate's hearing, at which Mrs Armstrong complained about the disappearance of her daughter, made her another ally—a man named Edward Thomas of the London Female and Preventive Reformatory Institute, who was in court that day on another case.

His precise role is still unclear. Stead saw him as a kind of 'Eminence Grise', acting for the brothels lobby, guiding Mrs Armstrong to form a weapon against him. Thomas denied this hotly in a letter to *The Times*. Presenting himself as a campaigner for justice for an innocent individual who had been trampled roughly by these starry-eyed Puritan reformers, he declared that he had been led 'carefully to investigate the allegation that Mrs Armstrong had sold her daughter and came to the conclusion that she had not done so, but had been duped by The Secret Commission—viz Jarrett'.

Thomas had met Rebecca in the past and was mildly sceptical about the story that:

> she was a changed character now and a truly converted woman . . . I can only say . . . that she has been to my knowledge, a person of the worst possible character and a most notorious liar.

Whatever his motives, Thomas—like *Lloyds Newspaper*—followed up the case and paid an early visit to Charles Street. It was Thomas who urged Mrs Armstrong to attend the opening hearing on 15 July of the committee of investigation—to whom Stead had agreed to reveal his evidence—at the Mansion House.

Crying profusely, Mrs Armstrong insisted to the panel of five stern men—two of whom were heads of their churches in Britain—that she had never sold her child and begged for news of her present whereabouts.

It was early days for Mrs Armstrong to be given any consideration at all. The last article of the series had been published only three days before and the public indignation that it had created was still inflamed.

The Reaction

No one at that hearing questioned the truth of the Lily story. Mrs Armstrong's protests were shouldered aside as the maudlin pleadings of an evil woman who had been exposed. However, Mr R. T. Reid, QC, the only lawyer on the investigating panel, gave her his assurance that Eliza was in safe hands—though still neither Mrs Armstrong nor Mr Thomas were informed of her address.

Together, they directed their efforts at the Salvation Army but, when she called at the headquarters building in Queen Victoria Street, Bramwell Booth refused to see her.

So once more, aided now by the support of the strange Mr Thomas, Mrs Armstrong returned to the magistrate and asked him again for help. As a result of this application the police were ordered to renew their investigation.

This time, Inspector Borner knew where to go. At Salvation Army headquarters, Bramwell Booth told him that the situation had changed since his last visit—although, in truth, it was exactly the same. Eliza Armstrong, he said, was now under his control and on the Continent with some friends of his. When Borner pointed out that he had been sent to see him by the magistrate, Booth insisted angrily that, if any move was made to return her to her home, he would apply to have her made a Ward of Court, no matter what it cost. This technical move—usually adopted in the case of death of both parents of a child—would have placed responsibility for her care in the hands of the court. 'I've investigated,' he told the inspector. 'The mother is a drunken woman and the neighbourhood is a bad one.'

Borner did not argue about the truth of what Booth said. In fact, his statement could hardly be challenged. Nor did he care probably if Booth had Eliza made a ward of court. But he had his orders from the magistrate. Clearly, it would help a great deal if Booth would agree to discuss the matter with Mrs Armstrong. Faced with this formal and clearly reasonable request by the police, Booth could no longer refuse to see her—even though still believing Stead's story to be accurate, he regarded her as a moral leper.

The next day, Inspector Borner returned to Salvation Army HQ with Mrs Armstrong. It must have been a highly daunting experience for her. For the first time, she actually faced an accuser, a man of

The Reaction

great power and influence, to whom she was the epitome of evil—a drunk who had sold her daughter.

Furthermore, from the testimony, she appears to have had little support from Inspector Borner. As the police always are, he was stolidly on the side of middle-class respectability. Mrs Armstrong was a working-class wife, who had been on charges before the magistrate's court on three occasions, either for drunkenness or the use of foul language. She was the kind of material that passed through the police stations every day.

For a few moments, after Mrs Armstrong had been ushered into Booth's office, there was silence. Faced as she was by the stiff, stern salvationist, and the inflexible police inspector, words—that never came very coherently to Mrs Armstrong—deserted her completely.

At last, when Borner told her impatiently to 'speak to Mr Booth,' she managed to stutter out: 'I've come to speak to you about my daughter—I want her back.'

Booth, sitting confidently at his desk, was calm enough. 'You can't have her back,' he said steadily. 'She's in the South of France, in good service, being well brought up and educated.'

'Why can't I have her back?' whined Mrs Armstrong, who appeared to be gaining a little assurance.

'Because I've been put to great expense,' answered Booth, estimating—according to Borner—that, if he was to bring Eliza back to England, the total outlay would be about a hundred pounds. 'Do *you* have a hundred pounds, Mrs Armstrong?' he asked—which was a pretty cool question, considering that no one in the Armstrong family had consented to Eliza being transported further than the suburb of Croydon.

'No,' she replied, 'I'm only a poor woman.'

'Well, why don't you let her remain where she is? I'll pay you her wages monthly . . . and I'll give you her address and you can communicate with her.' He turned to Borner. 'What do you think would be a fair wage, Inspector. Two or three shillings a week?'

'That's a question I can't interfere with,' said Borner. 'That's a question for the parents.'

Anyway, after all the accusations, Mrs Armstrong was not bargain-

The Reaction

ing about wage rates. 'No,' she insisted adamantly, 'I want her back.'

'She appears to be afraid that the child has been tampered with or outraged,' explained the inspector.

To Booth, this must have seemed an outrageous suggestion from a mother who had sold the girl for this precise purpose. 'Well I can assure you that the child was pure when she was brought to me,' he said tautly.

'Oh thank God for that,' she exclaimed and, according to the inspector, burst into tears.

Booth told Borner that he had a medical certificate to prove her virginity, if the magistrate would like to see it, but the inspector did not think this would be necessary.

Once again, Booth pressed her to let Eliza stay in France, but Mrs Armstrong would not even consider it. 'No, Sir,' she insisted through her sobs, 'I want my child back to take her before the magistrate to prove that I never sold her.'

'She wouldn't know whether she was sold or not,' argued Booth.

'Oh yes, she would,' insisted Mrs Armstrong. 'A girl of thirteen would know.'

Suddenly, according to his testimony, Booth changed his tactic of reasoning with her. 'Did you know something about Rebecca Jarrett?' he demanded sternly.

'Yes.'

'Did you know what sort of woman she was?'

'Yes,' answered Mrs Armstrong, though she possibly misunderstood Booth's meaning.

'Was it not a very extraordinary thing,' he asked, 'that you should let your child go with a woman like this?'

According to Booth, she made no answer. In fact, there was no point in arguing. She was completely adamant that the only way that life would be tolerable for her in Charles Street was to get Eliza back.

Booth shrugged his shoulders. He wrote Eliza's address on a piece of paper and handed it to Mrs Armstrong. She was a servant in a little town called Loriol, about 100 miles south of Lyon in France. 'You'd better consult your husband,' he said, 'and let me know if you'll let the child remain.'

The Reaction

The inspector returned with Mrs Armstrong to see the magistrate. Part of the mystery, at least, had now been solved. Even if her departure from Britain still seemed extraordinary, Eliza's whereabouts had now been established.

This time, however, the revelations in court not only alerted *Lloyds Newspaper* to the fact that the story clearly merited some additional coverage. It attracted the attention of the far more respectable *St James Gazette* that had attacked the *Pall Mall* so vigorously when the paper first started running the controversial series. Declaring that the *Lloyds* article was 'well worth the readers careful study', it highlighted the fact that certain members of the Salvation Army had been concerned strangely with 'the spiriting away' of Mrs Armstrong's little girl.

Backed now by this strong support, *Lloyds Newspaper* picked up the story once again. Its reporter, Mr Hales, took Mrs Armstrong to Winchester to explore the address from which Rebecca Jarrett had written to Nancy Broughton, and to probe the background of this strange woman with a limp who had taken Eliza from Charles Street.

Like Inspector Borner, they found that there was no one living at Hope Cottage—for which the neighbours were thankful. For evidently the 'fallen women' who were housed there often quarrelled noisily and, once a week when a Salvation army captain called to drill them, kept everyone 'awake through the night with Hallelujah choruses'.

Persistently, the reporter and Mrs Armstrong visited Josephine Butler's other home for ex-prostitutes. There, from the principal, they learned the full story of Rebecca Jarrett's life of vice, of her elevating spiritual experience and miracle cure that made her determined to devote herself to 'rescue work', and of her position as matron of Hope Cottage.

The facts, as *Lloyds* stated bluntly in a big two-column story in its issue, were indeed bizarre. Eliza Armstrong 'was decoyed from her parents by a professedly religious woman' who was 'matron of a Winchester home',

Moving carefully from reporting to campaigning, *Lloyds Newspaper* questioned if 'any body of religionists had the right to decoy a child

The Reaction

from its mother'. Furthermore, they queried, was it 'a religious act, when that child is enquired for by its parents, for them to hide that child's whereabouts and give false addresses?'

In fact, though Booth and Rebecca Jarrett had not been entirely truthful, they had given no false addresses. But the suggestion behind the *Lloyds'* report was that the statement that Eliza was in Loriol was a blind. She was still being kept concealed from her mother. Mrs Armstrong, it asserted, had written to her daughter on Monday. By Saturday night, she had received no reply—which was not surprising, for by then Eliza was no longer at Loriol.

During the next few days, in a move that was clearly linked with the newspaper criticism, the conflict was re-opened by the brothels lobby in the House of Commons. Cavendish Bentinck asked the Home Secretary if he had seen the *Lloyds'* article and whether he had directed any enquiries to be made. Promptly, another MP was on his feet demanding whether the decoying of a child under fourteen was not a felony?

From the viewpoint of these stubborn opponents of the Criminal Law Amendment Bill, the situation was marked with beautiful irony. Only a few weeks before, Stead had been sweeping all opposition from before him—the crusader for Britain's womanhood. Now, it seemed, the most dramatic aspect of his revelations was untrue—or, at least, open to serious challenge. The girl who, he claimed had been bought for rape for £5—one typical example of a trade that, he claimed amounted to thousands annually—had merely been employed as a domestic servant. The melodramatic examination of 'Lily's' virginity followed by the brothel scene that he had described in such vivid detail was all, it now seemed, based on a fallacy.

Not even Stead's enemies doubted the sincerity of his belief in the facts he described, but the obvious possibility that they were inaccurate —which was now emerging—had laid him wide open to attack.

Clearly, even Stead himself had begun to question whether the facts he had written were completely true—for, as early as the end of July, he ordered a check on the situation in Charles Street. He was told that Mrs Broughton did not run a brothel, as he had stated. Later, on being questioned, Rebecca Jarret insisted that she had never said she did.

Suddenly, Stead's position had become highly delicate—and not merely because he was vulnerable to criminal prosecution. If the 'Lily' story could be proved to be false, it would throw doubt on the whole series and he would become a target for laughter—an over-zealous journalist whose enthusiasm for his cause had caused him to overstate the facts to an extent that was absurd. In a more usual type of subject, this might not have been too serious. Newspapers often made mistakes. But in a controversial issue—so shattering that it had caused parliament to rush through legislation in a state of near-panic—it would be unforgivable.

Stead's only hope, both professionally and socially, lay in maintaining the fragile truth of the 'Lily' story—and stubbornly, blindly, emotionally he insisted on this for the rest of his life.

By the first week in August, none of the critics—either in the Press or in parliament—had charged that there was any connection between 'Lily' and Eliza. Ostensibly Stead was not involved in Mrs Armstrong's complaints about her daughter. All the heat was focussed on Bramwell Booth who, as a result of the Army's temperance campaigning, still had many enemies.

The pressure was causing such great alarm at Salvation Army headquarters that, after the attack in the *St James' Gazette*, Booth wrote to Stead asking for support. 'You might say a word tomorrow (in the paper),' he urged, 'to the effect that we took charge of the girl after having rescued her from what might have been a terrible fate. It only wants to be known that we (you) have really rescued the girl and are now being blackguarded for not giving her up by some unscrupulous people and the country will know who to believe.'

By then, Stead had realised that, against the growing and organised opposition, their case for holding the child was weak. On his urging, Booth telegraphed orders to France for Eliza to be brought to Paris where she was more accessible, should they have to bring her home.

By then, too, the two men had passed on to Mrs Armstrong the letter from Eliza that they had stopped at Salvation Army head-

The Reaction

quarters. In it was the same rhyme that she had sent to Rebecca Jarrett:

> As I was in bed
> Some little forths [thoughts] gave [came] in my head.
> I forth of one, I forth of two;
> But first of all I forth of you.

Clearly, Eliza's repertoire was rather limited, but it indicated an affectionate nature. Certainly, the rhyme was to prove very important in the climax towards which events were now moving.

Next Sunday, 16 August, *Lloyds Newspaper* again ran the story prominently. By now, they had enough new leads to fill several of the earlier gaps in the events of the night of Eliza's departure from Charles Street.

The most important new informant was the driver of the hansom cab that had taken Eliza and Rebecca to the brothel after her examination by Madame Mourey. At the time he had suspected the purpose for which the child was apparently destined. He remembered her clearly with her long black hair, her big red straw hat and high button boots, and he had noted with misgivings the tall woman with the limp and the black stick who had accompanied her. Naturally, as a 'cabbie', he knew the character of Poland Street, where he had been instructed to take them, and was aware that the address over the ham and beef shop was a brothel. Also, he had seen the two men who had followed furtively in a separate cab. It had worried him to such an extent that he had talked it over with his wife—and, when *Lloyds* had started running their articles on Mrs Armstrong, he had contacted the paper.

Exploiting his new leads, Hales, the *Lloyds* reporter decided to take Mrs Armstrong on a dramatic call on Madame Mourey. It developed into a scene of pure Victorian farce, which he described in detail in his paper.

Despite the respectability of her Milton Street address—which had so shocked Stead—Madame Mourey was part of the vice underworld of London and the reporter was taking no chances. As a precaution against a rough reception, he also took along the tough and aggressive Mr Armstrong—black faced and sooty-clothed, as Hales made clear, from somebody's chimney—who was left discreetly outside the house in case of need.

Cautiously, the reporter sent Mrs Armstrong to knock on the front door. Then when it was opened by a servant, he moved after her quickly into the house and asked to see the 'accoucheuse'.

'You can't see Madame without an introduction,' the servant told him.

'I'll introduce myself,' answered the reporter.

Scared by this new development, the servant ran down some stairs into what seemed to the newsman, who followed with Mrs Armstrong, to be a consulting room. The maid hurried out of another door and crossed a yard into a conservatory. 'There's a man in the house! There's a man in the house!' she screamed.

'A Frenchman appeared in a state of great excitement,' wrote the reporter, 'and was followed by a second female . . . A large dog of the Newfoundland type was panting, barking and tugging at his chain through the consulting room window that was open. I told the Frenchman that I only wanted quietly to ask Madame a few questions and, when she had answered them, we should both go away.'

At last Madame Mourey, also highly upset, came to see them. To start with she denied all knowledge of the visit by Rebecca Jarrett and Eliza but, under probing, she recalled the occasion and admitted she examined the child.

'Why was she examined?' asked the reporter.

'A gentleman wished it.'

She turned to Mrs Armstrong who had been introduced as Eliza's mother. 'She was a beautiful child.'

'Who was the man?' asked Hales.

'I don't know,' said Madame Mourey, 'I never saw him before.

The reporter must have pressed her a bit too hard, for he wrote that at this moment 'a fresh scene of excitement ensued and one of the servants raised the cry of "Police!" Mrs Armstrong, fearing that I was going to be attacked, or that the dog might be let loose, rushed out of the room and along the passage, calling to her husband: "Charley! Charley!" . . .'

The sudden appearance of the besooted, well-built Charles

The Reaction

Armstrong induced a state of shock in Madame Mourey and the occupants of the house. 'His demon-like appearance,' wrote the reporter, 'had an electrical effect. The female servants ran back. The Frenchman seemed paralysed, and the old lady threw up her hands, while her eyes remained fixed upon the black figure before her.'

'Well,' said Mr Armstrong. 'You're a fine colour all of you! Why, you're all as white as turnips. What's the matter?'

Mrs Armstrong was growing hysterical urging her husband to violence; and the *Lloyds Newspaper* reporter, deciding he had enough copy, hustled them out of the house.

Meanwhile, Bramwell Booth had answered the implied allegations that the papers had made against him. In a written statement, he said that Eliza Armstrong had been placed in his care by 'some person who wished to save her from the demoralizing surroundings in which she was placed'. He had offered to return her to her mother though he had advised her to let her stay where she was. She had left his office to consult her husband but had not since been in touch with him. Neither the home in Winchester nor Rebecca Jarrett were anything to do with the Salvation Army.

Finally, to show his 'bona fides', he offered to hand over the child to the editor of *Lloyds Newspaper* providing he would agree to take responsibility for her—an offer that the editor declined hastily.

'Detectives,' the paper announced darkly, had called on Mrs Armstrong on Saturday 'and directed her to attend at Scotland Yard on Monday, adding that afterwards she would have to go before the Public Prosecutor.'

In fact, Mrs Armstrong claimed that she had written to Booth after her meeting with him, asking him to return the child to her—but Booth insisted that the letter never arrived. He asserted, too—and this was not denied—that he had stayed very closely in touch with the police who were behaving very strangely.

Without a word to anyone, an inspector had left London for Loriol, taking with him Charles Armstrong, with the intention presumably of bringing Eliza home. By then, she had left the little French town on the first stage of a journey home. So their trip was wasted.

The Reaction

The police had kept Stead, also, very much at arm's length. Although they went through the motions of following up some of his statements in his articles, they did not ask the *Pall Mall Gazette* for any help with their enquiries—since they too, had been the target for attack.

Ironically, developments that were to place Stead and Booth on trial were approaching their climax at almost the precise moment that the national campaign of the combined Purity Movement reached its zenith. Only two days before the massive demonstration in Hyde Park, Stead was barracked as he spoke at a meeting in London with the chant of 'Armstrong! Armstrong!'

'I'll tell you about Armstrong . . . ,' he responded from the platform. 'We took that child from a place that was steeped in vice, from a mother who has admitted she was going to a brothel as she thought and instead . . . we placed her in good and Christian guidance.'

Stead's source for his allegations that Mrs Armstrong had admitted knowing about the brothel destination arose from Bramwell Booth's meeting with her, the exact details of which were to be vehemently contested. But Stead's performance on that platform was noteworthy because it was his first public utterance in defence of his actions.

By then, all the campaigners were fighting off attack. Old General Booth, speaking in London, asserted that 'nobody but arrant fools would believe' some of the newspaper allegations about the Salvation Army. 'The history of their actions for twenty years were a sufficient proof that they would do nothing which was not in accordance with truth and righteousness.'

And in Winchester, Josephine Butler—who had been abroad—moved into print in the local paper in strong support of Rebecca Jarrett. 'I cannot allow my friends to be slandered in my absence without a protest . . . The child will be restored to her mother in due time: but it will not be a happy day for the child, for her mother is a slave to drink and was seeking to sell her child.' This was a big assumption—and a libellous one at that. For although there was no doubt that drink was among Mrs Armstrong's problems, even Stead had been moved at the affection that 'Lily' had displayed for her mother.

The Reaction

Meanwhile, Edward Thomas was conducting his one-man campaign for the Armstrongs. 'It is true,' he declared in an appeal for funds for them 'that the Armstrongs are a poor family; it is equally true that they live in a low neighbourhood, forced to do so by their poverty . . . Now what has been the effect of all this on the Armstrong family? Simply an increase in their poverty and the poor woman's health is beginning to show signs of breaking down . . . It is a case demanding public sympathy and assistance.'

During that week of climax, while plans were being completed for the big demonstration in Hyde Park on Saturday, all the indications suggested that the police were preparing to act against Stead and his helpers. Stentoriously, the *St James' Gazette* was demanding prosecution so that Bramwell Booth could explain 'more precisely the circumstances under which he got possession of the child and the nature of his association with the woman, Rebecca Jarrett'.

Stead and Booth faced up to the fact that, against this pressure, they could retain custody of Eliza no longer. On Sunday—the day after the big demonstration—Sampson Jacques visited Mrs Armstrong in Charles Street and offered to take her the following morning to see her daughter, who was now at Stead's home in Wimbledon.

The next day, Eliza and her mother were re-united in Stead's big garden and Mrs Armstrong signed a formal receipt for her daughter. But they were not permitted to go straight home to Charles Street, where Eliza—still, of course, a virgin—could be paraded in front of the critical neighbours. With Inspector Borner—who had insisted on travelling to Wimbledon with the party—they went to see the public prosecutor.

The interview with Eliza, the principal prosecution witness, completed the crown's preparations for the case. The following week, a warrant was issued for the arrest of Rebecca Jarrett. Stead was on vacation in Grundewald in Switzerland when he heard of the charges against her and wired immediately: 'I alone am responsible. Rebecca Jarrett was only my unwilling agent. I am returning by the first express to claim the sole responsibility for the alleged abduction and to demand, if condemned, the sole punishment.'

Stead, however, was in no position to direct who was to be charged.

The Reaction

The following Monday, the preliminary hearings opened at Bow Street police court where a magistrate listened to the evidence of the prosecution to decide if the case should go to trial. Stead was charged, as he desired, but it did not help Rebecca Jarrett who, despite the editor's claim to responsibility, was held in jail. The other defendents were Booth, Sampson Jacques, Madame Coombe, the Salvation Army officer who had accompanied Eliza to Paris, and Madame Louise Mourey. The main charge was abduction but there was a secondary allegation—against Madame Mourey, Stead and some of the others involved with the examination of Eliza—of technical assault.

The heady weeks that had followed the publication of the series were over. A reaction in the public mood had set in that was fast exploited by the brothel interests. It was symptomatic of the sudden change in attitude that, on the Monday following the ecstatic mass demonstration in Hyde Park, General Booth was attacked when he arrived at Hull for a public meeting. 'The Police,' reported *Lloyds*, 'had great difficulty in preventing the mob getting at him.' And he was, in fact, struck by a stick.

The same kind of hostile crowds surged round the entrance to Bow Street magistrates court, close to Covent Garden fruit and vegetable market, when the hearings into the abduction of Eliza opened on 7 September. Stead and Booth had to be dragged through a surging, yelling mass of hooting Londoners to reach the entrance to the courtroom.

For Stead, in particular, his sudden transformation from the role of campaigning hero to that of denigrated villain on a criminal charge must have been bewildering. The noisy crowd—who could often be heard all day within the police court—carried effigies of the main defendants. And, one morning, Stead had the unnerving experience of waking up in Wimbledon and seeing a mockup of himself dangling from a tree in his own garden.

On the second day, the threats of the crowd became serious. When Bramwell Booth, disdaining an offer of police protection, walked away from the courtroom at the end of the hearing, he was followed and beaten up. After that, the defendants travelled to and from the court every day in a police truck.

The Reaction

The prosecution of Stead sparked off a massive spate of correspondence to the Home Office from the purity movement throughout the country. How was it, letters and memorials demanded repeatedly, that the editor who had disclosed the facts of the vice underworld—and even caused the law to be changed—was now in the dock facing his accusers while the guilty men he had exposed went free? Why did no criminal proceedings follow the revelations in the *Pall Mall Gazette*?

It was an embarrassing question that the ministers had to face, too, in the House of Commons. For the answer—that there was inadequate evidence to support any prosecutions—branded the police either with inefficiency or, as Stead had charged, with connivance with vice interests, who had bought their inactivity with liberal bribes.

In fact, in the official but private investigation that had followed Stead's bribery allegations, the police had vigorously pleaded their innocence. The East End brothels, asserted one division, were far too poor to pay out protection money on the scale that Stead had suggested. From the more affluent West End, Superintendent Dunlap protested that the fact that he had prosecuted more than a thousand prostitutes, every year, for the past five years, did not surely suggest inactivity.

Meanwhile, as the hearings in the Armstrong case proceeded, the administration was nervously watching the newspaper that Stead was still editing. When the *St James Gazette* suddenly exposed its competitor's secret plans to run a new series on English girls in foreign brothels, alarm gripped the Home Office.

Treasury counsel were asked hurriedly if there was any way of stopping the new series if the *Gazette* started publishing. And counsel's response that there was no way of checking publication—though there might possibly be grounds for subsequent charges for obscene libel—did not bring comfort to anyone.

Lord Hallsbury, the ex-Lord Chancellor, wrote a blistering letter to the Home Secretary urging that the reasons that had deterred the government from prosecuting Stead for obscenity in July would not apply to a series that was about the Continental brothels. For in this case, no one could accuse the government of shielding the depraved

The Reaction

rich at the expense of the poor. The clients of the foreign brothels were outside the control of the British authorities.

Had Stead proceeded with the series—which since the *St James Gazette* claimed to have a copy of his contract with a German detective, he appeared to be considering—then he would clearly have faced a serious new attack.

Cautiously, a Home Office official ordered the CID at Scotland Yard to keep a careful watch on the *Pall Mall Gazette* for any warnings of future revelations.

It is doubtful, now that the threats that were facing Stead and Booth had grown so much more serious, if there was much for the government to fear in the way of new sensations. For by then, the hearings before the magistrate—that had lasted for three gruelling weeks—were over. The case was sent for trial at the Central Criminal Court in Old Bailey, near St Paul's Cathedral. There, a month later on Friday, 23 October, Stead and his co-defendants arrived to face a jury.

10
The Trial

The rain and the cold grey sky of that Friday morning provided Stead, as he arrived at the gloomy stone entrance of the Old Bailey, with a fitting setting for yet another role in his seemingly endless repertoire of parts—this time, a martyr for his cause.

The crusading editor saw himself as nothing less than a victim of political persecution, as a sacrificial offering to a society that he had outraged by exposing its vices. He believed adamantly that the CID and the public prosecutor's department had searched keenly for an excuse to bring him to trial—and that, when they did, they had acted on a technicality.

In regarding the export of Eliza as so trivial an offence, Stead was displaying the arrogance that was a feature common to all the puritan sex reformers. Because they believed they were serving God as opposed to the Devil, they were all so sure they were right. When in their zeal they made errors such as Stead had made, they dismissed them as mere details. If their critics raised these as issues, the moralist campaigners saw them as enemies, with Satanic motives.

There is, however, some evidence to support Stead's belief that he was a political victim, that the administration were, at least, pleased that they could bring charges against him.

Although the instruction to Treasury counsel to consider prosecution still exists, it is fairly clear that at least one Home Office file, covering the preparation of the case, is missing from the records—removed, maybe, by some tactful civil servant.

Certainly, the judge in the trial displayed a partiality for the prosecution—acting at times as though he was its counsel—that was clearly open to criticism.

The Trial

The fact that the Establishment press, led by *The Times*, were almost unanimous in their attacks on the editor conforms with a picture of revenge. Perhaps there was a basic need in the society of Victorian London—perhaps there is always this need in any society—to demand retribution from a man who had trampled so defiantly on their code of behaviour.

On the other hand, once the government had rejected its obvious opportunity to act on the grounds of obscenity, it is hard to see how they could have exacted this toll if Stead himself, with his unchecked 'Lily' story, had not given them a clear opening for prosecution.

Also, if the facts about Eliza's eventful, and at times unpleasant, journey from Charles Street to France were as the Armstrongs stated, then clearly the public prosecutor would have been neglecting his duty if he had not promoted charges. For if the vice setting that Stead had described did not exist, then his treatment of Eliza was an atrocious attack on the liberty of an individual, and the public assaults on the Armstrongs that the campaigners had launched, once they were under pressure, amounted to persecution.

The dock in the New Court of the Old Bailey was large. It was more than ample for the six defendants in the Armstrong case who, when the court was called to its feet, stood up to face their judge, Mr Justice Lopes, as, clad in full wig and crimson robes, he took his place on the bench before them.

The government clearly regarded the case as important—which tends to support Stead's claim of political motivation—for the Attorney General himself, Sir Richard Webster, who had helped to push the Criminal Law Amendment Bill through the House of Commons, was leading the prosecution. On the other hand, the brothels lobby MPs, too, were waiting poised to attack if there was any sign of weakening on the part of the crown.

In all there were twelve counsel involved in the case in which the main charge was that the defendants had unlawfully taken an unmarried girl under the age of sixteen out of the possession of her mother and father. All the accused pleaded not guilty.

In a sense, although they were not in the dock, the Armstrongs, and

The Trial

even the residents of Charles Street, were also on trial. For at this stage, although the issues became a little more complex as the trial progressed, the case hinged on the question: did Mrs Armstrong sell Eliza or had she merely permitted her to leave home to take a job as a domestic servant?

Even Stead, for all his protestations, could not be absolutely certain of the answer to this question because his sole source of information was Rebecca Jarrett. However, if he and the others were going to win acquittal, it was vital that the Armstrongs should be completely discredited as witnesses and displayed as cynical suppliers of the vice market—displayed, in short, to be like so many of the other parents whom Stead had featured in his series.

Certainly, the trial was marked by irony, for it was one of the first cases to be brought under a section of the Criminal Law Amendment Bill that Stead himself had forced through parliament. In fact, had not his series—with its story of 'Lily'—achieved the result it did, the particular charge he was now facing could not have been brought.

From the start, too, his personal case was hampered by the fact that the crown lawyers insisted skilfully that they were not challenging his 'high motives'. These, however—so they argued—did not justify the offence and there was, they contended, no point in his calling witnesses in support of them.

Eliza—pretty, demure, with her long black hair—was the first witness. For nearly four hours, under the gentle guidance of junior Treasury counsel Harry Poland, she told the story of what had happened to her from the moment on 2 June when Rebecca Jarrett had called at the Broughton's home in Charles Street.

Very little of what she said was in dispute—since even Rebecca agreed that, in front of Eliza, she had pretended that the purpose for which she needed the child was domestic service. Indeed, most of the narrative she was now relating had appeared in the *Pall Mall Gazette*. It formed a quiet start to the trial, with no distressing scenes of vehement cross-examination.

When Eliza was eventually allowed to step down from the witness box, after four hours of testimony, her place was taken by her mother for what would clearly be a gruelling session.

The Trial

To begin with, as prosecuting counsel took her through the events as she recalled them; she was calm, telling the story that *Lloyds Newspaper* had already published. It sounded reasonable enough. Her eldest daughter was in service, so that it was fairly natural that Eliza should want to do the same.

She was adamant on the key question: she had not received any money from Rebecca, except for the shilling she borrowed.

At first, when Sir Charles Russell QC—Rebecca's highly eminent attorney—rose to cross-examine, he handled her relatively gently. He questioned her about her relations with Mrs Broughton, about what she had been told about Rebecca, and whether she was satisfied that Eliza had been well treated in France. Then he moved into more controversial areas and asked her what happened when she met Rebecca on Derby Day.

'She asked me whether the girl was pure,' Mrs Armstrong conceded under the lawyer's probing. 'I said to her: "What do you mean?" She said: "Is she fast? Has she been running about with boys?" I said: "Certainly not." And she said: "Because my husband is a very particular man." '

When Russell asked her about the money she received, she answered that Rebecca had given her a shilling 'for the baby'.

'Will you swear that was all?' he demanded. 'Will you swear that it was not a sovereign that was given to you?'

'I do swear it,' she insisted, 'and call God to witness it.'

Bramwell Booth's counsel took over from Russell and focussed his cross-examination primarily on her meeting with Booth and Inspector Borner. He was hoping to force an admission from her that, on that occasion, she conceded that she knew Rebecca was a procuress.

'Did Mr Booth say to you,' he asked, after several similar questions, 'that it was rather peculiar that you let your child go with a gay woman?'

'No,' she insisted firmly, 'he said nothing of that kind to me. If I'd known that Jarrett was a gay woman, I shouldn't have let my child go with her, *I* can assure you.' And, on this, she was to be supported later by the respectable testimony of Inspector Borner.

So far, Mrs Armstrong had stood up well to the cross-examination.

The Trial

But now it was the turn of Stead—who was defending himself—and a great deal depended on his attacking her story successfully.

He stood in the dock, his voice, with its North of England accents, seeming loud in the courtroom. 'When you saw Inspector Borner,' he asked, 'did you tell him you thought your daughter was Lily?'

'No.'

'Why not?'

'I'd no reason for telling him. I might have told him. But I don't remember whether I told him or not.'

'Did you tell your husband?'

'No.'

'Why not?'

'I knew what a violent man he was. I didn't read it [the article] to him because it was too disgusting. It would have shocked him and I was afraid he'd strike me if I told him I thought that Lily was Eliza.'

'Although you identified Lily as Eliza, you never thought of making any enquiry of me?' asked Stead.

'I didn't know where you lived.'

'But Inspector Borner would have told you.'

'There were so many mixed up in it,' she said, 'I didn't know the address.'

'Didn't you know that it was printed in the paper?'

'No, I didn't know it was printed in the paper.'

She was beginning to bend under his attack. Her voice was growing louder, her answers more defiant. Already, tears were beginning to trickle down her cheeks.

'When you saw the articles in the *Gazette*,' Stead went on, 'what made you think that Lily was Eliza?'

'One reason . . . was a little verse because that was in a letter I received from my daughter.' This was the rhyme—'As I was in bed'—that Stead had published in his first article. 'I didn't know she knew the verse until I got her letter.'

'But as you didn't receive the letter until August,' Stead, his voice icy, queried sharply from the dock, 'how could you possibly have identified Lily by the verse on 9 July.'

The Trial

The tears streamed down Mrs Armstrong's face as she fought to find the words to answer him. 'I was uneasy before I got the letter' she sobbed... 'Well after seeing the verses, I was more uneasy.'

Before Stead could press her further, the judge intervened. As he understood it, Mrs Armstrong thought Lily was Eliza when she first read the articles and, when she got the letter with the same verse, her suspicions were confirmed.

Mrs Armstrong looked at the bench gratefully, 'Yes, My Lord,' she said with relief, 'that's right. That's what I meant.'

Stead switched his line of questioning, but he sustained his attacking technique. Now, he focussed on her pattern of behaviour after she had read the articles. Sobbing, she answered his cold critical questions about Mrs Broughton. 'Yes,' she thought she *had* got Eliza away for immoral purposes, though she did not think so any longer. Now, she knew that Rebecca Jarrett was to blame.

Then Mrs Armstrong broke down completely, her body shuddering. For a few moments, she was unable to answer any questions.

Despite his harrying of her, Stead seemed almost sympathetic. 'I'm sorry,' he said, 'but my questions are directed against Mrs Broughton rather than you.'

'There's nothing objectionable in your questions, Mr Stead,' declared the judge.

At last, Mrs Armstrong recovered enough of her shattered self-control to continue. In fact, her case so far was quite good, though marred by certain obvious weaknesses. It was unusual, for example, to purchase new clothes for a child who was going into service, in which she would presumably be given a uniform—and, from the viewpoint of the defence, the fact that Rebecca had taken her out shopping was an important aspect of the Derby Day events. This was why Stead now concentrated on it.

'How much did you expect a girl of Eliza's age would get as wages as a servant?' he asked.

'About half a crown a week,' she answered.

'Could the clothes bought for Eliza have been bought out of a month's wages?'

'I don't know.'

The Trial

'Did you not know that the clothes bought for Eliza cost nearly a sovereign?'

'I should want two suits for that.'

The judge interposed: 'Just answer the question Mrs Armstrong.'

'I don't know,' said Mrs Armstrong. 'They wouldn't be very expensive—a penny and three farthing tie and three and eleven boots.'

In fact, as was to be proved, Eliza had also been bought a new dress and a coat and a hat as well—and Stead had scored a good point. Now, he questioned her about another part of her testimony on which she was vulnerable: she had been charged by the police that night with being drunk. Where had she got the money if Rebecca had not given her a sovereign? He approached the key question carefully, establishing first the background of a cash shortage on Derby Day.

'Did you not ask Mrs Broughton to lend you sixpence the morning Jarrett was in her room?' he demanded.

'No, I asked her to lend me a penny to get some sweets for the baby. Jarrett then pulled out her purse and handed me a shilling for the baby.'

'Then,' asked Stead carefully, 'if Mrs Broughton says you came into her room to borrow sixpence (as testified in the magistrates court earlier) she is telling what is untrue?'

'Yes.'

'You're charging Mrs Broughton . . . with telling lies. You realise what you're doing?'

'I asked her for a penny,' asserted Mrs Armstrong adamantly.

'You got a shilling anyway,' commented Stead drily.

'Yes,' she answered defiantly. 'I bought a comb for Eliza and a pair of socks for the baby.'

'How much did you pay for the comb?'

'Sixpence.'

'How much for the socks?'

'Fivepence three farthings,' she replied, adding sarcastically, 'and I got drunk with the remaining farthing.'

'Mrs Armstrong,' said the judge, 'you must answer the questions.'

'Yes, I will, My Lord,' she said, 'but look at the character I've got with these people.'

The Trial

'Listen to the questions, Mrs Armstrong,' ordered the judge, 'and answer them temperately and moderately. Do you *mean* you got drunk with that farthing?'

'They say I got drunk with that shilling,' she retorted. 'I couldn't be very drunk with a farthing.'

But Stead wanted the attention of the court on the sovereign that Rebecca had insisted to him that she had paid her. 'Where *did* you get the money?' he demanded.

'I had some,' she answered sullenly.

'If that is so, how came you to borrow a penny to buy sweets for the baby?'

'My husband gave me the money.'

'To get drunk with?'

'Oh, no, certainly not.'

'Did you use your housekeeping money to get drunk with?'

'I'm *not* going to tell you.'

Knowing he had her cornered, Stead pressed her relentlessly. 'How did you get the money to get drunk with that night?'

'I'm not going to make you any answer.'

Again the judge cut in: 'Answer the question. You've already said you got drunk.'

'Well,' conceded Mrs Armstrong, 'I took a glass of beer after my husband struck me.'

Again the judge remarked drily: 'Whatever might be the general habits of the witness there was no doubt she was drunk on the night of 3 June.'

'This isn't the first time you've been locked up for being drunk, is it Mrs Armstrong,' asked Stead. 'How many times have you been fined?'

'Three times,' she replied sullenly.

'For drunkenness?'

'Yes.'

'You frequent public houses?'

'Yes.'

'Do you sometimes send Eliza or the other children for drink?'

'Yes.'

'No, further questions.'

Mrs Armstrong was no longer doing so well. The Attorney General himself rose to re-examine her about the key issue of the clothes that Rebecca had bought Eliza. 'Were they "swell" in the character?' he asked—meaning silk, as suitable for a seduction victim.

'No,' answered Mrs Armstrong quickly, 'they didn't look flash. They were like we'd have dressed her in to send her to Sunday School'—a comparison, suggesting as it did a good Christian home, that must have pleased the crown lawyers.

When Sir Richard Webster read the *Pall Mall Gazette* article about Lily as evidence, it gave Stead another opportunity to cross-examine. Once more he ferreted for her reactions to Mrs Broughton, for he clearly believed that her behaviour after the *Gazette* arrived in Charles Street was incriminating. Did she believe that Mrs Broughton had sold Eliza into immorality, he asked once more?

'I believed that Mrs Broughton *might* have let her go for a wicked purpose,' she conceded.

'Did you say so to her?'

'No . . . I didn't know what to think.'

Once more, the judge interrupted—this time to inquire where Stead's cross-examination was leading.

'I put these questions to show that the witness said nothing to Mrs Broughton because she had a guilty conscience, My Lord,' answered the editor. 'I want to bring out that her conduct was inconsistent with what any honest mother would have pursued towards a neighbour whom she believed to have sold her child into infamy.'

The judge was not convinced—but he allowed him to continue.

'You will be entitled to urge that on the jury,' he said a little dubiously.

Stead addressed Mrs Armstrong again about the five pounds that the article reported had been paid for Eliza. Mrs Broughton had admitted receiving one pound, which left four pounds unaccounted for. 'Did you in any way accuse her of getting the four pounds?' he asked.

'No.'

'Did you in any way ask her for what she got that money?'

'No.'

The Trial

'Why did you say nothing to her?'

'If I had as much sense as you perhaps I might,' she retorted—and laughter spread through the courtroom.

Stead did not think it was funny. 'But when a woman has lost her child and finds a story in the newspapers stating that she has been ruined,' he persisted, 'she wouldn't want much sense to go and make inquiries.'

'I've told you what I know and I'm very tired.'

This time Stead displayed no sympathy. Relentlessly, he flung question after question at her. Why did she not ask Mrs Broughton about that extra money? Why did she not ask if Rebecca Jarrett was a woman who was an old hand at procuration—which the article stated—and got young girls for immoral purposes?

'You never asked a single question of Mrs Broughton,' demanded Stead, 'which would have led you to identify this girl as your daughter?'

Mrs Armstrong was weakened by emotion and by pressure. 'I don't understand you,' she whimpered.

'Here,' explained Stead, 'are six or seven distinct statements that you've made . . .'

'I dare say there are a lot of lies as well as truths,' Mrs Armstrong interjected.

'And yet,' continued the editor remorselessly, 'you never took the trouble to ascertain what were lies and what were truths.'

'I had trouble enough!' exclaimed Mrs Armstrong.

'You never asked Mrs Broughton what was true or what was false?' pressed Stead.

'What's the use of talking to a woman who can't read or write?' pleaded Mrs Armstrong.

'Did it never occur to you to read it [the article] over to Mrs Broughton and say "Is this Lily . . . Eliza?"'

'No.'

At last, the judge stopped the inquisition. 'I've listened to enough, Mr Stead,' he said, 'to raise the question of whether the witness' conduct is consistent with that of an affectionate, honest mother.'

'Very well, My Lord,' answered Stead.

The Trial

And so Mrs Armstrong was at last allowed to leave the witness box. There was clear damage to the crown case. Where had she got the money to get drunk with if she had not received a sovereign from Rebecca? Why had she not remonstrated with Mrs Broughton (although, in fact, at a later stage she had) when she suspected she might have sold her child—*unless* she was party to the deal? Why had it been necessary to spend a pound on new clothes for Eliza if she was merely going into service?

All these questions would clearly be probed some more as Nancy Broughton now stepped into the witness box to take the oath.

By contrast with Mrs Armstrong, whose emotionalism led her into tears and loud and sudden exclamations of sarcasm, Nancy Broughton was by nature a cheerful, gregarious chatterer. Words—a flow of minute gossipy details—spilled from her in a torrent, words that were sometimes meaningless and incoherent and occasionally ill-advised.

Under the careful examination of Harry Poland—who must have found her a very hard witness to control—she told her version of Rebecca's two visits to Charles Street and, in particular, of the controversial reason for her payment to her of a sovereign—although Rebecca claimed that this was two sovereigns.

'She said: "Nancy, I'm going to stop to dinner—You've got no money to get it," I said: "Yes, I have. There's bacon in the cupboard, potatoes on the fire and money in the cup." She held out her hand to me and said: "Take this, Nancy, take it, you have a shawl in pawn."'

'How did she know that?' asked Poland.

'Because I told her I hadn't got a shawl to my back. She said: "Well, Nancy, I promised you I'd try to pay you some day for the kindnesses towards me..."'

This evidence gave strong support to the crown's case that the reason for the payment of the money was a good one. Rebecca truly was in her debt from her hard times that Mrs Broughton had helped her through, and some months before her visit to Charles Street she had written her a letter of gratitude—that was produced in court— in which she assured her: 'I have a little money to give you directly I see you.'

The Trial

However, for all the garrulous stream of detail that poured from her, she was absolutely adamant that there had been no doubt at all as to why Rebecca wanted a girl. There had been no hint of immoral purposes. She had, she said, married a commercial traveller. She lived in a six-roomed house in Croydon and needed a girl for service 'to clean around the oil-cloth and carpets, as she was afflicted and couldn't kneel'.

On the night of Rebecca's first visit, she met Mrs Armstrong again. Even though she had a baby in her arms, she was drunk and abusive. 'I'm not going to let my child go for a tart,' she said.

Even Mrs Broughton realised at once that this was a bad slip. When Poland questioned her again, she corrected herself. Now, as she recollected the incident, Mrs Armstrong had said that she wouldn't let her child go to be a servant.

The next morning—on the important Derby Day—Mrs Armstrong had apologised for the way she had spoken to her the night before. A little while later, she had come over to Mrs Broughton's home to talk to Rebecca. 'My child shall go,' she had told her, Mrs Broughton testified, 'if it's as a servant you want her.'

Mrs Broughton's chatty evidence gave the defence some good material to work with—for there was a clear implication that Mrs Armstrong had, at least, suspected that Rebecca Jarrett wanted Eliza for immoral uses. And this was something that, throughout her gruelling cross-examination, for all her tears and emotion and sarcasm, Mrs Armstrong had never conceded.

It was only a small gap in the prosecution, but Stead and the defence lawyers worked actively to widen it.

Under grilling by Russell, Mrs Broughton—clearly realising the danger to which she had made herself vulnerable—insisted that Rebecca had never mentioned to Mrs Armstrong in her hearing anything about Eliza being pure. Under pressure she conceded that she had asked her if she had seen her romping about the street with boys, and she had replied that she had only seen her with boys and girls. Adamantly, she asserted that Rebecca had never mentioned anything about wanting a pure girl for a gentleman or starting a house.

Then support for the defence came from an unexpected quarter. The foreman of the jury rose to his feet. 'My Lord, the jury wish to

The Trial

put a question to the witness. She stated that on the Tuesday Mrs Armstrong abused her and . . . said she would not let her daughter go for a tart. This was heard by all the jury but one. In a repetition of the answer, the witness substituted a servant. We wish to know whether Mrs Armstrong said she wouldn't let her daughter go for a tart.'

'I said servant,' insisted Mrs Broughton indignantly. 'I didn't say the . . . the other word.'

But the court shorthand writer said she did use it and, although Mrs Broughton still denied it angrily, it was a mark against her as a witness.

One after another, witnesses for the prosecution supported the story of the two women—Jane Farrer and Charles Armstrong from Charles Street, Inspector Borner and the police officer who had taken Charles Armstrong on the abortive trip to Loriol to find Eliza.

Five days after the start of the case, the prosecution rested—mainly on the testimony of their two dubious witnesses. Now the focus of the trial would be on Rebecca Jarrett, the only other person who *knew* the terms on which Eliza was taken away from Charles Street.

Sir Charles Russell rose to his feet to open the defence case on her behalf. 'There is,' he declared, 'no attempt at denial . . . that she was the active party in the taking away of the child from Charles Street on 3 June . . .' Briefly, he gave the court a resumé of Rebecca's background. And he made no attempt to make it sound better than it was. 'She had passed the greater portion of her life alternating between the desire to lead a better life and the relapse into immorality. She has kept at Bristol, at Liverpool, at Manchester and in London what are called "gay houses".'

Briefly, he provided a run down of her reformation, her trip to London to see Stead and his assignment to buy him a girl. Russell mocked the two main defence witnesses. 'It is inconceivable that Mrs Armstrong and Mrs Broughton, from their own statements, did not know the purpose for which the child was taken away.'

As Rebecca took the oath, she appeared an austere, unattractive person—tall and a bit heavy, with her hair cut in a fringe under a hat that, according to one newspaper, resembled a Salvation Army cap without actually being one.

The Trial

Her testimony was in direct contrast to that of Mrs Armstrong and Mrs Broughton. She had made it completely clear why she wanted a girl. She had said nothing about living in a six-room house in Croydon or wanting a servant to scrub the oil-cloth because she could not kneel. She swore that she had told Mrs Armstrong that 'if she is a pure girl, I shall keep her, but if she is not I shall return her the same as she is.'

She had, she insisted, paid a total of £5 for Eliza.

Moment by moment, she related the story of Stead's melodramatic arrangements for Eliza on the night of Derby Day—very little of which, after the departure from Charles Street, was in dispute.

Then Sir Richard Webster, the Attorney General, stood up to cross-examine. There are many ways of discrediting a witness and it is clear that, by this time, Sir Richard had formed the judgment of Rebecca's character that was to be the crux of his case—namely that her background of vice was not nearly so murky as she had drawn it, that, although it was marked by a degree of immorality, she did not have the underworld contacts that she had led Stead to believe. Fabrication, therefore, had been vital.

The Attorney General questioned her about the 'gay houses' she had run, probing where they were and who she ran them with. He asked in particular about a house she claimed to have operated at 23 High Street, Marylebone—not far from Charles Street—at the end of 1882 and the beginning of 1883. She answered him with hesitation and only under pressure did she concede that this house was leased by a man named Sullivan, whom she was living with at the time. It was to prove an important part of the case although at the time it seemed so remote from Eliza Armstrong that neither *The Times* nor *Lloyds* reported it at all.

Meanwhile, Sir Richard questioned her about the *Pall Mall Gazette* account of the negotiations in Charles Street. Insisting firmly that 'I believe I told Mr Stead as truthfully as I could all that had passed', she conceded that he had 'made some slight mistakes in the article'.

One by one, Sir Richard took her through the mistakes—among them the statement that the child was bought from a woman who was a brothel keeper, that she had been purchased for £5 on Tuesday rather than on Wednesday, that the father was a drunken man, that he was informed that she was going away, that the brothel keeper had first offered the mother a sovereign for her child. All these, she suggested, were misunderstandings by Stead of what she had told him.

Late in the afternoon, the court rose for the weekend, during which the police were clearly busy checking up on Rebecca's evidence. For, when she entered the witness box on Monday, the Attorney General said: 'Now, Rebecca Jarrett, you said on Friday that you kept a gay house at 23, High Street Marylebone at the end of 1882 and the beginning of 1883.'

Rebecca realised what was coming, for she had given a false address —if, indeed, she had ever run a brothel anywhere—to protect Sullivan, her ex-lover. 'I'm not going to tell you where I did live,' she said defiantly. 'I am willing to go through any punishment but I am not going into my past life. Anything concerning the case I'm ready to answer you truthfully.'

The judge glared at her, for a refusal to answer a relevant question was close to contempt of court. 'All I can tell you,' he said, 'is that I think it is a proper question...'

'Well, Sir...' interposed Rebecca.

'Will you listen,' thundered the judge continuing. '... and a question that ought to be answered and, if not answered, the jury will draw their own inference.'

'I caution you,' warned the Attorney General. Then repeated his question about her statement that she had kept a gay house at 23, High Street, Marylebone—which, it was now obvious, was untrue. 'Do you adhere to that answer?'

Emotionally, she cried out: 'You forced that lie out of me. I'm not going to tell.'

There was a 'sensation', as *Lloyds Newspaper* put it, in the courtroom, as once more Sir Richard put the question: 'Do you adhere to that answer?'

'I'm not going to give any other answer.'

From that moment, since she was admitting she had lied under oath, it was clear that Rebecca's chances of acquittal were remote; and, since the main part of the defence case rested on the jury's belief in

The Trial

her evidence, her false testimony had threatened gravely the situation of the other defendants.

As Stead made his opening speech, the judge stopped him repeatedly because he was speaking of his motives in organising the purchase of Eliza. Again, the editor saw this as political repression but, seen in retrospect, it seems a consistent view for the judge to take. 'What the prosecution say is this,' he said to Stead at one moment. 'Assuming your motives to have been honest and high minded and pure, still you overstepped the law in what you did.'

When the Archbishop of Canterbury entered the court, to take the box as a witness for Stead, the judge invited him courteously to sit with him on the bench, but he refused to allow him to testify. For what personal knowledge could His Grace possibly have about the abduction of Eliza? All he could support was Stead's purpose and this was not under challenge.

At last, Stead himself walked across the courtroom from the dock and entered the witness box to face the Attorney General.

From the start, the government lawyers had designed their strategy around a picture of events in which Stead was a respectable, honourable man who had been careless and overtrusting, who had been drawn to break the law by his enthusiasm for what he believed to be a good cause. The real criminal in the case, they implied, was Rebecca Jarrett. This was sound tactics, for an all-male Victorian jury were not likely to sympathise with a 'fallen' woman, whereas they might well feel a lot of respect for Stead.

For this reason, Sir Richard's highly aggressive cross-examination of Stead was truly aimed at Rebecca. Systematically, covering the same ground as he had pursued with her, he took the editor through the Lily article, pointing up the inaccuracies which still Stead—unlike the judge—did not seem to think were very important.

These arose, he said—as indeed Rebecca had testified—through misunderstandings between them.

'The keeper of the house,' said the Attorney General at one point, reading from the article, 'offered the mother a sovereign for her daughter.'

'I have no doubt that Jarrett told me that,' said Stead.

The Trial

'Did you hear Jarrett swear in her testimony that she did not?'

'I heard Jarrett swear a great many things about the Lily story which surprised me.'

'Why did it surprise you?' asked the judge.

'Because they don't agree with what she told me.'

'I gather then,' said the Attorney General 'that till I was able to put the questions I did, you implicitly believed in Jarrett?'

'Yes,' admitted Stead.

'Shaken at all now?' queried the judge.

'I think it is a defective memory, rather . . .'

'Answer the question, please,' he demanded.

'Are you shaken at all as the veracity of Jarrett?'

'Well, of course,' said Stead, still being evasive, 'I will say that I don't believe Jarrett as implicitly as I did.'

'Then I may say you are somewhat shaken?'

'Yes,' answered Stead doubtfully, 'I have less confidence in her.'

'Less faith?'

'Her memory seems defective, but I think she intends to tell the truth.'

The judge was now clearly supporting the prosecution to an extent that revealed clear partiality. These two eminent men—the most senior lawyer in the government and a High Court judge—were grilling Stead on the weakest link in the defence case. If Stead could be forced to admit that Rebecca had lied to him about what had happened in Charles Street, how could he or the other defence counsel insist that her version of the story was true as against that of Mrs Armstrong and Mrs Broughton?

Sir Richard put the lead question for what was clearly going to be another attack. ' "The father," ' he read out from Stead's article, ' "who was also a drunken man, was told that his daughter was going to a situation." Did Jarrett tell you that?'

'Yes, as far as I remember.'

'Did she tell you?' demanded the judge, as though everyone's memory was infallible.

'To the best of my memory.'

The Trial

'Have you any doubt?'

'I would not have had any doubt if it were not for her memory.'

'If you had not heard Jarrett's evidence,' insisted the judge, 'would you have had any doubt that Jarrett told you this?'

'Not in the least. To the best of my memory what I wrote is an exact transcript of what Jarrett told me.'

Stead was not giving the admission that the crown needed and the Attorney General was growing exasperated. 'You are a master of English,' he declared acidly, 'you can understand this question. I cannot attempt the dictation of the *Pall Mall Gazette*, but I can put a plain question.'

'You ought to answer these questions,' chided the judge. 'You are a highly educated man.'

The Attorney General read out another passage: ' "The father received the news with indifference without even enquiring where she was going to" ' He faced Stead coolly, challenging him to be evasive. 'Did she say that?'

'Yes.'

He asked two more questions, based on the article, and each time Stead conceded the single answer 'yes', though they were minor points that did not reflect the same conflict with Rebecca's testimony as the earlier issues.

There were several more witnesses for the defence—including Josephine Butler and Howard Vincent—though the judge curbed much of the testimony on the same old grounds that it merely supported Stead's motive.

Since Rebecca's exposure as a liar, the defence case was badly cracked but, finally, the judge crushed what little remained of it with a ruling that astonished Stead and his supporting counsel.

Shaen, the solicitor whom Stead had consulted before embarking on his project, was testifying—confirming he had advised the editor that, providing he could show that he had no criminal intent, he would not be committing a breach of the law.

'I don't agree with that view of the law at all,' said the judge, 'I shall tell the jury that the taking of the child away against the will of the father was a criminal offence.'

The Trial

Stead could barely believe that he had heard correctly. None of the defence lawyers had challenged the fact that Charles Armstrong had hit his wife for allowing Eliza to leave home without his permission. Even the article in the *Pall Mall Gazette* conceded essentially that the father had not been consulted. The transaction had clearly been with the mother.

Hurriedly, as he wrote later, Stead consulted Sir Charles Russell on strategy. For an important possibility had occurred to him: what if the Armstrongs were not, in fact, married—as many working class people were not? What if Charles Armstrong was not the legal father? Should they not ask permission to recall Mrs Armstrong to put this question to her?

But this was too much for Russell. The question was improper to put in open court to an apparently married woman without strong reason to support it.

It was a pity he was so squeamish. For, as they discovered later, the Armstrongs were *not* married. The consent of Charles Armstrong was not needed. If they had put the vital question, it could have shattered an important aspect of the crown case.

As it was, the trial continued to what was now an inevitable conclusion. The defence fought as hard as they could—but it could only be a defiant last stand.

Russell insisted that, since Stead 'took no notes or memoranda till he made his preparations for writing the article . . . it is unfair and unjust to attribute to Jarrett discrepancies very possibly due to Stead himself.' He asserted that there was little doubt that Mrs Armstrong had sold her child but even he was forced to admit that there was no evidence that this was done with the permission of the father.

In making his final speech, Stead was in his element. A verdict of guilty was now almost certain and it gave him ample scope for the dramatic technique that he could deploy so well. His performance in that quiet courtroom was deeply moving.

'I'm told,' he said, 'that Jarrett is discredited but . . . I believe she told me a true story . . . She may have been a stupid witness, but she is not a fraudulent witness, in regard to this particular case. I maintain the possibility of a fallen woman's conversion.'

The Trial

'I believe in Jarrett as I do in the Bible. I honour her, driven and harassed as she was in her evidence here, for refusing to answer questions that would incriminate her old friends...'

On the question of the factual conflict between them, he spoke of the immense strain his researches had set up on him: 'I'd been obliged to drink champagne and smoke which I did not do before, and although I didn't get drunk, too much champagne is not good for anyone, least of all for a teetotaller. My memory might consequently have gone astray on some of the things told me by Jarrett. Her memory was not so strained as mine and she might have recollected better than I did after the strange and exciting crisis through which I passed...'

Stead took upon his shoulders the guilt of everyone who had been involved with him—except Madame Mourey, the accoucheuse for whom he had no sympathy at all. 'If I'm found guilty,' he told the jury simply, 'I shall make no appeal. By your verdict, I shall stand; and, if in the opinion of twelve Englishmen—sons of English mothers, fathers possibly of English girls—if they say I am guilty, I will take my punishment and I shall not flinch.' As he finished, a spontaneous burst of applause broke out in the court.

As the clapping died down, the Attorney General stood up. 'If Mr Stead's speech had been made by counsel,' he complained, mildly, 'much of it would have been stopped by law...'

His case was now so strong that he was not too concerned that the judge had not curbed the eloquent editor. He merely had to ensure that the perspective of the jury was clear. He drew a picture of the Armstrongs as a respectable Christian family—apart from the mother 'being given at times' to drink. 'The father was not black hearted,' Sir Richard insisted, 'because he had a black face.' They had been grossly libelled by a woman of appalling character who had admitted lying under oath.

Rebecca Jarrett, he said, had been posing as a 'repentant Magdalen ... It is clear she is one of those women who had been led to exaggerate her guilt for the purpose of glorifying herself and exaggerating her merit at the present time ... She was introduced to Stead as a woman who had been steeped in iniquity and sin who was now

The Trial

repentant . . . such a woman that Stead told her she deserved to be hanged and damned . . .'

'Jarrett's position,' the Attorney General went on, 'depended on her power of keeping up the story she had told Stead . . . Jarrett started out to buy girls who were in stock and it was essential she should get a girl, else she would soon have been discarded by Mr Stead and possibly discarded by Mrs Butler as well . . . She went to brothels in Whitechapel and failed absolutely. Her position as a Magdalen was at stake and so she went to her old friend in Lisson Grove (a main road adjoining Charles Street).'

'Nothing,' he declared, 'can justify what the girl was subjected to.'

The judge summed up—again displaying the bias he had revealed when grilling Stead, even describing Rebecca, still unconvicted, as 'that abominable woman'—and the jury considered their verdict for three hours.

It was nearly half past seven when they returned to the courtroom. Stead and Rebecca Jarrett, the foreman announced, had taken Eliza against the will of her father. Her mother had *not* consented to her going 'to be used for immoral purposes'. Bramwell Booth, Sampson Jacques and Madame Coombes of the Salvation Army were declared not guilty of the abduction charges.

Stead, the jury had decided, had been deceived by his agents. They recommended mercy and wished to put on record their high appreciation of the services he had rendered the nation by securing the passage of a much needed law for the protection of young girls.

It was not yet the end. The charge of indecent assault—the examination by Madame Mourey—was still to be tried before another jury, although the verdict was a foregone conclusion. The facts had all been admitted in Stead's article.

At last, on Tuesday 10 November, the judge prepared to pass sentences in both trials. 'I am prepared to give you credit,' he told Stead, 'for good motives from your point of view. But at the same time I cannot disguise from my mind that you have acted throughout recklessly . . . Believing in the existence of the most horrible depravity, it appears to me that you made statements which, when challenged, you were unable to verify. You then determined to verify the truth of

The Trial

your assertions by an experiment on a child who was to be bought and subjected to all that a real victim would have been, but who was to be rescued before any harm was done . . . You chose your own agent and, as might have been anticipated from her antecedents and as you might have known, that agent deceived you . . .'

'The result is that your experiment . . . has absolutely and entirely failed because the jury have affirmed that Eliza Armstrong, the girl subjected to that experiment, was never bought for immoral purposes at all.'

Stead, stated the judge, had published a distorted account of the case of Eliza Armstrong that was a disgrace to journalism. He had subjected the parents to 'unutterable scandal and ignominy'. The child herself had 'been dragged through the dirt, examined by a woman who . . . bore a vile character'.

And he sentenced him to jail for three months. He was more fortunate than poor Rebecca who, like Madame Mourey, was condemned to twice as long. Jacques was to be imprisoned for only one month.

Already, after the verdict of the jury was known, Stead had written a leader in the *Pall Mall Gazette* praising English justice and stating that the trial had been fair—which provoked an angry outburst from Josephine Butler against her 'dear friend'. Perhaps Mr Stead 'may think he himself was courteously treated', she wrote, 'but what of the courtesy or even decent fairness shown in regard to Rebecca, upon whom the utmost vituperation permissible in a court of law was vented.'

The treatment of Rebecca did not seem to weigh too heavily on Stead's conscience. He appeared to regard her, like Eliza, as an unavoidable casualty in his cause.

Meanwhile, the sentencing removed the last curbs from Stead's competitors who, until the verdict, had been able to publish nothing more outspoken than factual reports of the trial—which they covered at great length.

Once, when the *Pall Mall Gazette* was running his series, Stead had accused the press of 'a conspiracy of silence'. Of that, at least, he could complain no longer. The attack that was now directed at him was universal—a unanimous cry of outrage.

11

A Society Outraged

'Nothing less than imprisonment,' thundered *The Times* the next morning, 'would have been an adequate warning to fanatics of all kinds'. As it was, it declared, 'on the charge not before the court—the charge of having, on insufficient evidence, published statements on which no amount of evidence would have justified the publication . . . he has nothing to say except to glory in having done it in a cause which he believes to be good. The zealot bows to the law, but is none the less a zealot.'

'The wonder grows,' commented the *Standard* severely, 'that it should ever have been possible for a moment to conceal such atrocious proceedings under the mask of a holy purpose.'

The *Morning Post* was not satisfied that Stead's punishment was severe enough. 'It would have been more consonant with the principles of justice,' it reflected, 'to have awarded heavier sentences to Stead, Jarrett and Jacques than to Madame Mourey who 'did not do one-hundredth part of the injury to the child that was done by the other defendants.'

The disapproval went way beyond newspaper journalists. 'We backed him up over "The Maiden Tribute",' Bernard Shaw wrote later to J. W. Robertson Scott, 'only to discover that the Eliza Armstrong case was a put-up job of his. After that, it was clear that he was a man who could not work with anybody; and nobody could work with him.'

As a body, the press rallied to the support of the Armstrong family, depicting them—as the Attorney General had presented them—as a Christian family that had been victimised, as *The Times* put it coldly, by 'those who believe themselves to be engaged in saving souls'. A

A Society Outraged

public subscription was announced and Harry Poland, junior counsel for the prosecution, declared that he would receive money that anyone cared to send in, for the benefit of the Armstrongs.

There was some public pressure on the family to mount suit for damages—and there is little doubt that these would have been substantial—but clearly the Armstrongs' legal advisers decided that the issue had been aired for long enough. The funds raised in 'the ready and liberal response' to Mr Poland's appeal, so *Lloyds Newspaper* reported, would be used 'to take a house for the Armstrongs away from Charles Street and to endeavour to benefit the children by seeing that they are warmly clothed and kept at school. Several persons have offered to provide a home for Eliza but Mr Poland is strongly of opinion that she should have an opportunity of completing her education and that she should be properly trained for good service.' If there was any cash left over, it would provide Eliza with 'a small dowry . . . as some recompense for the outrageous wrongs inflicted upon her'.

Against the unanimous hardline attitude of the press, the telegrams and petitions with which the Purity Movement bombarded the government made little impact. In fact, on that November day, when Stead was confined for the first day of his sentence in his prison cell—from which he was permitted to continue editing the *Pall Mall Gazette*—it seemed as though the public reaction of Victorian England was complete, as though Society had formed a united front to fight off Stead's assault on public decency and had now returned to normal.

The appearance was deceptive. The impact of the long campaign of the 'Soul Savers'—climaxed so dramatically as it was by Stead's attack—was to colour the moral attitude of Britain and much of Western Society for generations. Their views were not far removed from those of the stark and joyless widow in Buckingham Palace who had so great an influence on the social mores of her time. Sex became even more sinful than it had been before.

The Criminal Law Amendment Bill—rushed through, as it was, so fast—did more than raise the legal seduction age of young girls. It outlawed homosexual acts between consenting adults in private—a

A Society Outraged

law that was not amended until the 1960s. It provided that boys who had sexual intercourse with girls under sixteen should be thrashed—even when they were younger than their partners. Only a few years were to pass before George Alexander, the actor-manager, was to be arrested in London on a charge of misconduct for giving a 'poor, miserable, starved and ill-clad whore a half crown'. He was acquitted, but it was a sign of the times.

Inevitably, in the new climate, Mrs Jeffries was a marked target for social vengeance. Although Stead had developed a reluctant sympathy for her—which was reflected in his series—Benjamin Scott was determined she should pay due penalty. In November, when Stead was in jail, he wrote to the Home Secretary, informing him that he had received a complaint that the 'nuisance', in Church Street was 'as bad as ever'. The police were ordered to investigate and, although they could not trace any immoral activities in Church Street, they reported that 15, Brompton Square, which was registered in Mrs Jeffries' name, seemed to be a disorderly house.

It was barely enough for official action, but Sir Godfrey Lushington, Permanent Under Secretary in the Home Office, gave vigorous instructions. 'I think the Commissioner should be ordered to spare no trouble or expense,' he ordered, 'in getting evidence against her if she is keeping a brothel at any place in London.'

It took them a long time and, even then, their proof was sparse. In November, 1887, she was charged with keeping a disorderly house—even though the house had been occupied during the period in question by a series of sub-tenants—and sentenced to prison for six months.

It was obvious that Stead felt that the move was vicious.

> Mrs Jeffries will probably die in jail. She is 72, suffering from diabetes ... We wonder what the Kings, Princes, Peers, and officers, who found the old lady so convenient for the gratification of their pleasures, think of her now. Probably, if the truth be told, they never spare a thought for their fallen flesh broker. Yet, if the truth must be told, so far as she deserves to be there, much more do they to share cells by her side ... She was but their go-between. They were the principals. They go forth scot-free, honoured by men and women ... She, despised broken and dying, is hurried off to end her days in jail.

A Society Outraged

Despite the harsh and derogatory criticism of his peers in other newspapers, Stead retained a firm belief that his 'Maiden Tribute' series was his greatest campaign—and was intensely proud of it for the rest of his life. 'It is not often,' he was to write, 'that a man can look back upon his conviction and sentence as a criminal convict with pride and exultation.'

Being Stead, he was not content with looking back. On 10 November every year, the anniversary of his conviction, he travelled his daily commuter route by train to the office in London, wearing his convict's uniform. Yet another role!

Professionally, he survived the appalling distortions of his Lily story, probably because the world of journalism—and the power élite with whom editors consort—accepted the judge's view: it was Rebecca Jarrett who told the lies, not Stead. It is a judgement that does not bear close study. A journalist, writing a sensational story is always tempted to exaggerate, to play up his highlights. The wording of the Lily article, when considered against a background of Stead's exultant researching, carries all the signs that he gave way to this temptation. He was, after all, no impartial reporter. He was campaigning. He was presenting facts to support a cause.

Perhaps, Rebecca told him *some* lies. Maybe the question of the purpose for which Eliza was taken from Charles Street was left just a little vague, so that there was a degree of scope for misunderstandings. But she did not tell *all* the lies, even though Stead himself had misunderstood her; and the impression remains that he could have done more for her later than he did, that in practice he permitted her to take the blame.

Certainly, he himself soared to higher and higher peaks. He continued campaigning. He went to St Petersburg, interviewed the Tsar, and strove to make Russia seem less ominous to the suspicious people of the West. He visited America and launched yet another morality assault in a book, *If Christ Came to Chicago*, that fast became a bestseller. New Yorkers, too, became a target in a series of articles headlined *Satan's Invisible World Displayed*.

When crisis gripped South Africa in 1899, he attacked the British government with great vigour, demanding 'Shall I slay my brother

A Society Outraged

Boer?'—a campaign that did not seem to spoil his great friendship with Cecil Rhodes, who was staunchly behind the administration in its Africa policy.

He left the *Pall Mall Gazette* to edit a journal *The Review of Reviews*, then, though still running the review, he launched a daily paper that was a disastrous failure.

He remained a stern moralist. When a report reached him that Prince Edward—later King Edward VII—had seduced a governess at the royal home at Sandringham, he resigned from freemasonry because the prince had just been appointed the Grand Master.

Rather vaguely, as he grew older, he probed around for a new subject for sexual campaigning. He had now at last entered the dreaded portals of a theatre and even grown to like it. But those pretty actresses, with their free-living ways, tempted his journalist's instincts. He even wrote to Bernard Shaw about it—to be answered with a stinging retort:

> What do you mean, you foolish Stead, by an immoral actress? I will take you into any church you like and show you gross women who are visibly gorged by every kind of excess . . . to whom money means unrestrained gluttony and marriage unrestrained sensuality; but against whose characters—whose 'purity' as you call it—neither you nor their pastors dare level a rebuke. And I will take you to a theatre and show you women whose work requires a constant physical training, an unblunted nervous sensibility . . . and yet when you learn that they do not allow their personal relations to be regulated by your gratuitously unnatural and vicious English Marriage Laws, you will not hesitate to call them 'immoral!' . . . When you sit in the stalls, think of this and . . . humble your bumptious spirit with a new sense of the extreme perversity and wickedness of that uncharitable Philistine bringing-up of yours.

At last, in 1912, Stead died—by a means that was suitably dramatic—in the disaster he had predicted, even before the Armstrong case. He was drowned in the tragic sinking of the Titanic.

Without question, the campaigns—started by Josephine Butler and Dyer and the Booths—were a great triumph for the sexual moralists. But, viewed with hindsight from an age in which sexual freedom is interlocked with the new image of the independent female, there lingers a certain irony.

A Society Outraged

For the campaigns, conducted as they were under a motivation of devout anti-sexuality, were also the first triumph for feminism in the more modern sense—the first display of mass female strength, the first assault on the previously unchallenged double standard, the first move towards Women's Liberation.

Bibliography

ACTON, DR WILLIAM. *Prostitution Considered in its Moral, Social and Sanitary Aspects, etc.* 1857, 1869
BELL, E. MOBERLEY. *Josephine Butler*, 1962
BOOTH, BRAMWELL. *Echoes and Memories*, 1925
BOOTH, BRAMWELL. *These Fifty Years*, 1929
BOOTH, CATHERINE. *Bramwell Booth*, 1933
BOREL, THOMAS. *The White Slavery of Europe*, 1880
BOWLEY, SIR ARTHUR. *Wages in the United Kingdom in the 19th Century*, 1900
BUTLER, JOSEPHINE. *Personal Reminiscences of a Great Crusade*, 1896
BUTLER, JOSEPHINE. *Rebecca Jarrett*, 1887
CHARRINGTON, FREDERICK. *Battle of the Music Halls*, 1885
COLLIER, RICHARD. *The General Next to God*
(I am particularly indebted to this excellent book for much of the material in Chapter 5)
DAVIES, OLWEN. *Florence, the Home Maker*, 1962
DEACON, RICHARD. *The Private Life of Mr Gladstone*, 1965
DYER, ALFRED. *The European Slave Trade in English Girls*, 1885
DYER, ALFRED. *Plain Words to Young Men on an Avoided Subject*, 1885
FLEXNER, A. *Prostitution in Europe*, 1913
FRYER, PETER. *Private Case—Public Scandal* 1966
Hansard, Parliamentary Report, 1870–1885
KINGSMILL, HUGH. *After Puritanism*, 1929
KRONHAUSEN, EBERHARD and PHYLLIS. *Walter—My Secret Life*, 1967
LAVER, JAMES. *English Costume of the 19th Century*, 1929
LAW, JOHN. *In darkest London*, 1891
Lloyds Newspaper, 1885
LONDON COMMITTEE ON THE TRAFFIC IN ENGLISH GIRLS. *Six Years Labour and Sorrow*, 1885
LORDS, HOUSE OF. *Sessional Papers*, 1881
MACGLASHLAN, W. *England on her Defence*, 1885
MAYHEW, HENRY. *London's Underworld*, 1950
NEVILL, RALPH. *Mayfair and Montmarte*, 1921
NEVILL, RALPH. *Piccadilly to Pall Mall*, 1908
Pall Mall Gazette, 1870–1885

Bibliography

PEARL, CYRIL. *The Girl with the Swansdown Seat*, 1958
PEARSON, HESKETH. *Bernard Shaw—His Life and Personality*, 1961
PLAYFAIR, GILES. *Six Studies in Hypocrisy*, 1970
QUENELL, PETER. *Mayhew's London*, 1949
RAILTON, GEORGE. *The Truth about the Armstrong Case*, 1885
ROBERTSON SCOTT. J. W. *The Life and Death of a Newspaper*, 1952
St James' Gazette, 1869–1885
SCOTT, BENJAMIN. *A State Iniquity*, 1890
SCOTT, G. R. *History of Prostitution*, 1936
Sentinel, The, 1879–1888
SHAW, DONALD. *London in the Sixties*, 1908
Shield, The, 1869–1885
STEAD, ESTELLE. *My father*, 1913
STEAD, W. T. *Mr Stead Before His Countrymen*, 1886
STEAD, W. T. *W. T. Stead in the Central Criminal Court*, 1885
STEAD, W. T. *My First Imprisonment*, 1886
STEAD, W. T. *The Life of W. T. Stead*, 1886
STEAD, W. T. *The Maiden Tribute*, 1885 (re-print in book form of articles in the *Pall Mall Gazette*)
STEAD, W. T. *If Christ Came to Chicago*
STEAD, W. T. *Satan's Invisible World Displayed* (re-printed articles)
TERROT, CHARLES. *The Maiden Tribute*, 1959
Times, The, 1870–1885
TREVELYAN, G. M. *English Social History*, 1946
TUCKER, F. de L. B. *The Life of Catherine Booth*, 1893
UNSWORTH, MADGE. *The Maiden Tribute*, 1949
"WALTER". *My Secret Life*, 18?? (date uncertain)
WATSON, AARON. *A Newspaperman's Memories*, 1925
WATSON, BERNARD. *A Hundred Years War—The Salvation Army*, 1964
WAUGH, BENJAMIN. *W. T. Stead—A Life for the People*, 1885
WAUGH, ROSA. *The Life of Benjamin Waugh*, 1913
WHYTE, FREDERICK. *The Life of W. T. Stead*, 1925
WILLIS, W. M. *The White Slaves of London*, 1912

Index

Accommodation houses, 27
Acton, Richard, 66
Agar, Rachel and Louise, 90, 93
Age of consent, 25, 26
   raised to sixteen, 164
   Royal Commission's recommendation, 73
   Salvation Army's campaign, 163
Amsterdam, 77
Anet, Leonard, 40, 42, 51, 80
Armstrong, Charles, 150, 171
   as portrayed by Stead, 155
   gives evidence at trial, 202
   not married to Eliza's mother, 208
   reaction to Eliza's disappearance, 168–9
   visits Mme Mourey, 183–4
Armstrong, Eliza, 34, 147, 148–55
   case sent for trial, 189
   court hearings, 187–9
   disappearance causes local comment, 168–9
   in South of France, 177–8
   moved to Paris, 181
   questioned in court, 192
   re-united with mother, 186
Armstrong, Mrs, 34, 148–50
   disagreement with husband, 150, 168–9
   gives evidence before committee of investigation, 175–6
   goes to magistrate for help, 171, 176
   her version of Eliza's departure, 172–3
   not married to Charles Armstrong, 208
   questioned in court, 193–200
   re-united with Eliza, 186
   seeks Eliza's return from Booth, 176–8
   visits Mme Mourey, 182–4
Association for the Control of Prostitution by Government Regulation, 61

Bellchamber, George, 107
Bentinck, William Cavendish, 144, 157, 161

filibusters Criminal Amendment Bill, 114–15
   launches attack on Stead, 180
Besley, Edward, 111
Bond, Louisa, 44–7, 48, 49, 54, 78
Booth family, 20, 83, 84
   see also Salvation Army
Booth, Bramwell, 86, 88–9, 91–2
   charged with abduction, 187
   found not guilty, 210
   interviews Mrs Armstrong, 176–8
   investigates white slave traffic, 95–8
   involved in Stead's researches, 142
   questioned by Inspector Borner, 172
   seeks Stead's support, 181
Booth, Catherine, 87–8, 162–3
Booth, Florence, 95
Booth, Kate, 94
Booth, William, 84–90, 92–5
   break with Methodism, 85
   counters attacks on Salvation Army, 185
Booth-Tucker, F. de L., 90
Borner, Police Inspector, 176–9, 186
   gives evidence at Stead's trial, 202
   goes to Winchester, 172
Bright, Ursula, 63
Bromwich, Elizabeth, 108
Brothels
   legal position, 25
   numbers in London, 25
   state support, 19, 20, 36, 61
   see also Accommodation houses; Brussels brothels; Dress houses; Night Houses
Broughton, Nancy, 128, 147–50, 169–71
   accused of running brothel, 171
   her version of Eliza's departure, 172–3
   questioned in court, 200–2
Brussels brothels, 21, 36, 39–52, 77–81
   extent of prostitution, 77
   owners tried and convicted, 80–1
   police connivance alleged, 78, 81
Butler, Josephine, 19–20, 21, 34, 51, 58–83, 162
   activity at Colchester by-election, 67–8
   begins public campaign, 57, 63

Index

Butler, Josephine—*cont.*
  gives evidence at Stead's trial, 207
  gives evidence to Royal Commission, 69–73
  involved in Stead's researches, 142
  provides home for prostitutes, 60
  social background, 58–9
  supports Rebecca Jarrett in press, 185
  visited by Bramwell Booth, 97

Canterbury, Archbishop of, 155, 162
  see also Church of England
Carpenter, Frank, 143
Child prostitution, 20, 21, 26, 28–31, 112, 134
  attacked by Josephine Butler, 79
  encouraged by parents, 29, 141
  exploitation by parents stopped, 164
  exposed in *Pall Mall Gazette*, 158
  protest march to Hyde Park, 165–6
  Rebecca Jarrett's information, 131
  sources of supply, 131
  Stead's research, 137–8, 141, 142
  see also Prostitution
Church of England
  supports Stead's campaign, 159
  see also Canterbury, Archbishop of
Colchester by-election (1870), 66–8
Committee of investigation, 164, 175–6
Contagious Diseases Act, 58, 60–1
  movement for repeal, 63–4
  Royal Commission, 68–73
Coombe, Mme, 152
  charged with abduction, 187
  found not guilty, 210
Criminal Law Amendment Bill, 82, 113–15, 144
  passed into law, 164
  promoted by Conservative government, 158, 159, 162
  provisions, 213–14
Cross, Sir Ralph Assheton, 157

Dress houses, 27
Dunlap, Joseph, 26, 28, 33, 133, 188
Dutton, T. D., 110
Dyer, Alfred, 35, 36–57, 73, 78
  character, 37
  evidence to House of Lords Committee (1881), 82
  letters to London press, 41
  praised by *Methodist Times*, 166
  prints Minahan's report, 104
  visits Brussels brothels, 44–7
Edlin, P. H., 114

Edward, Prince of Wales, 106, 109, 113, 160–1, 216
Ellen, Emily, 51
The European Slave Trade in English Girls, 44

Farrer, Jane, 147, 148, 170
  gives evidence at Stead's trial, 202

Gillett, George, 43–5, 82
Girls Friendly Society, 134
Gladstone, William Ewart, 25, 74
  backed by Stead, 119–20
  friendship with Olga Novikoff, 124
Gospel Purity Association, 113
Granville, Lord, 82

'Hallelujah Lasses', 90–1, 94
  see also Salvation Army
Harcourt, Sir William, 133
Haynes, Eliza, 91
Hennessey, Louisa, 49, 53–6, 81
Higgleton, Ada, 41, 43, 49
Hope Cottage, 130, 179
Hopkins, Ellice, 21, 114
House of Lords committee report (1882), 82, 112
Household Words, 24

Jacques, Sampson, 132–3, 151–2
  calls on Mary Jeffries, 138
  charged with abduction, 187
  found not guilty, 210
  sentenced on other charges, 211
  takes Mrs Armstrong to Eliza, 186
Jarrett, Rebecca, 127–32
  characterised at trial, 208–10
  charged with abduction, 187
  sentenced, 211
  converted to salvationism, 130
  goes to Salvation Army shelter, 129
  her version of Eliza's departure, 173
  interviewed by Stead, 127–8
  obtains girl for Stead, 136–7, 146
  public support from Josephine Butler, 185
  questioned in court, 202–4
  sent to Josephine Butler, 129
  writes to Nancy Broughton, 170
Jeffes, Thomas, 41–2, 48, 57
Jeffries, Mary, 99–111, 158
  arrested and tried, 109–11
  evidence of ex-coachman, 107
  extent of business, 102
  gives information to Stead's Secret Commission, 138

221

Index

imprisoned, 214
prosecuted for brothel-keeping, 100
trial questioned in House of Commons 161
Jones, Ann, 48

Kingsmill, Hugh, 17
Kitching, Theodore, 91

Ladies National Association for the Repeal of the Contagious Diseases Acts, 63
Laws affecting prostitutes, 19, 25
Lenaers, Edward, 41, 78–9, 81
Lewis, Rosa, 106
'Lily', *see* Armstrong, Eliza
Lloyds Newspaper
supports Mrs Armstrong's case, 174–5, 179–80
takes Mrs Armstrong to find Rebecca Jarrett, 179
takes Mrs Armstrong to Mme Mourey, 182–4
London
City Solicitor arrests newsboys, 160
East End conditions, 85–6
extent of prostitution, 23–7
London Committee for the Suppression of Traffic in English Girls, 105
London Female and Preventive Reformatory Institute, 175
Lopes, Mr Justice, 191
Loriol, 178, 180
Lumley, Sir Saville, 47–8
Lushington, Sir Godfrey, 162, 214

McLoughlin, Mary, 50
The Maiden Tribute, 106
The Maiden Tribute of Modern Babylon, 153
Manning, Cardinal Henry Edward, 112, 134–5, 145, 155, 162
Martineau, Harriet, 63
Massey, William, 69
Masturbation, 37
Mayhew, Henry, 24, 32
Merrick, G. P., 32
Middle classes
attitudes to poverty, 11
obligations to tenants, 11
Miller, Mary, 108
Minahan, Jeremiah, 100–12
bribed by Mary Jeffries, 102
employed as investigator, 105
report submitted on brothels, 102
printed by Alfred Dyer, 104
resigns from police force, 104

Morals police
in Belgium, 40, 41, 78, 81
in Britain, 62, 65, 73
in France, 76, 81
see also Police
Morley, John, 120, 121
Morning Post, 212
Mourey, Louise, 138–9
charged with abduction and assault, 187
sentenced, 211
examines Eliza Armstrong, 151
visited by the Armstrongs, 182–4
Music halls, 24
My Secret Life, 27
see also 'Walter'

Nash, Lucy, 81
La Nationale, 81
Newland, Ellen, 39–41, 80
Night houses, 24
Nightingale, Florence, 63
Northern Echo, 119–20
Novikoff, Olga, 123–5

Pall Mall Gazette, 13, 15, 105, 115, 116
articles accepted by committee of investigation, 164
articles published abroad, 162
articles read as evidence at trial, 198
offices attacked, 159–60
runs series on prostitution and white slave traffic, 153–62
reactions, 156
series on foreign brothels rumoured, 188–9
Paradis, Mme Evariste, 54–6
Parent, Josephine Ann, 51, 76
Perversions, 27, 83, 106
Philadelphia, 75–6
Plain Words to Young Men on an Avoided Subject, 37
Poland, Harry, 192, 200
collects money for the Armstrongs, 213
Police, 61–2
attitudes to Mary Jeffries, 101–3
attitudes to prostitutes, 25–6, 135–6
behaviour in retrieval of Eliza Armstrong, 184–5
corruption charges, 77, 162, 188
enquiry ordered, 162
enabled to raid brothels, 164
see also Morals police
Portsmouth, 130
Procurers, 31
in Stead's investigation, 139–40

222

Procureur du Roi, 45–6, 57
Prostitutes
  levels of income, 33–4
  medical inspections, 18–19, 58, 64
  place in London society, 25
  rescued by Josephine Butler, 60
  sale by parents, 141
Prostitution
  Bill filibustered, 16
  extent in European cities, 77
  extent in London, 23–7
  levels of operation, 26–7
  middle class philosophy, 11–12, 18
  see also Child prostitution
Purity Leagues, 20, 75

Quakers, 20, 36, 75
  committee against state-supported brothels, 73

Reform movement, 12–14
Reid, R. T., 176
Reynolds, Mrs, 151
Robertson Scott, J. W., 120, 121, 212
Royal Commission on the Contagious Diseases Acts, 68–73
Russell, Sir Charles, 193, 208

St James Gazette, 156
  takes up Eliza Armstrong's case, 179
St Louis, Missouri, 75
Sallecartes, Jean, 42–3, 49, 54, 76, 81, 144–5, 162
Salvation Army, 20, 84–98
  attacked by clergy, 92
  'Hallelujah Lasses', 90–1, 94
  international spread, 93–4
  night patrols in Oxford Street, 162–3
  provides decoy for Stead researches, 142–3
  psychological impact, 89
  role of women, 89–90
  sets up home for prostitutes, 95
  women attacked by publicans' mobs, 93
  see also entries under 'Booth'
Saturday Review, 23, 24
Schultz, Max, 76–7
Scott, Benjamin, 34, 38, 73, 80, 82, 104–5, 115–16
  attacks Mary Jeffries, 214
  meets William Stead, 15–17, 20–22
  visited by Bramwell Booth, 97
Secret Commission, 126, 137, 172, 175
The Sentinel, 111, 112
Shaen, William, 145
  gives evidence at Stead's trial, 207

Shaftesbury, Earl of, 112, 155
Shaw, George Bernard, 122, 212
  sells copies of *Pall Mall Gazette*, 156
  writes on the character of actresses, 216
Shepherd, Kate, 90, 93
The Shield, 64, 79
'Skeleton Army', 93
Snagge, Thomas, 50, 82, 144
Society of Friends, *see* Quakers
Splingard, Alexis, 45–6, 78–9, 80–1
Stead, Emma, 123
Stead, William Thomas, 13–14, 33, 58, 115–17, 118–46
  assistant editor of *Pall Mall Gazette*, 120
  attempts to obtain girls for researches, 134–46
  career after release from prison, 215–16
  character, 18–19, 118
  charged with abduction and assault, 187
  sentenced, 211
  claims responsibility for Eliza Armstrong's disappearance, 186
  creates Secret Commission, 126
  cross-examines Mrs Armstrong, 194–9
  editor of *Northern Echo*, 119–20
  extra-sensory perception, 122
  facts in articles proved inaccurate, 180–1
  first contact with Salvation Army, 90
  historical judgement, 13–14
  interviewed by Home Secretary, 157
  investigates white slave traffic, 143–6
  journalistic attack on Mary Jeffries, 105
  love affairs, 123–5
  meets Benjamin Scott, 15–17, 20–2
  meets Eliza Armstrong, 151
  questioned in court, 205–7
  reconstruction of white slave operation, 152–3
  research into prostitution, 137–43
  sent for trial, 189, 190–211
Storks, General Sir Henry, 66, 68
Stuart, James, 114
Suffragette movement, 19, 59
  see also Women's rights

Tanner, Adeline, 49, 50, 51, 57, 76, 77, 80
Temperance movement, 24, 92
Terrot, Charles, 106
Thomas, Edward, 175, 176
  campaigns for the Armstrongs, 186

Index

The Times, 212
Titanic, 122, 216

United States of America
    Salvation Army meets opposition, 94
    state control of prostitution voted out, 74–75

Vincent Howard, 23, 25, 26, 76–7, 135
    gives evidence at Stead's trial, 207

'Walter', 12, 27–30, 32–3, 52–3
Watt, Maria, 108
Webster, Sir Richard, 160
    cross-examines Mrs Armstrong, 198
    cross-examines Rebecca Jarrett, 203–4
    cross-examines Stead, 205
    leads prosecution against Stead, 191
    makes closing speech for prosecution 209–10
White slave traffic, 38, 42–3, 133
    action by British and Belgian governments
    Bramwell Booth's enquiries, 95–8
    new penalties introduced, 164
    organisation, 50
    Stead's investigation, 143–6
Williams, Anne, 49
Williams, Montagu, 101, 109, 111
Women,
    attitudes of society, 11–12, 17
    in the Salvation Army, 89–90
    organised against state-supported brothels, 63–5
Women's rights, 12, 16, 217
    Josephine Butler's campaign begins, 59–60
Wookey, James B., 113
Working classes, 11

HQ
356
.P36
1972